Alexander Broadie is Professor of Logic and Rhetoric at Glasgow University – a Chair once occupied by Adam Smith – and is a Fellow of the Royal Society of Edinburgh. He holds an honorary doctorate from Blaise Pascal University (Clermont-Ferrand), conferred in recognition of his contribution to Franco-Scottish philosophical relations. He has published many books on Scottish thought and is currently completing work on his *History of Scottish Philosophy*.

The Author of the Wealth of Nations

Alexander Broadie

THE SCOTTISH
ENLIGHTENMENT

The Historical Age of the Historical Nation

BIRLINN

This edition first published in 2007 by
Birlinn Limited
West Newington House
10 Newington Road
Edinburgh
EH9 1QS

www.birlinn.co.uk

ISBN 13: 978 1 84158 640 3
ISBN 10: 1 84158 640 4

British Library Cataloguing-in-Publication Data
A catalogue record for this book is available from the British Library

Typeset by Palimpsest Book Production Limited,
Grangemouth, Stirlingshire
Printed and bound by Cox & Wyman, Reading

opposite:
David Hume by James Tassie
(The Scottish National Portrait Gallery)

'I believe this is the historical Age
and this the historical Nation'

Hume in a letter to his publisher
William Strahan, August 1770

Contents

	List of Plates	ix
	Preface	xi
ONE	Introduction	1
TWO	The Enlightenment in Scotland	6
	1 The problem of origin	6
	2 Thinking for yourself	14
	3 Theory and practice	20
	4 Light and darkness	22
	5 The literati	25
	6 The age of criticism	32
	7 Improvement	38
THREE	History and Enlightenment	43
	1 Why study the past?	43
	2 The dynamic of society	54
	3 History and national identity	58
	4 History and moral philosophy	61
	5 Conjectural history	64
	6 The course of history	75
FOUR	Morality and Civil Society	78
	1 Some key concepts	78
	2 Nature and society	79
	3 The fragility of freedom	85
	4 Patriotism as a passion	94
	5 Sympathy and education	100
	6 A general education	108
FIVE	Enlightened Religion	113
	1 Religion and Enlightenment	113
	2 *The Natural History of Religion*	119
	3 Why dialogue?	126
	4 *Dialogues Concerning Natural Religion*	130
	5 Kames in trouble	140
	6 The view from the pulpit of St Giles	146

SIX   Enlightenment in the Arts   151
       1 Whaur's yer Wullie Shakespeare noo?   151
       2 Scots in Rome   153
       3 Painting and education   156
       4 Portraiture   164
       5 The craft of painting   167
       6 Hutcheson's aesthetics   175
       7 Hume on the standard of taste   178
SEVEN Science and Enlightenment   186
       1 Science and its unity   186
       2 The psychology of scientific discovery   191
       3 Theology and Newtonian science   198
       4 The blind geometer   203
       5 The age of the earth   209
       Epilogue The End of the Scottish Enlightenment?   219
       Bibliography   223
       Index   231

List of Illustrations

Adam Smith, cartoon by John Kay   Frontispiece
David Hume, medallion by James Tassie   v
Lord Kaimes, Hugh Arnot and Lord Monboddo,
    cartoon by John Kay   222

Plate Section

1 Edinburgh New Town in the form of a Union Jack, by James Craig

2 'West Street, called Trongait', by Robert Paul and William Buchanan

3 'The Origin of Painting', by David Allan

4 'The Connoisseurs', by David Allan

5 'Aberdeen Literati' – an eighteenth-century cartoon

6 Self-portrait of John Kay, greatest of Scotland's Enlightenment cartoonists

7 Playbill advertising John Home's *Douglas*

8 A page of the Minute Book of the Glasgow Literary Society

9 A page from a lengthy manuscript by Thomas Reid

10 Thomas Reid, by Sir Henry Raeburn

11 David Hume, by Louis Carrogis

12 Elizabeth Gunning, Duchess of Hamilton, by Gavin Hamilton

13 David Hunter of Blackness, by Sir Henry Raeburn

14 Margaret Lindsay (Mrs Allan Ramsay), by Allan Ramsay

15 Mrs Colin Campbell, by Sir Henry Raeburn

16 James Hutton, by Sir Henry Raeburn

17 'Unconformity at Siccar Point, Cockburnspath'
18 Front elevation of William Adam's design for Arniston House, from *Vitruvius Scotus*
19 The main entrance to Glasgow College in the 1700s, when Hutcheson, Smith, Reid et al. taught there

Preface

The Scottish Enlightenment was a wondrously rich cultural movement in eighteenth-century Scotland, and I was faced with a thousand choices regarding what to discuss, or at least mention, and what to omit. The problem of choice was the more difficult because the very concept 'Scottish Enlightenment' is contested. Some say that essentially the movement consists of a range of eighteenth-century Scottish contributions in the fields of political economy, moral philosophy and history, while others argue that writings on mathematics and the natural sciences were also an essential part. My own sympathies are with the inclusivists, and I chose to follow my sympathies in writing this book. Since in addition to these fields it is easy to argue that the fine arts were no less a part of the Scottish Enlightenment, I included them also in my narrative, and, having to choose among the fine arts, I have paid particular attention to painting, though theatre and other arts are given at least walk-on parts. Finally, religion had a bearing on almost everything that was accomplished during the Age of Enlightenment, and this fact prompted me to give religion a prominent place in my discussion.

An enormous number of people contributed to the Scottish Enlightenment, and choices regarding whom to focus on were difficult. Many of my own favourites are here, such as David Hume, Adam Smith, Adam Ferguson, Thomas Reid, James Hutton and Henry Raeburn, but I have also included a large supporting cast. Sadly, many who made a valuable contribution are hardly, if at all, mentioned. There are simply too many. My aim, however, was not to compile an encyclopedia, but instead to convey an idea of what the Scottish Enlightenment was all about and why it is now perceived to have been such an important moment in European culture.

The Scottish Enlightenment boasts an extraordinary number of brilliantly creative persons. As well as their ideas there were the people themselves, a highly sociable group who spent a great deal of time in each other's company, attending societies, clubs and taverns, enjoying good wine, good food and good conversation, and this side of their lives is important as contextualising their work. These highly sociable people wrote highly original works on society, sociability and the nature of good citizenship, and in this book I have therefore attended to the thinkers as real, live flesh-and-blood participants in the society they analysed so acutely. I wanted to make the point that they were speaking from rich experience. Nevertheless, the fundamental reason why there is now a large and growing industry centred on the lives of these great thinkers is simply that they had thoughts that were startlingly original in their own day, and that still today have the power to hold our attention and to enlarge our intellectual horizons. This fact is acknowledged in these pages by the predominance of discussion on the ideas themselves.

Not all the ideas of the Scottish Enlightenment are readily intelligible to the non-specialist. I have done my level best to be as clear as possible on matters where clarity is not easily achieved. That my level best is better than it might have been is due largely to the kind offices of Patricia S. Martin, who read the whole book in typescript and, in the name of clarity, made many suggestions, almost all of them acted on.

A.B.

Glasgow, June 2007

ONE

Introduction

During a period of a few decades on either side of 1760, Scotland was home to a creative surge whose mark on western culture is still clearly discernible. That creative surge is now known as the Scottish Enlightenment. It was a moment when Scots produced works of genius in chemistry, geology, engineering, economics, sociology, philosophy, poetry, painting. The list is long. These works can be examined largely in abstraction from their historical context and treated, as nearly as is possible, as statements of universal significance that somehow transcend the individual circumstances of their production. That indeed is how they are sometimes examined. The aim of this book is to give an account of some of the great achievements of the Scottish Enlightenment, treating them not in abstraction but instead within their historical context, as works produced by people who were in constant contact with each other, and who were among the leading movers and shakers in those great centres of Scotland's high culture, the ancient universities, the church and the law. Since those institutions survived the Union of 1707 with their Scottish identity fully intact and protected by law, and since they therefore constituted a major principle of continuity for Scotland during the period when the country was being integrated into the new British political system, the Scottish Enlightenment is inextricably bound up with the country's identity, which reaches back to the Reformation and beyond that to the great cultural achievements of medieval Scotland.

I begin by focusing on what I take to be the two essential features of Enlightenment. The first is its demand that we think for ourselves, and not allow ourselves to develop the intellectual vice of assenting to something simply because someone with authority has sanctioned it. Secondly, Enlightenment is characterised by the social virtue of tolerance, in that, in an enlightened society, people are able to put their ideas into the public domain without fear of retribution from political, religious or other such authorities that have the power to punish those whose ideas they disapprove of.

With these two criteria in mind, I seek to demonstrate that Scotland across the eighteenth century was indeed an enlightened country, at least relatively speaking. It is shown, first, that many people were engaged in highly innovative thinking; the thinkers not only refused to settle for accepting the word of earlier authorities but argued that some of the great authorities of earlier times were simply wrong. In subsequent chapters, aspects of their destructive critical thinking and of their constructive alternative proposals are fleshed out at length. Secondly, it is shown that some whom certain authorities found a serious irritant were able nevertheless to get on with their lives, suffering no more than minor inconveniences, pinpricks, for their irritating behaviour. The example on which I focus is David Hume, whose ideas on religion appalled sections of the Kirk, but whose presence in Edinburgh was treated by many there as a cause for celebration.

Hume is perhaps now the most famous of the thinkers of the Scottish Enlightenment, but I discuss the work, and the lives, of many others also who contributed to the movement. These include a remarkable group, Francis Hutcheson, Adam Smith and Thomas Reid, who successively occupied the chair of moral philosophy at Glasgow University. At Aberdeen were formidable academics, including the Newtonian mathematician and physicist Colin Maclaurin, the philosopher and art historian George Turnbull, and the rhetorician George Campbell. In Edinburgh were Hugh Blair, Adam Ferguson, Dugald Stewart and James Hutton. However, these are only a very few of those who could be named here; for one of the most remarkable things about the Scottish Enlightenment is the sheer number of people who participated actively in the movement. Chapter 2 contains a discussion of the relations, both personal and intellectual, between these men, and focuses on the fact that their sociability was an important aid to their work. One factor in their sociability was the large number of clubs and societies that sprang up in Scotland during the period, especially in the main cities, and I attend to their role in the grand scheme.

Thereafter in successive chapters there is detailed discussion of some of the great figures and their ground-breaking theories. The starting point is the strong interest in history shown in eighteenth-century Scotland. I respond to the fact that some of the most prominent writers, such as David Hume, William Robertson, Adam Smith and Adam Ferguson, wrote extensively on history, and in Chapter 3 this interest in history, and in the writing of it, is explored, with particular regard to the relation between Scottish historical writing and national identity, and between the study of the past and the sense of the dynamic of society. Finally, and in light of the fact that the eighteenth-century Scottish historians employed scientifically respectable methods of enquiry, I consider whether their scientific approach committed them, any of them, to a belief in historical determinism.

Many of those who wrote histories also commented extensively on the nature of society and on its values, both civic and moral. Their knowledge of history was of course essential if they were to write illuminatingly on the dynamics of society and on the prospects for progress. In Chapter 4 I pursue these themes, relying particularly on Adam Ferguson as my guide. Ferguson attends to the idea of civic freedom and to the question of whether it is not only enshrined in law but really protected by it. For he holds that adjudications can be according to the letter of the law while yet totally against its spirit, and that the possibility of a gap between the letter and the spirit gives a corrupt magistracy room to act to curtail the civic freedoms that were thought to have legal protection. For this reason Ferguson speaks of the need for there to be citizens who resolve to be free and who 'having adjusted in writing the terms on which they are to live with the state, and with their fellow-subjects, are determined by their vigilance and spirit, to make these terms be observed'. (Ferguson, *Essay*, p.239) I explore the issues implicit in this quotation, and explain why Ferguson could not really bring himself to trust the leaders of the Enlightenment, the 'superior geniuses' who, in his opinion, were well capable of acting to curtail civic liberties, even while proclaiming their dedication to the very liberties they were curtailing.

Among the civic liberties that seemed at times most under threat in the Scottish Enlightenment was the liberty to say publicly whatever one wanted on matters of religion. In Chapter 5 I discuss the difficulties that some leading writers on religion had with sections of the Kirk, and show that the course the difficulties took demonstrates how very enlightened Scotland had become within a relatively short period of time. These large social points provide the context within which I explore some of the ideas on religion produced in Scotland during the eighteenth century, particularly ideas associated with David Hume, Lord Kames, and also Hugh Blair, who occupied the pulpit of the High Kirk of St Giles for four decades.

Eighteenth-century Scotland boasted a richly and diversely talented artistic community, and it is to the achievements of the artists that much of Chapter 6 is dedicated. Many Scottish artists studied abroad, particularly in Rome, with the result that there was always a community of Scottish artists there during the eighteenth century. In this chapter the work of the most outstanding figure in that community, Gavin Hamilton, is considered, especially in its relation to some of the big ideas of the Scottish Enlightenment, ideas such as George Turnbull's doctrine that a properly slanted education in painting can enhance civic virtue. Since there was a major dispute in the Scottish Enlightenment about the objectivity of aesthetic judgments, about for example whether there is a standard we can agree on by which to measure the aesthetic worth of a painting, I probe this dispute, attending in particular to the philosopher Francis Hutcheson and to David Hume's famous essay 'Of the standard of taste'.

During the Scottish Enlightenment, science flourished no less than did the arts, and in Chapter 7 I explore some of the singular achievements of the period. Among them is one, Thomas Reid's development of a non-Euclidean geometry, that seems to have escaped the notice of nineteenth-century mathematicians who were developing that same field. Reid's remarkable discovery has only recently begun to receive the attention which is its due. I present Reid's main findings in this area and discuss their significance. Attention is also paid to the epochal work by James Hutton, 'father of modern geology', whose theory of the earth introduced people to the concept of 'deep time', a concept matching that of the astronomer's 'deep space', and no less stupendous for its effect on our view of our place in the grand scheme of things. Chapter 7 has a particularly important place in this book, because as we look about us in Scotland we see everywhere examples of the triumph of the Scottish Enlightenment in the field of the visual arts – I have in mind especially painting and architecture. In addition we all know about Hume's reputation as a philosopher and Adam Smith's as an economist. It is therefore easy, too easy, to think that the achievements in these fields were *the* great success stories of the age. But among the achievements of the scientists were many that were awesome, and certainly Joseph Black's work on the chemistry of heat, and Hutton's on the geological processes that shape continents, bear comparison with the greatest works of the philosophers, economists, historians and others who contributed to the Scottish Enlightenment. It was therefore necessary in this book to celebrate loudly those scientific advances.

Given that the Scottish Enlightenment was one of the greatest moments in the history of European culture, it is natural to think it a great pity that it came to an end. At the close of the book I wonder aloud whether it did come to an end, and conclude that from one perspective, that provided by my initial discussion of the nature of Enlightenment, it has not yet done so. The good news therefore is that we are, in a quite robust sense, still living in the Age of Enlightenment that was initiated in Scotland in the early eighteenth century by such thinkers as Hutcheson, Turnbull and Maclaurin.

TWO

The Enlightenment in Scotland

Section 1: The problem of origin

The explosion of creativity that composed the Scottish Enlightenment is an awesome thing. It is also a matter of surprise that it happened. One reason for surprise is that, by the early years of the eighteenth century, the country was bereft of a court and a parliament and had become impoverished. It had lost its royal court to London at the time of the Union of the Crowns in 1603 when James VI of Scotland became also James I of England. It is true that, in the later seventeenth century, James, Duke of York, established a miniature court in Edinburgh, but it had a very brief lifespan. Scotland had also lost its parliament to London at the time of the Union of the Parliaments in 1707 when both the parliament of Scotland and the parliament of England ceased to exist, and the British parliament came into existence and began to sit where the English parliament had previously sat. Each of these events might have spelled disaster for high culture in Scotland, since a royal court and a parliament are both major centres of patronage. And, even if it was still a Stewart king who ruled (as it was until the revolution of 1688 which brought William of Orange to the throne), the fact that the throne was in London was bound to result in less royal patronage for Scotland than would otherwise have been the case. And so we find that, from the start of the Enlightenment period, a number of star Scottish performers, who would in all probability have spent their lives in Scotland contributing significantly to the cultural ambience of the country, spent instead a significant part of their working lives in England, especially in London, working for southern patrons. For obvious reasons this is particularly true of painters. For example, William Aikman (1682–1731), the leading Scottish portraitist of his generation, went to London in search of patronage and there he stayed. And the painter John Smibert

(1688–1751), a native of Edinburgh, practised in London, before eventually going to America. His honorific title 'father of American painting', indicates the magnitude of Scotland's loss. And Allan Ramsay (1713–84), unsurpassed as a portraitist among Scottish painters, also spent many years of his adult life in London, and whatever the significance of Hogarth's apparently slighting reference to Ramsay as 'another face painter from abroad', Ramsay enjoyed great success in London. As well as painters, writers also gravitated to London. A conspicuous example is James Thomson (1700–48) from Ednam in Roxburghshire, who during his own lifetime had a considerable reputation as a poet. He went to London in 1725 and never returned. He is now best known as the author of *Rule Britannia* though his greatest literary achievement was a long nature poem, *The Seasons*. There were, however, many others who made their home in England, for example David Mallett (described by Dr Johnson as 'the only Scot whom Scotchmen did not commend'), James Beattie, Tobias Smollett, James Macpherson and James Grainger. There were many others.

Besides the departure of the two great centres of patronage, a further reason why Scotland's breathtaking achievements in the eighteenth century are so much against the run of history is the fact that, at the beginning of the Enlightenment, Scotland was in an impoverished state due in part to the failure of the Darien scheme to establish a Scottish colony in the Isthmus of Panama, a failure that cost Scotland approximately a quarter of the country's liquid capital. There had also been a series of disastrous harvests in the 1690s. A country in such a low economic state could not be expected to produce a high culture, even less a high culture on the world-beating scale achieved by Scotland in the eighteenth century. What then can be said that might contribute to an explanation of the occurrence of the Scottish Enlightenment?

As a first step to the answer, we should avoid exaggerating the negative factors at work in Scotland in the late seventeenth century and early eighteenth. The departure of the royal court did not lead to the departure of a high proportion of the aristocracy. Moreover the departure of parliamentarians to London did not mean the end of political activity in Scotland, especially as the Scottish MPs were comparatively few; by the Treaty of Union, sixteen aristocrats went to the House of Lords and forty five men were elected to the Commons (a rather small proportion of the total number of 586 MPs). With the united parliament sitting in Westminster, Scotland in large measure continued to be ruled by Scottish aristocrats living in Scotland. For decades the third Duke of Argyll governed Scotland from Scotland. It is true that British, and therefore Scottish, foreign policy was made in London. But after 1707 Scotland was in large measure an autonomous region, left to look after itself so long as it did not threaten to destabilise Britain (which it did in 1715 and 1745). After the Union of the parliaments these centres of political power in Scotland were major centres of patronage for the universities, the church, the legal institutions and the arts. Scotland therefore, though fast becoming 'unionised' in many details as well as in the grand political scheme, preserved highly visible and genuinely potent symbols of its distinctive identity. The country was narrowly spared what would have been a remarkable symbol of the Union when draft plans for Edinburgh New Town were drawn up by James Craig in the 1760s. There is compelling evidence that one of Craig's draft plans envisioned the New Town in the form of a Union Jack with a central square from which the spokes of the Jack radiated (see Plate 1; also McKean, 'James Craig', pp.48–56). Perhaps the plan was revised because of the bad design of rooms that was implicit in the tight angles of the buildings near the centre square. Nonetheless the Hanoverian agenda is plain. Indeed that agenda triumphed in the final version of the plan when the streets of New Town received their names: George Street, Queen Street, Frederick Street, Hanover Street; and Charlotte Square. New Town, in nomenclature though not in shape, was and is a celebration of the Union. But the triumph should not be allowed to mask the preservation of Scottish identity. Hence if there was going to be an Enlightenment in Scotland there was good prospect that it would have a Scottish character.

That there was a possibility of something special happening in the eighteenth century is suggested by the impressive level of cultural achievements that existed in the country prior to the Union.

Scotland had been at least as civilised as most other European countries and it possessed an intellectually vigorous, well-educated and outward-looking class, looking outward particularly to the European continent. This perspective was deeply ingrained by the seventeenth century. The three Scottish universities founded in the Pre-Reformation period had always been strongly oriented towards Europe. St Andrews (founded 1411/12) and Glasgow (founded 1451) had been modelled on the universities of Paris and Bologna respectively, and in their early decades almost all the teaching staff at St Andrews and Glasgow, and also at King's College, Aberdeen (founded 1495), had been foreign-educated Scots, with Paris providing the great majority of the Scottish teachers for the Scottish universities. In the sixteenth century this state of affairs continued, with Scots working at the highest levels in the universities of continental Europe before returning to posts in Scotland, including posts at the University of Edinburgh (founded 1583).

Thus, for example, John Mair (c.1467–1550), from Gleghornie near Haddington, rose to be professor of theology at Paris, and was described as the university's 'prince of philosophers and theologians'. His lectures at Paris were attended by Ignatius Loyola, John Calvin, Francisco Vitoria, George Buchanan and François Rabelais. During his early years in Paris, Mair lived in the same house as Erasmus. While provost of St Salvator's College in St Andrews, he tutored John Knox, who declared of him that 'his word was then held as an oracle on matters of religion'. (Knox, *John Knox's History of the Reformation in Scotland*, vol.1, p.15) Mair also spent five years from 1518 to 1523 as principal of Glasgow University. There was at that time no more distinguished an academic in Europe. He was at the centre of things, teacher of some of the great movers and shakers of the age. His friend and fellow logician and theologian, Hector Boece (c.1465–1536) from Dundee, who was also a student and then professor at Paris, became the first principal of King's College, Aberdeen; and George Lokert (c.1485–1547) of Ayr, another friend and fellow logician and theologian, who had likewise been a student and then a professor at Paris, returned to become dean of Glasgow. Robert Galbraith (c.1483–1544) was professor of Roman Law at Paris before returning to take up the post of senator of the College of Justice in Edinburgh. William Manderston (*c*.1485–1552), a Glasgow graduate, was successively rector of the universities of Paris and St Andrews. We know of many other foreign-educated Scots who likewise returned to Scotland to contribute to the rich cultural scene. Demonstrably Scotland was culturally as much in Europe as France was.

In the Post-Reformation period also there was a substantial flow of young Scots to the universities of continental Europe, many of whom returned to Scotland to take up academic posts. One consequence is that students in sixteenth- and early-seventeenth-century Scotland were no more in an educational backwater than their predecessors had been. They were receiving high-quality education that kept them abreast of latest developments across the spectrum of subjects, such as physics, medicine, philosophy, theology and law. Among the Scots who went to continental Europe to deepen their education was the mathematician and astronomer Duncan Liddel (1561–1613) of Aberdeen, who studied in Gdansk, Frankfurt and Breslau, discussed astronomy with Tycho Brahe, and rose to be pro-rector of Helmstedt. He was the founder of the mathematics chair at Marischal College, Aberdeen. Thomas Seget of Seton near Edinburgh studied at Edinburgh, Leiden and Louvain before moving to Padua in 1598 where he knew Galileo. He subsequently stayed at Prague and worked with Kepler. The two carried out astronomical observations together in 1610 in search of confirmation of some of Galileo's observations. Another of Galileo's Scottish acquaintances was John Wedderburn (1583–*c*.1654) of Dundee who matriculated at the University of Padua in 1598, and who published a mathematically strong defence of Galileo. Wedderburn later went to Prague, where Kepler speaks of him as *mihi amicissimus*, 'my very dear friend'. Somewhat against the trend of Scots scholars travelling abroad, the greatest contribution to science made by a Scot during this period was John Napier's (1550–1617) who did not, so far as we know, train abroad. His *Description of the Wonderful Canon of Logarithms* (1614) was taken up by a delighted Kepler, who was quick to see the value of Napier's tables of logarithms. In addition to his invention of logarithms Napier's invention of a slide-rule was to have a substantial impact.

Speaking generally, it is evident that Scotland of the fifteenth and sixteenth centuries was an outward-looking country, well aware of European high culture and wide open to its new ideas. It is also demonstrable that Scots of the period contributed substantially to that shared European culture.

Throughout the seventeenth century, Scots were intellectually very active at home and abroad, as witness Thomas Forbes (c.1629–1688), philosopher and academic medical doctor at Pisa (1659–62), and Robert Sibbald (1641–1723), who went to Leiden in 1660 to study medicine and subsequently became first professor of medicine at Edinburgh University. His interest in botany (and particularly his interest in the medicinal properties of herbs) led him in 1670 to co-found, with Andrew Balfour (1630–94), the Physic Garden (later the Royal Botanic Gardens) in Edinburgh. Edinburgh's pre-eminence during the eighteenth century as a centre of medical studies was presaged by the foundation of the Royal College of Physicians of which Robert Sibbald was a founder. Another of the co-founders was Archibald Pitcairne (1652–1713) who, like Sibbald, had trained at Leiden. A further distinguished scientist of the Pre-Enlightenment period was James Gregory (1638–75) from Drumoak, Aberdeenshire, the first professor of mathematics at Edinburgh, chiefly known now for his mathematical account of the reflecting telescope. I mention these men (though many others also could have been named) to illustrate the fact that during the seventeenth century Scotland's universities boasted a strong science base. The amazing advances that were made by Scottish scientists during the eighteenth century were possible only because Scotland was already strong in the sciences. Throughout the seventeenth century Scottish professors had been cognizant of work that was being carried out elsewhere in Europe and they had passed their knowledge on to their students. As mathematicians, experimenters and informed observers, Scots had also been contributing substantially to the Europe-wide scientific enterprise, and had done so both in Scotland and abroad – it is possible that at least as much science was done by Scots living abroad as by Scots at home.

I have stressed the interest that Scots took in science and mathematics, but they were active across the whole range of fields of high culture, including theology, philosophy and law. Among the outstanding theologians were Robert Leighton (1611–84), Gilbert Burnet (1643–1715), and Henry Scougall (1650–78) whose *The Life of God in the Soul of Man* was a key text. But none of the theologians was of the stature of James Dalrymple, the first Viscount Stair (1619–95), the outstanding figure in Scottish law during the Pre-Enlightenment period and one of the greatest thinkers on law that Europe has produced.

Dalrymple graduated from Glasgow University in 1637 and was a Regent in Arts there from 1641 till 1647. The following year he became an advocate and thereafter was appointed a judge. From 1661 Dalrymple, by now titled Viscount Stair, was active in the Court of Session and sat on many commissions through which he was connected to important moments in Scottish History. He is also connected to a great moment in Scottish literature since, owing to the events of her tragic final weeks, his daughter Janet was the model for Lucy Ashton, in Walter Scott's *The Bride of Lammermuir*, who attempted to murder her new husband and died in a deranged state shortly afterwards.

Above all, however, the reason Stair is important to Scotland is his treatise *The Institutions of the Law of Scotland, deduced from its originals and collated with the civil, canon and feudal laws, and with the customs of neighbouring nations*, first published in 1681, with a revised and longer edition appearing in 1691. The word 'deduced' works hard in this informative title. The book has the structure of a deduction or inference. In the dedication to Charles II, Stair writes: 'you have governed this nation so long and so happily, by such just and convenient laws, which are here offered to the view of the world, in a plain, rational and natural method . . . There is not much here asserted upon mere authority, or imposed for no other reason but *quia majoribus placuerunt* [because most people liked them]; but the rational motives, inductive of the several laws and customs, are therewith held forth.' The *Institutions*, which set the practice of law in Scotland on a sound philosophical base, almost certainly helped to ensure that Scots law would remain in force as a distinct entity after the Union of 1707. For with Stair's *Institutions* in use, everybody knew that Scotland had a distinct system of law and knew, or could easily find out, what its content was. English law therefore could not be imposed on Scotland by default.

The fact just demonstrated, that from the beginning of the fifteenth century to the beginning of the eighteenth there were many Scots of the highest intellectual calibre working creatively across the entire range of high culture, is crucial if we are to understand how the Scottish Enlightenment came into existence. The enlightened Scots – they called themselves 'literati' and I shall follow them in this – were the beneficiaries of an immensely rich cultural heritage. They took up their inheritance with gratitude and exploited it to the full. It is implausible to suppose that that amazing surge of the human spirit in the eighteenth century would have been so magnificent if the intellectual patrimony of the literati had not itself been so magnificent. The outcome makes David Hume quite boastful in a letter to Gilbert Elliot of Minto: 'Is it not strange that, at a time when we have lost our Princes, our Parliaments, our independent Government, even the Presence of our chief Nobility, are unhappy, in our Accent & Pronunciation, speak a very corrupt Dialect of the Tongue which we make use of; is it not strange, I say, that, in these Circumstances, we shou'd really be the People most distinguish'd for Literature in Europe?' (*Letters*, vol.1, p.255)

There is a common view that, during the eighteenth century, two Scottish cultures are distinguishable. One (to which Hume refers in the passage just quoted) was a high or polite culture to which the geniuses belonged. It was literary, was based on the universities, the Kirk, the legal institutions and the country's many literary and scientific societies, and was international, at least in the sense that its members were in constructive dialogue with their counterparts in other countries. The other culture was popular or vernacular; it was primarily oral, had a wide base, and was more nationalistically Scottish, as can be gathered from the many popular ballads that were an important conduit for the ideas and sentiments of the people.

The distinction seems clear; but there is room for doubt about its usefulness as an analytic tool for historians, since the reality is much more complex than the abstract categories would suggest. For example, in the field of poetry it is not easy to categorise Allan Ramsay senior, Robert Burns and Robert Fergusson in terms of the distinction; nor James Macpherson, whose translation of *Ossianic* poetry from Gaelic brought into Enlightenment society an epic, claimed to be of ancient origin, describing the Gaels in a primitive stage of society. There is a similarly complex situation in the music of Scotland during the eighteenth century, as witness the difficulty in classifying the great fiddler Niel Gow (1728–1807) and his brother Nathaniel whose music, primarily dance music, straddles the divide between art music and popular music, or rather is firmly placed on both sides of the divide. Nevertheless, while recognising that the classification of Scottish culture into 'high' and 'popular' is problematic in its application, there is no doubt that at least most of the major figures of the Enlightenment in Scotland, the geniuses and the large supporting cast of fellow academics, scientists, lawyers, ministers and medical doctors, were unequivocally on the side of high culture.

Section 2: Thinking for yourself

The literati formed part of an international community of thinkers who saw themselves as citizens in the Republic of Letters, somewhat like workers in a multinational corporation whose aim is to place intellectual property in the public domain. These citizens addressed each other across as well as within national boundaries. Citizenship depended not on place of birth but solely on the writings with which a person put his thoughts before the public for discussion, dispute and improvement. The literati therefore did not just write for each other, they wrote for anyone anywhere willing to read them, and in fact some had a large international readership. A few Scots, such as David Hume and Adam Smith, were among the most widely read and influential members of this international community. The international dimension of the Scottish Enlightenment was therefore crucial to it, just as it was essential to the Pre-Enlightenment Scottish culture.

Nevertheless in several ways the Scottish Enlightenment had a distinctively national character. This will be spelled out in subsequent chapters, but it is in any case plain that Scots who think about politics, economics, social structures, education, law or religion are bound to have in mind the politics, economics, society, education, law or religious life of Scotland, and these national considerations are bound to influence what they write. It is not simply that Scottish models are the ones that the Scottish thinkers naturally light upon as a starting point for their reflections. The point is that Scottish thinkers write as Scots, that is, as people who have lived in, worked with, and in substantial measure been formed by, these same institutions. Hence, in so far as there is something distinctively Scottish about the institutions on which the thinkers reflect (and demonstrably there is), there will also be something distinctively Scottish about those reflections upon the concepts embodied in the institutions, and upon the values that the institutions were created to serve.

There are therefore two elements or aspects of the Scottish Enlightenment that need to be considered, namely what was enlightened about it, and what was Scottish. I shall deal with these matters in turn. The question, 'What was enlightened about the Scottish Enlightenment?', calls for an analysis of the concept of enlightenment. With the analysis to hand we will also be able to tackle the question, which will be considered in the Epilogue, of when the Scottish Enlightenment ended. As to the analysis of enlightenment my account will be roughly according to that found in the essay 'What is enlightenment?' by the greatest of Europe's Enlightenment philosophers, Immanuel Kant (1724–1804) from Königsberg in East Prussia. There are Post-Enlightenment accounts of enlightenment, but it is worth paying special attention to contemporary accounts, for it may reasonably be supposed that those living through the historically conditioned experience of the Enlightenment will have particularly apposite insights into the concept. Though Kant's account is and has always been controversial, it is the most famous, and probably also the most widely accepted. It also fits well the Scottish experience.

The term 'enlightenment' suggests emergence from darkness. To claim enlightenment is therefore to congratulate oneself on not being, or no longer being, benighted. But if the eighteenth century was the Age of Enlightenment, what was it about previous ages that constituted their darkness? We need to unpack these metaphors 'light' and 'dark'. From the perspective of the eighteenth century, what previous ages suffered from was the dead hand of authority, especially political authority and even more especially religious authority. Of course political and religious authorities were hardly if at all less in evidence in the eighteenth century than in the Middle Ages, but the scope of those earlier authorities was perceived to be different. Among thinkers of the Middle Ages, religious authority was conspicuous in at least two ways.

First, the philosophers and theologians knew well that mistakes could have deadly consequences for them. Two examples will serve. The first concerns John Duns Scotus (c.1266–1308), a native of Duns in Berwickshire and arguably the greatest philosopher that Scotland has produced. In 1307, while living in Paris, he wrote a short passage on the immaculate conception of the Virgin Mary. Some theologians were appalled at what he had written, one even declaring that 'one should proceed [against Scotus] not by arguments but otherwise'. (Frank and Wolter, *Duns Scotus*, p.8) The menace behind the words did not need to be spelled out. News reached Scotus, and he fled the city, in such haste that he did not even go to his rooms to collect the manuscripts he was working on. The fact that the teaching in that passage was shortly thereafter adopted as the official doctrine of the Church should not detract attention from the risk Scotus took in placing in the public domain an idea that was at the time heterodox. The second example concerns David Guild, a student at the University of St Andrews. In 1541 he was charged with heresy on account of assertions he had made in an exam. With the support of John Mair, then provost of St Salvator's College, St Andrews, Guild survived the accusation and indeed went on to become dean of the Arts Faculty. But the risk he ran was plain to all. It had been only a few years previously in 1528 that Patrick Hamilton, proto-martyr of the Scottish Reformation, had been burned at the stake before St Salvator's College, on account of his heretical views. That Hamilton had been burned and Guild threatened with the same punishment distinguishes the Enlightenment from what the Enlightenment stood out against, the lethal authority of a Church in its dealings with those who contradicted its doctrines.

The second role that should be emphasised as regards the place of authority in the Middle Ages is the routine widespread use of so-called 'arguments from authority'. These are arguments in which the justification offered for affirming a given proposition is that the proposition has the support of an authority in the relevant field. For example, everything that the Bible says, and everything that follows from what the Bible says, must be true because the Bible is the word of God. No conceivable argument for a proposition could be stronger than the argument that a given proposition must be true since God affirmed it or affirmed something that implied it. And likewise, from around the middle of the thirteenth century, Aristotle, the greatest thinker of ancient Greece, was thought to be an authority on almost everything, and hence the fact that he had affirmed a given proposition was often taken as proof that the proposition was true.

I dwell on these two roles played by authority in the Middle Ages because it was against these more than against anything else that the Enlightenment defined itself. Enlightenment is a movement or process away from the constraints of such forms of authority. This aspect of the self-image of the Enlightenment is negative in so far as it concerns what people have escaped from and stand out against. It is hardly necessary these days to say what is wrong with authority so far as it threatens the lives of those tempted to say something theologically off-message. But what is wrong with arguments from authority? The short answer is that they appear to rule out major intellectual progress. In particular, it is difficult to see that much progress is possible if there is a climate of intellectual passivity in which the authorities on which people rely are not themselves called to account. Why after all should the authorities not be called to account? What is the proof that they are speaking truly? Might Aristotle not be wrong about something? Should there not be some means of answering this question other than by taking on trust the word of a later authority to the effect that Aristotle speaks with authority on this matter? And while it might seem bizarre that the word of God should be called to account, his word is interpreted for us by human authorities and accepted on their interpretation, and we ought to be able to call those interpreters to account. In any case the word of God comes down to us in humanly edited versions, and the editions can also be called to account. We can therefore ask: 'Is this really what God said?' and 'Is this really what God meant?'. Intellectual progress appears not to be possible except in an intellectual climate in which people are not overly respectful of authorities. This shift in climate was a major feature of the Enlightenment.

It has to be said that the comments just made regarding the medieval use of arguments from authority are totally unfair. While those philosophers and theologians did indeed rely on the authority of the Bible, of Aristotle, of St Augustine, and so on, they also sought to reach the truth by bringing before the tribunal of reason the propositions derived from the authorities; and a good deal of philosophy and theology was written by brilliantly creative thinkers such as Thomas Aquinas, Duns Scotus and William Ockham, men whose insights into human nature, morality and the nature of existence are still unsurpassed. How can they be thought to have laboured under the dead hand of authority if they made such profound and original contributions to their disciplines? Nevertheless, from the perspective of the Age of Enlightenment (and that is the perspective that concerns me here), there were during the Middle Ages strict limits to the autonomous use of reason, for the bottom line was laid down by the Church – as witness Scotus's flight from Paris to Cologne and Patrick Hamilton's burning. In the sense just outlined therefore the word of authority did not merely set the agenda for thinkers; it also set the limits of what dare be said.

If we do not rely on authorities to tell us what to think, what is the alternative? The one emphasised in the Enlightenment is this, that we do the thinking for ourselves. To determine the answer to a question we go and look for ourselves, or experiment for ourselves or reason for ourselves. In this way we gain freedom from the oppressive authority of another's thinking. This freedom is the space that our spirit needs if we are to grow intellectually and morally. Habitual respect for authority, where in effect we simply leave the authority to do the thinking for us, is a slavery of the mind. Since this slavery, even more than slavery of the body, constrains and distorts the humanity of the enslaved person, it follows that to cut oneself free from such slavery is to take a step towards one's flourishing as a human being and it is therefore to make an assertion on behalf of a morally sound conception of humanity. On this account of the matter, to think freely is morally superior to leaving others to do our thinking for us, and it is therefore little wonder that the enlightened ones employed 'Enlightenment' as a term of self-congratulation. Freedom from intellectual servitude is celebrated by Robert Burns when he lauds the stance of 'the man o' independent mind' ('A man's a man for a' that' v.3, line 7).

Church leaders tell us what to think, so do politicians, so do many others. We never need to look far to find guardians of the truth who are forever trying to be helpful by saving us from the difficult and potentially dangerous task of independent thinking. As distinct from these kindly acts by church leaders and politicians, these guardians of the truth, there is at the heart of the entire Enlightenment project, and represented a thousand times in the Scottish Enlightenment, the idea of autonomous reason, not our reason going down tramlines that others have laid for us, but instead our reason following through lines of thought according to its own dictates, saying 'yes' to propositions because it can see them to follow logically from things that it can see to be true.

This is not to say that the voice of authority has no role to play; it has a crucial one, that of setting the agenda. The enlightened person accepts the word of authority not as something to which he has to say 'yes', but as something which it is appropriate to subject to critical analysis. The question for the enlightened person therefore is whether the word of authority can stand up to cross-examination before the tribunal of reason. If it can then it is accepted because it is sanctioned not by authority but by reason. If on the other hand it cannot withstand the cross-examination then it has to be discarded, however exalted the source. The Enlightenment was an age of criticism in the sense of 'critical analysis' or 'critical reflection'. It was through critical reflection that people were to gain their freedom – I do not say 'secure' it, because our freedom is never secure. Any position gained from the dead hand of authority has to be defended. Without an effective holding operation the position is lost.

This emphasis on independent thought, or autonomous reason, might suggest that the ideal of the Enlightenment is the solitary thinker working things out for himself. But any such suggestion should be resisted, for there was nothing solitary about the enlightened ones of the eighteenth century. It is one thing to think *for* yourself, another to think *by* yourself, and the enlightened ones were not much given to thinking by themselves. On the contrary, thinking was regarded as essentially a social activity. People thought with each other; that is, they *shared* their thoughts. I now therefore wish to emphasise a second feature of enlightenment, namely its distinctive form of sociality. Earlier I mentioned the Republic of Letters, a notion that gained common currency during the Enlightenment. Citizens of this Republic, writers who committed their writings to the public domain, discussed and disputed with each other in public, and did so in freedom, in the sense that they were not constrained by fear of what might become of them if their ideas met with the disapproval of the political, religious, or other authorities. In this respect there is a sharp contrast between on the one hand the enlightened countries of the eighteenth century and on the other the Church and the countries of medieval Europe.

Section 3: Theory and practice

I do not wish to imply that in an enlightened country freedom of speech would be accompanied by unbounded freedom to act in the direction dictated by the freely spoken words. According to the concept of enlightenment here being expounded, a minister of the Church should be able, without fear of punishment, to publish a book in which he criticises doctrines of his own Church. But this does not imply that he should be at liberty to stand before his congregation in the course of a religious service and criticise those same doctrines, nor that he should consider himself free to teach children in the congregation doctrines that the Church would reject. In short, whatever he says as a citizen of the Republic of Letters, he must do what the Church does. On entry to the ministry he undertook to teach and preach within the doctrinal framework laid down by the Church, and to teach or preach otherwise would be to betray his oath of commitment. Likewise a member of the public can, as a person of ideas, write a treatise attacking the country's system of taxation, but he must do what citizens are bound to do, namely pay their taxes. And likewise as regards a soldier who is also a person of ideas. In the latter role he can publish a scholarly article criticising the strategic thinking of the military high command, but of course he must do as soldiers do, obey orders.

Enlightenment, as so understood, might seem of limited value because it seems to be on the side of theory not of practice. But this is an inaccurate assessment for it presents the literati as living in their ivory towers while the world proceeds as if their influence could not pass through ivory. In reality, if the literati did not have their hands directly on the reins of power, they had lines, direct or otherwise, to those who did. For example, governments certainly attended to Adam Smith's arguments against monopolies and in favour of free trade. There is a strong tradition, which accurately reflects attitudes even if it is not verbally correct, that when Smith entered a room in which William Pitt the Younger, William Wilberforce and others were sitting, they all rose, and Smith asked them to be seated. Pitt's reply is reported to have been: 'No, we will stand till you are first seated, for we are all your scholars.' (Ross, *Life of Adam Smith*, p.376) Pitt was later to pay tribute to Smith in referring to 'the writings of an author of our own times, now unfortunately no more, (I mean the author of a celebrated treatise on the Wealth of Nations,) whose extensive knowledge of detail, and depth of philosophical research, will, I believe, furnish the best solution to every question connected with the history of commerce, or with

the systems of political economy'. (Ross, *Life of Adam Smith,* p.378)
There is likewise evidence that Smith's strongly argued support for
American independence also affected government action. In other
fields also the literati exercised power directly or indirectly.

As regards the religious life of Scotland, among the literati were
a number of ministers of the Kirk who disapproved of the harsh
message and harsh discipline of traditional Scottish Calvinism.
They formed a grouping, the Moderate Party within the Kirk,
pro-Hanoverian, Whig, and preaching a softer Calvinism that
contained an important element of humanism and respect for
civic virtue. These ministers, led by men of the calibre of William
Robertson and Hugh Blair, came to dominate the General Assembly
for many decades, and had a profound influence on the teaching and
practices of the Kirk. It was through their efforts that the Kirk was
on the side of the Enlightenment, and indeed was a major driving
force behind it. There is no doubt that the Moderates exercised
considerable power in Scottish society. They were certainly not
ivory-towered, demonstrably not when one considers that Hugh
Blair, as well as being the first occupant of the chair of rhetoric
and belles lettres at Edinburgh University, was also minister of the
High Kirk of St Giles, and used his pulpit week by week to provide
intellectual underpinning for the values of the Enlightenment.

One other way in which the literati exercised power must
be mentioned, as being as important as any of the others. The
reason why the industrial revolution developed so fast in Scotland
compared with other countries in Europe was the creativity of
Scotland's scientists and engineers in formidable alliance with the
entrepreneurial skills and drive of its commercial community. In
several ways therefore and in substantial measure the leaders of
the Enlightenment in Scotland were not ivory-towered thinkers but
thinkers who also changed society.

Section 4: Light and darkness

The idea that light is somehow on the side of the good and that
the dark is to be avoided has been around for a long time. As
regards the eighteenth-century Enlightenment, the reality behind

the metaphors of light and dark can best be expressed in terms of speech. To live in the light it is not enough that one be capable of autonomous or independent thought; one must also be able to publish one's thoughts without living in fear for having published them. There is of course such a thing as freedom of thought; it is the freedom possessed by a person whose thinking does not run down tramlines. But it is freedom of speech, not freedom of thought, that characterises an enlightened country. Enlightenment, on this account, is therefore a moral category, for tolerance is a moral virtue, and in an enlightened country the authorities practise that virtue on the country's writers. This way of unpacking the metaphors also makes it clear that enlightenment is not a passive state, a state of having a light shining on one, for this would be to imply that it is the source of illumination that is doing the work. Nor is enlightenment a state of having knowledge, for that might have been given to us by someone else, so that beyond barely understanding what we have been told we have contributed nothing to the acquisition of that knowledge. Enlightenment is on the contrary to be understood, first, as mental activity, engaged in by a person committed to the values of truth and validity as the sovereign values of reason. He reflects critically and creatively and, motivated by these sovereign values, goes to the places to which his arguments take him; he is not mentally passive, as are all those who live in the grip of a habit of mind. Secondly, without fear, and therefore freely, he places the fruits of his thought in the public domain. Granted that there are these two sorts of freedom, freedom of thought and of speech, what is the relation between them?

The answer helps to explain the sociability, indeed the clubbability, of the Scottish literati. It might be thought that it is easier to suppress freedom of speech than of thought, that however much we are constrained by authorities who simply terrorise people into public verbal acquiescence, people can still, in the solitude and privacy of their own heads, think what they want. Well, perhaps it is easier in that a person terrorised into silence might none the less think the thoughts that he is too frightened to articulate aloud. Nevertheless someone brought up not under conditions of freedom but under a regime of terror, and therefore never able either to share with another his thoughts on the regime or to gain access to the thoughts of another (for they also will have been suppressed), will be limited in his ability to engage in independent thinking on this matter. It is not that such thinking will be impossible for him but that it will be more difficult. In addition there is a question of how good his independent thinking would be even if he were capable of such activity, for in the absence of feedback from others who have had the opportunity to reflect critically upon those thoughts he lacks a proper standard by which to measure the quality of his own thinking. We are always 'trying out our ideas' on others. By such means we find out not only what others think of our ideas but what we think of them also. Thinking, though it seems to go on essentially in our heads, is in fact a social or communal activity. In that sense an attack on freedom of speech is also an attack on freedom of thought. Freedom to put ideas into the public domain is therefore requisite for enlightenment. It is with such considerations as these in mind that the Aberdeen regent George Turnbull (1698–1749) wrote: 'Liberty or a free Constitution is absolutely necessary to produce and uphold that Freedom, Greatness and Boldness of Mind, without which it cannot rise to noble and sublime Conceptions. Slavery soon unmans and despirits a People; bereaves them of their Virtue and Genius, and sinks them into a mean, spiritless, enfeebled Race that hardly deserves to be called "Men"'. (*A Treatise on Ancient Painting*, p.99) This was a commonly expressed sentiment in eighteenth-century Scotland.

By thinking with others, that is, by engaging in discourse with them, not only do others have the opportunity to react intellectually to me, but I have the opportunity to react to their reaction. So I tell them of a thought of mine, attend to their criticism and in the light of it seek to modify the thought. They disprove and I improve. The Republic of Letters provides almost a guarantee of intellectual improvement, because it presents us with intellectually lively readers who can produce improvement in us, first by providing criticism to which we have to respond, and secondly by just being there. For the very thought that the readers are out there waiting to think through what we have to say forces us to reach deeper into our souls in an effort to find ideas that will better withstand critical survey by such lively protagonists. The mechanism is clear. While writing we see our words through the eyes of others. This gives us a new perspective, stimulates fresh thinking, enables us to anticipate lines of attack and lines of development; and the other literati, though present to the writer only in his imagination, are there, helping to improve the text while it is being written.

Section 5: The literati

The literati would have had no trouble imagining the reaction of the readership for whom they were writing. The literati knew each other, they lived in each other's intellectual pockets, and were forever visiting each other. There were many close friendships, for example those between David Hume and Adam Smith, between Adam Smith and John Millar, and between Lord Kames and Thomas Reid. There were also many family ties, such as, at Edinburgh University, the father–son relation of Alexander Monro *primus*, first professor of anatomy, and Alexander Monro *secundus*, who was also professor of anatomy, and the father–son relation of Matthew Stewart, professor of mathematics, and Dugald Stewart, who succeeded his father in the mathematics chair before transferring to the chair of moral philosophy. There were other such happy coincidences in Edinburgh, and also in Glasgow, for example Principal Davidson and his son Robert, regius professor of civil law, and at Aberdeen, for example Alexander Gerard, professor of moral philosophy, who was succeeded by his son Gilbert. The only major literatus who seems not to have been more or less closely related by blood to another literatus was Adam Smith.

The literati set up societies, scores of them, in which they could further enjoy each other's company and could discuss and debate. The societies are found widespread across Scotland though especially in Glasgow, Edinburgh and Aberdeen, which were the three chief university towns of the eighteenth century and the great centres of Enlightenment activity. St Andrews, and in particular the university, made little impact upon the Scottish Enlightenment, perhaps in part because its university was not surrounded by a bustling commercial, legal or ecclesiastical life with which it could interact. To appreciate the significance of this last point it is sufficient to note the extent to which Adam Smith was aided in his work on the *Wealth of Nations* by his numerous conversations with the Glasgow merchants who had already established many trading links with North America, links which were then adding to the wealth of the city, and which gave the merchants insights into, for example, the strengths and weakness of a policy of free trade.

As regards Edinburgh one society of particular importance was the Rankenian Club, founded in 1717 and named after Thomas Ranken, the owner of the hostelry on the west side of Hunter Square where the Club convened. *The Scots Magazine* for May 1771 affirmed: 'It is well known, that the Rankenians were highly instrumental in disseminating through Scotland freedom of thought, boldness of disquisition, liberality of sentiment, accuracy of reasoning, correctness of taste, and attention to composition; and that the exalted rank which Scotsmen hold at present in the Republic of Letters, is greatly owing to the manner and spirit begun by that Society.'

Even allowing for a measure of exaggeration in this judgment, it is plain from the membership list that the Club contained a heady mix of intellectuals whose discussions and disputes were almost bound to have a creative outcome. Among the members were William Wishart (c.1692–1753) (principal of Edinburgh University), John Stevenson (1695–1775) (professor of logic at Edinburgh), George Turnbull (1698–1748) (professor of moral philosophy at Marischal College, Aberdeen), Colin Maclaurin (1698–1746) (professor of mathematics at Edinburgh), John Pringle (1707–82) (professor of moral philosophy at Edinburgh and later president of the Royal Society of London), Sir Alexander Dick (1703–85) (president of the Royal College of Physicians) and Alexander Boswell of Auchinleck (1706–82) (a Lord of Session). The Select Society, another prominent Enlightenment club, was founded in Edinburgh in 1754 by the portrait painter Allan Ramsay (1713–84) jointly with David Hume and Adam Smith. Among the membership were Lord Elibank (1703–78), Hugh Blair (1718–1800) (professor of rhetoric and belles lettres at Edinburgh), Lord Dundas (1742–1811) (president of the

Court of Session), William Cullen (1710–90) (professor of chemistry at Glasgow), Adam Ferguson (1723–1816) (professor of natural philosophy and then of moral philosophy at Edinburgh), William Robertson (1721–93) (principal of Edinburgh University), the Earl of Dunmore (1730–1809) and David Hume's kinsman Henry Home (1696–1782), who was raised to the Bench as Lord Kames. It was instituted as a debating society, in which any topic could be debated 'except such as regard Revealed Religion, or which may give occasion to vent any principles of Jacobitism'.

In the latter part of the Scottish Enlightenment the Oyster Club was formed in Edinburgh. John Playfair, professor first of mathematics and then of natural philosophy at the university, composed a brief but affectionate portrait of the club:

> This club met weekly; the original members of it were Mr Smith, Dr Black, and Dr Hutton, and round them was soon formed a knot of those who knew how to value the familiar and social converse of these illustrious men. As all the three possessed great talents, enlarged views, and extensive information, without any of the stateliness and formality which men of letters think it sometimes necessary to affect; as they were all three easily amused; were equally prepared to speak and to listen; and as the sincerity of their friendship had never been darkened by the least shade of envy; it would be hard to find an example, where every thing favourable to good society was more perfectly united, and every thing adverse more entirely excluded. The conversation was always free, often scientific, but never didactic or disputatious; and as this club was much the resort of the strangers who visited Edinburgh, from any object connected with art or with science, it derived from thence an extraordinary degree of variety and interest. (Playfair and Ferguson, 'James Hutton & Joseph Black', p.98)

Among its members, apart from the three founders already mentioned, were John Playfair himself, Robert Adam, Dugald Stewart, Henry Mackenzie, Sir James Hall and John Clerk of Eldin.

Glasgow likewise could boast such societies. Alexander Carlyle, the most important autobiographer of the Scottish Enlightenment, reports that during his days as a student at Glasgow, 1743–5, the city was bustling with intellectual clubs. (See K. Holcomb in Hook and Sher, *The Glasgow Enlightenment*, p.95) Among the members of the Literary Society of Glasgow (founded 1752) were Joseph Black (1728–99) (professor of chemistry at Glasgow), William Cullen, Thomas Reid (1710–96) (professor of moral philosophy at Glasgow), William Leechman (1706–85) (professor of divinity), James Watt (1736–1819) (inventor of the improved version of the Newcomen steam engine) and John Anderson (1726–96) (founder of Anderson's Institute, later the University of Strathclyde). Aberdeen's Philosophical Society included Thomas Reid, George Campbell (1719–96) (principal of Marischal College), Alexander Gerard (1728–95) (professor of moral philosophy at Marischal College), and James Beattie (1735–1803) (professor of moral philosophy and logic at Marischal). Finally, the Philosophical Society of Edinburgh, one of the most prominent of the societies of the literati, became in 1783 the Royal Society of Edinburgh, whose founder members included William Robertson (1721–93), William Cullen, John Robison (1739–1805) (professor of natural philosophy at Edinburgh), Hugh Blair, Adam Ferguson and Adam Smith.

Most of these men will feature in the following chapters. I mention them here to indicate the extent to which clubs and societies figured in their lives. The point to be stressed, which will assume greater significance in the later stages of this book, is the disparateness of their fields of expertise, mathematics, physics, geology, chemistry, medicine, logic, rhetoric, moral philosophy, theology, classical languages, sociology, economics, commerce, history, painting, architecture, town planning. Discourse in such disparate, brilliant company is bound to provide new perspectives and yield new insights. It was community thinking at its dazzling best, a perfect outcome of the Enlightenment imperative: 'Think with others.'

It might be added that the lists of names of members of the Enlightenment societies and, even more, the lists of those who were known to have been the leading lights in them, point up the fact that the societies were largely composed of professional men rather than aristocrats. Many of the 'lords' who figure in them were law lords who had worked their way up through their profession. The Scottish Enlightenment was a triumph of the Scottish middle class.

The reference just made to the 'men' of the Scottish Enlightenment was intentional. There were no women among the first rank of contributors, though there were many women who made a significant contribution. The place of women in Scottish culture is a topic that surfaces often during the century of Enlightenment, for example in Allan Ramsay's play *The Gentle Shepherd* (1725). Mause, an educated woman, is accused by Bauldy of being able to 'o'ercast the Night, and cloud the Moon, / And mak the Deils obedient to her Crune'. She replies:

> This fool imagines, as do mony sic
> That I'm a Wretch in Compact with Auld Nick,
> Because by education I was taught
> To speak and act aboon their common Thought.
>
> (Ramsay, *Works*, vol.2, p.232)

And if we turn now to Allan Ramsay the painter, son of Allan Ramsay the poet, in *A Dialogue on Taste* (1755) the painter's mouthpiece Colonel Freeman gives a 'professorial kind of discourse' and then, out of deference to the feelings of the ladies present, proposes a change of subject. Lady Modish objects immediately: 'And truly, Colonel, you ought to make us some apology for breaking off a serious conversation on our account; as if we were incapable of being entertained by anything but trifles! It is true we are seldom tried with anything else, but that is not so much our fault as that of you men; who think, no doubt, to preserve your authority the better by keeping us in ignorance.' It is nice to see father and son so much in agreement, even if they are discussing a disagreeable phenomenon. Nevertheless in literature and painting, and other fields also, there were women who produced notable work. But not in philosophy unless one

includes Lady Mary Shepherd (1777–1847), daughter of the third
Earl of Rosebery, who wrote, however, very much at the tail-end
of the Scottish Enlightenment.

A striking feature of the societies was the fact that besides
the wide range of disciplines represented by the membership as
a whole, very many of the literati were themselves a master of
many disciplines. Reflecting the tradition, which survived into the
eighteenth century in Scottish universities, of the regent master
who would guide his students through the entire arts faculty
syllabus, Adam Smith produced work of major importance on
moral philosophy, economics, jurisprudence and rhetoric. He was
also a brilliant social historian and in addition wrote knowledgeably
on the history of science. Thomas Reid, perhaps the deepest of the
philosophers of the Scottish Enlightenment, wrote masterpieces on
the nature of mind and on human action. He was also a powerful
mathematician and wrote extensively on the life sciences, and in
addition he wrote on rhetoric and jurisprudence. His disparate
talents reinforced each other to great effect. In the course of his
first book, *An Inquiry into the Human Mind*, on the philosophy of
perception, he develops in detail a non-Euclidean geometry which
he then deploys in a formidable argument against Hume. Lord
Kames wrote numerous books on the law, but also composed
large works on aesthetics, moral philosophy, religion, education,
history and agriculture. Sir John Sinclair (1754–1835), apart from
his massive compilation, *The Statistical Account of Scotland*, also
wrote extensively on banking, agriculture and town planning (he
planned the new town of Thurso).

The situation here described invites contrast with the context of
scholars of the previous century, men such as Robert Leighton,
Henry Scougall, Robert Sibbald and Archibald Pitcairne for whom
the country did not provide anything remotely comparable with the
richly and complexly interwoven cultural context enjoyed by the
literati. And above all what the seventeenth-century scene lacked
were the numerous, varied and intellectually vibrant societies that
proved in the eighteenth century to be such a powerful catalyst
for creative thinking.

There is no evidence that the Government looked askance as these clever men argued their way through the decades of Enlightenment, taking up any and every subject, debating and disputing, putting their thoughts into the public domain with a view to persuading, or being persuaded by, others. The Government did not think to close down the clubs when government policy was criticised. And while many (or perhaps most) of the high flying evangelical churchmen believed that some of the clubs harboured dangerous atheists, the Kirk did not move to secure the closure of any club, and would certainly have failed had it so moved. In any case the Kirk was not a monolith. As spectacular testimony of this fact, though many churchmen were appalled at the very idea of theatre, thinking it a focus of immorality and unbelief, it was a churchman no less, the Reverend John Home, minister of Athelstaneford, who wrote *Douglas* (1756), the most famous play of the Scottish Enlightenment, and four prominent figures in the Church, William Robertson, Hugh Blair, Alexander Carlyle and Lord Kames, worked to ensure its performance.

I think that it is in the light of considerations such as these that we should read Hume's statement in the Introduction to his *Treatise of Human Nature*: 'So true it is, that however other nations may rival us in poetry, and excel us in some other agreeable arts, the improvements in reason and philosophy can only be owing to a land of toleration and liberty.' The liberty of the country is emphasised at the end of Hume's *History of England* where, writing of the period after the Glorious Revolution of 1688, he writes '. . . we, in this island, have ever since enjoyed, if not the best system of government, at least the most entire system of liberty, that ever was known amongst mankind.' (vol.6, p.531) Elsewhere Hume writes: 'Nothing is more apt to surprize a foreigner, than the extreme liberty, which we enjoy in this country, of communicating whatever we please to the public, and of openly censuring every measure, entered into by the king or his ministers. If the administration resolve upon war, it is affirmed, that, either wilfully or ignorantly, they mistake the interests of the nation . . . If the passion of the ministers lie towards peace, our political writers breathe nothing but war and devastation.' (Essay: 'Of the liberty of the press', opening lines, in *Essays*, pp.9–13) For Hume this 'extreme liberty', which he describes as a 'peculiar privilege', is grounds for celebration.

It should be noted however that he speaks of 'extreme' liberty only in relation to political authority; and not also in relation to ecclesiastical. As regards ecclesiastical authority, enlightened Scotland had some way to go, as we shall see in due course from a consideration of Hume's career. But the great progress made, post-Union, by the Kirk in the direction of attaching high value to liberty is evidenced by the words of Moderator of the General Assembly, William Robertson, at the close of his *History of Scotland*: 'And the Scots, after being placed during a whole century [1603–1707], in a situation no less fatal to their liberty than to the taste and genius of the nation, were at once put in possession of privileges more valuable than those which their ancestors had formerly enjoyed; and every obstruction that had retarded their pursuit, or prevented their acquisition of literary fame, was totally removed.' (Robertson, *History of Scotland*, vol.2, p.260) For Robertson the period between the Union of the Crowns and the Union of the Parliaments had been a catastrophe, with Scotland's aristocracy suborned and the Scots become as if a conquered nation. There was, in Robertson's judgment, some light in that dark century. Notably there was Andrew Fletcher of Saltoun, 'the patriot', who railed against the Union of the Crowns as destructive of Scottish liberties; though it has to be added that Robertson disagreed with Fletcher about essentials, for Fletcher was convinced that liberty of the citizens would not be recovered except by an independent Scotland, whereas Robertson was a committed unionist.

Section 6: The age of criticism

Reference was made earlier to the Age of Enlightenment as an age of criticism in the sense of 'critical reflection or analysis'. Nothing was reflected on or analysed more closely than religious belief, in particular, belief in the existence of God. Were there any sound arguments for God's existence, and for his attributes, such as omniscience, omnipotence and omnibenevolence? And what of other religious beliefs? Which of them could withstand cross-examination before the tribunal of reason? At one time or another many of the leading literati, for example, David Hume, Adam Smith, Lord Kames and James Hutton, were berated by the Kirk, or at least by sections of it, for cutting across Kirk doctrine, and in at least one important case the person's reputation for unbelief was an effective bar to a university post.

The fact that this happened does not suggest to us an era of 'extreme liberty', but it must have seemed just such an era to the literati themselves. For in order to get a sense of the perspective of the literati we should compare Enlightenment Scotland with the country during the preceding decades, and we must therefore note the career of an Edinburgh student Thomas Aikenhead. He matriculated at Edinburgh University in 1693, and proceeded to the study of arts. In November 1696 he was charged with blasphemy. According to depositions against him, some of them made by fellow students, he held that theology 'was a rapsidie of faigned and ill-invented nonsense, patched up partly of the morall doctrine of philosophers, and partly of poeticall fictions and extravagant chimeras'. And he is also reported as saying that the New Testament is 'the History of the Impostor Christ', and it is claimed that he 'learned magick in Egypt'. He was also held to have said that 'God, the world, and nature, are but one thing, and that the world was from eternity.'

Aikenhead was indicted under two laws, the first, of 1661, prescribing the death penalty for anyone who, while of sound mind, 'shall rail upon or curse God, or any of the persons of the blessed Trinity'. The second law confirmed the 1661 law and in addition covered those who 'shall deny, impugn or quarrel, argue or reason, against the being of God, or any of the persons of the blessed Trinity, or the Authority of the Holy Scriptures of the old and new Testaments, or the providence of God in the Government of the World'. On Christmas Eve 1696 he was found guilty and sentenced to death. On 6 January 1697 the General Assembly of the Church of Scotland encouraged the king to execute vigorously the laws restraining 'the abounding of impiety and profanity in this land' (Hunter, 'Aikenhead the Atheist', p.237) and just two days later Aikenhead was hanged. He was the last person to be executed in Britain for heresy, and Lord Macaulay was moved to describe the hanging as 'a crime such as has never since polluted the island'. (Hunter, 'Aikenhead the Atheist', p.221) It was a bad decade for Scotland; a year after Aikenhead's death six were found guilty in Paisley of the charge of witchcraft, and five were hanged.

In the 1740s, and therefore well into the Age of Enlightenment in Scotland, there were many in the Kirk whose attitude resembled that of Aikenhead's accusers. William Leechman, elected professor of divinity at Glasgow in 1743, with the support of the university's moral philosophy professor, Francis Hutcheson, was charged with heresy almost immediately upon his appointment. Hutcheson himself had already been in trouble because of his alleged liberalism on matters of religion, but his problems were fewer than Leechman's. The latter wrote about his predicament to a friend:

> I don't believe it is possible for one in your Situation to imagine to what hight bigottry and nonsense in Religion prevails in this Country, especially in this part of it: There is not one Man in the Presbytery of Glasgow, with whom I can use any freedom in discoursing on Religion, or from whom I can expect friendship in the present affair [Leechman's trial on a charge of heresy], except one intimate Companion, who is quite disregarded by the rest of them. From this view of my present Situation, you may easily perceive, how difficult a task it must be to teach pure and genuine Christianity, and at the same [time] not to expose myself to the fury of Bigots. (quoted in Ross, *Life of Adam Smith*, p.59)

Yet Leechman was a deeply religious man, this notwithstanding Hume's description of him as an atheist. Hume read Leechman's sermon *On the nature, reasonableness, and advantages of prayer; with an attempt to answer the objections against it. A sermon* (1743), and declared to his close friend William Mure of Caldwell, a former student of Leechman's at Edinburgh: '. . . I am sorry to find the

Author to be a rank Atheist. You know (or ought to know) that Plato says there are three kinds of Atheists. The first who deny a Deity, the second who deny his Providence, the third who assert, that he is influenc'd by Prayers or Sacrifices. I find Mr Leechman is an Atheist of the last kind.' (*New Letters*, p.11) Of course there is a certain irony in Hume, of all people, describing Glasgow's professor of divinity as an atheist. But indeed, using Plato's third account of what an atheist is, Hume would say that all of the elders in the Presbytery of Glasgow were atheists. Leechman's problems arose because his beliefs were thought not to coincide with those of most of the elders in the local Presbytery. But if the Presbytery's judgment of Leechman was so harsh then what would they think of David Hume, who was widely regarded as an atheist? Nothing tells us more about the level of toleration in Scottish society than Scotland's treatment of Hume, and I should like now to say something about this matter as a way of illustrating the extent to which Scotland had become an enlightened place by the middle of the eighteenth century.

Though Hume had a reputation for moral scepticism as well as for atheism the worst that happened to him was that he failed in his attempt first to become professor of moral philosophy at Edinburgh in 1745 and then professor of logic and rhetoric at Glasgow in 1752. His failure in both cases was due principally to the Kirk which managed without difficulty to stop his candidacy in its tracks. In both cases there were other factors, aside from his alleged atheism, working against Hume's candidacy. One such was his views on morality. Of particular importance was the opinion of Francis Hutcheson who accused Hume of 'lacking warmth in the cause of virtue'. But it was mainly Hume's reputed views on religion that were the express cause of his failure. Hume's letters tell the story. In August 1744 he was able to write: 'The accusation of Heresy, Deism, Scepticism, Atheism &c &c &c. was started against me; but never took, being bore down by the contrary Authority of all the good Company in Town'. (*Letters*, vol.1, pp.57–8) But eight months later he writes: 'I am inform'd, that such a popular Clamour has been raisd against me in Edinburgh, on account of Scepticism, Heterodoxy & other hard Names, which confound the ignorant, that my Friends find some Difficulty, in working out the Point of my Professorship, which once appear'd so easy.' (*Letters*, vol.1, p.59) The advice of the fifteen ministers of Edinburgh was sought by the town council and it proved decisive. Twelve voted against Hume and three in favour. Things fared no better in Glasgow where his candidacy for the logic and rhetoric chair had to face many obstacles, including the right of the Glasgow Presbytery to give advice on Hume's religious and moral fitness for the post. (*Letters*, vol.1, p.164)

Although none of this bespeaks 'extreme liberty' Hume was never charged with heresy, even less was he hanged for it. On the contrary, immediately after his failure to secure the Glasgow chair a move was made to have him appointed librarian of the Advocates' Library in Edinburgh. Once again he was opposed by men concerned about his views on religion. But this time, as he reports: 'I carried the election by a considerable majority, to the great joy of all bystanders.' (*Letters*, vol.1, p.165) Hume was no doubt telling the plain truth in reporting the popularity of his success. For despite the hostility of many ministers, he was a popular man whose presence in Edinburgh was widely regarded as grounds for celebration, not regret. He was much more than merely tolerated, and this indicates the moral distance covered since the Aikenhead affair, though there was a considerable distance yet to be covered.

This is easily demonstrated, for on Hume's death in 1776 Adam Smith wrote a letter, published shortly afterwards, in which he said of Hume: 'Upon the whole, I have always considered him, both in his lifetime and since his death, as approaching as nearly to the idea of a perfectly wise and virtuous man, as perhaps the nature of human frailty will permit.' (*Correspondence*, no.178) The letter provoked a ferocious response from a variety of Christian sources, so much so that Smith was driven to remark: 'A single, and as, I thought, a very harmless Sheet of paper, which I happened to Write concerning the death of our late friend Mr Hume, brought upon me ten times more abuse than the very violent attack I

had made upon the whole commercial system of Great Britain.'
(*Correspondence*, no.208)

As hinted earlier, to demonstrate that a country enjoyed an Age
of Enlightenment it is not necessary to demonstrate that during
that period all the citizens were enlightened. Instead the question
is whether, and if so then to what extent, writers could put their
ideas into the public domain without fear from the political or
religious authorities. There were still bigots in the second half
of the eighteenth century in Scotland, and they would certainly
have silenced Smith had they had the power. But they were far
from powerless. Hume's last work, *Dialogues Concerning Natural
Religion*, on which he worked intermittently for about twenty-five
years, was not published till after Hume's death, because he did
not wish to stir up more opposition than was necessary. In one
of his last letters to his publisher William Strahan he wrote of
the book: 'I have hitherto forborne to publish it, because I was
of late desirous to live quietly, and keep remote from all Clamour:
For though it be not more exceptionable than some things I had
formerly published; yet you know some of these were thought very
exceptionable; and in prudence, perhaps, I ought to have suppressed
them.' (*Letters*, vol.2, p.323) Hume left to Adam Smith the task of
seeing the *Dialogues* through the press, but Smith demurred and
in the end it was left to Hume's nephew David to see to the
publication of the work. It is probable, though not certain, that
Smith was simply looking for a quiet life and was reluctant to stir
up stridently hostile reactions such as had greeted the affectionate
portrait of Hume that he published shortly after Hume's death. But
in any case it is clear that there were segments of the Kirk who at
least had the power to make life very unpleasant for people they
thought heterodox.

It might be thought that the Enlightenment was essentially
anti-establishment, on the grounds that the Enlightenment thinkers
were engaged in critical thinking in which much of the target of their
negative criticism was the dead hand of authority, and especially
the authority of the Church and of the State. Arguably in some
countries, such as France, the Enlightenment was anti-establishment,

but things were different in Scotland, perhaps for the reason that Hume had highlighted, namely that to a degree exceptional in Europe this was a country of toleration and liberty. The Kirk was no doubt part of the establishment, but it has to be recalled that it was not a monolith and that while many ministers were intolerant of expressions of Enlightenment values, other ministers, such as William Robertson and Hugh Blair, were spokesmen for just such values. The same may be said of the legal institutions, which were certainly part of the establishment and yet which boasted leaders of the Enlightenment.

Section 7: Improvement

It is commonly held that the drive for improvement was central to the Enlightenment project, and in a sense it was, but as regards realistic prospects for progress the general stance among the literati was that of a guarded or qualified optimism. The exercise of autonomous reason was seen as enabling people to break out of the constraints of old technologies and old ideas of how to manage our physical circumstances, and to secure advances in ideas relating to such things as agriculture, transport, manufacture, all of these being areas of economic activity that were seen as impacting directly on the standard of living and therefore on the quality of life of the citizens. It is no accident that one of the masterworks written during the Age of Enlightenment in Scotland was Adam Smith's *An Inquiry into the Nature and Causes of the Wealth of Nations*. Smith's work was not of merely theoretical interest; he wanted to know how wealth was produced, because he believed that such knowledge would enable people, and especially governments, to plan more efficiently for wealth creation. Smith's motive for writing the *Wealth of Nations* was therefore not far removed from the motive of Sir John Sinclair, who in the 1790s compiled the multi-volume *Statistical Account of Scotland* which provides a detailed picture of everyday life in every parish in the country, and especially of the economic, educational, ecclesiastical and other resources available in the parishes. Sinclair tells us what he means by 'statistical': 'the idea I annex to the term, is an enquiry into the state of the country, *for the purpose of ascertaining the* quantum *of happiness enjoyed by its inhabitants, and the means of its future improvement.'*

Smith and Sinclair were key figures in the Scottish Enlightenment, and the fact that both were practical men intent on showing how improvement was practically possible signifies an essential feature of the thinking of the literati. But improvement is one thing and utopianism is another, and there is no suggestion in this that there was a serious streak of utopianism in the thinking of the literati. Whether or not Calvinist preoccupations with depravity were a stumbling block to utopian aspirations in Scotland, the fact is that the literati in general held that progress had to be fought for, and that while we could indeed achieve it by our own efforts, improvements would not remain unless we fought to preserve them. We shall meet with many examples of this attitude to improvement. Two will suffice here.

Adam Smith argued that the greatest improvement of the productive power of labour was due to the division of labour. Where such a division is made, a complex task is shared out between a number of workers each of whom performs repeatedly one of the simpler tasks out of which the complex task is composed. To take Smith's famous example, the making of a pin is composed of at least eighteen sub-tasks. If these are shared among ten men, each doing the same thing repeatedly, the team can produce 48,000 pins in one day, whereas one man working entirely by himself could scarcely produce even one. Hence division of labour looks like good economics. But Smith saw that such a system of labour had bad consequences for the workers. Their work 'is so simple and uniform as to give little exercise to the understanding; while, at the same time, their labour is so constant and so severe, that it leaves them little leisure and less inclination to apply to, or even think of anything else'. (*Wealth of Nations*, p.785) This state of affairs bears down on the spirit of the worker: 'The torpor of his mind renders him, not only incapable of relishing or bearing a part in any rational conversation, but of conceiving any generous, noble, or tender sentiment, and consequently of forming any just judgment concerning many even of the ordinary duties of private life.' (p.782)

In the early stages of the industrial revolution therefore Adam Smith saw what would in due course prove to be one of the great problems that it engendered. But he also prescribed the solution, namely a system of state-funded education, designed primarily to counteract the mind-numbing effects of the systematic application of the principle of the division of labour. I shall consider an important aspect of this point in Chapter 4. For the present, the point to be emphasised is that though the national economic progress through which Smith was living was built on the division of labour, he regarded the progress as a mixed blessing. Indeed his view was that the division of labour had consequences that were not only morally but also economically undesirable, since a demoralised workforce was likely to be inefficient. There is no hint in Smith's writings that economic development is ever sure. Two steps forward might be followed by one step, or even two steps, back, and in so far as economic solutions generate problems, gains have to be protected; furthermore those protective means have themselves to be watched lest their impact too prove morally damaging.

Undoubtedly the Enlightenment movement saw itself as directed towards improvement, and saw the autonomous use of reason as the chief instrument in the struggle. But the literati were well aware of the limitations of reason, none more so than David Hume, ever sceptical about its power to deliver solutions, and particularly sceptical about its power in the field of religion. This takes me to the second example of qualified optimism about the power of reason to deliver improvement. Hume recognised the need to use reason to fight 'bigotry and superstition', but he did not believe in the possibility of a total victory in this field, for there are principles in human nature that work towards the defeat of reason. In *An Enquiry Concerning Human Understanding* Hume argues against the possibility of decisive evidence in support of miracles. He claims to have found an argument which 'if just, will, with the wise and learned, be an everlasting check to all kinds of superstitious delusion, and consequently, will be useful as long as the world endures. For so long, I presume, will the accounts of miracles and prodigies be found in all history, sacred and profane'.

(sect.10, part 1, p.110) It should be emphasised that Hume believes that his argument, if just, will have a salutory effect on the 'wise and learned'. This is a highly qualified judgment of the power of his argument, for how many of us are wise and learned? Plainly Hume thinks that as long as the world endures there will be others who are neither wise nor learned, and who will be impervious to Hume's powers of persuasion.

Which is not, of course, to imply that time spent battling against superstition is time wasted. It was, after all, to that battle as much as to anything that Hume dedicated his life. He was even fighting it on his death bed. Practically the last thing he wrote was a paragraph to be inserted in part 12, the final part, of the *Dialogues Concerning Natural Religion*. In that paragraph he argued (in the person of his mouthpiece Philo) that the dispute between theist and atheist is at base merely verbal: 'Where then, cry I to both these antagonists, is the subject of your dispute? The theist allows, that the original intelligence is very different from human reason: The atheist allows, that the original principle of order bears some remote analogy to it. Will you quarrel, Gentlemen, about the degrees, and enter into a controversy, which admits not of any precise meaning, nor consequently of any determination?' Hume was not in an unqualified sense anti-religion, but he was in an unqualified sense against what he identified as superstition, superstition being a form of religion unable to survive cross-examination before the tribunal of reason. Hume would not object to a rational religion, a religion which exists entirely within the bounds of reason and which is therefore able to survive such a cross-examination. Its content would be primarily, or even solely, moral, and observance would lead to or perhaps consist in the exercise of civic virtue. It would not engender a church some of whose members have the power to coerce others; on the contrary, all motivation to live according to the practical principles of a rational religion must derive from the individual's own recognition of the validity of those principles. In this sense each adherent is his own authority, and in consequence this religion is one without hierarchy. There is no doubt that Hume would find such a religion fully congenial, and in a sense he dedicated himself to promoting it. In accepting it he was in accord with the spirit of the Enlightenment, but he was however also in accord with the Enlightenment in his pessimism over whether such a religion could ever replace superstition. The author of *A Treatise of Human Nature* believed that he understood human nature sufficiently well to recognise an irrepressible irrationalism at home in the human soul.

THREE

History and Enlightenment

Section 1: Why study the past?

In Chapter 2 I emphasised the fact that the Scottish Enlightenment was heir to a rich cultural tradition that included a wide range of profound contributions to disciplines which were in due course to become key disciplines of the Scottish Enlightenment. I believe that the failure to acknowledge this inheritance has led to a serious distortion in the received history of Scottish culture, a distortion that ill serves our understanding not only of the earlier periods but also of the Enlightenment. It ill serves the former because it fails to acknowledge the many brilliant achievements of earlier times, and it ill serves the latter because it closes off lines of enquiry whose pursuit would disclose new depths and subtleties in the complexly woven texture of the Scottish Enlightenment. The lines of enquiry I have in mind particularly concern the manifold relations, conceptual and historical, between the earlier and later periods. Familiarity with the earlier writings can lead one to see with fresh eyes the perhaps over-familiar writings of the Enlightenment; and with fresh eyes one sees new and valuable things.

One key discipline of the Scottish Enlightenment is historiography, the writing of history, and to avoid the distorted view that it was in the eighteenth century that Scottish historiography came into its own, it has to be stressed that that century was the second of the two great periods of Scottish historiography, the first being the sixteenth century during the decades on either side of the Scottish Reformation. The sixteenth century is notable for major histories by, among others, John Mair (*Historia Maioris Britanniae*), Hector Boece (*Scotorum Historiae*), George Buchanan (author of the wide ranging *Rerum Scoticarum Historia*) and John Knox, historian of the Scottish Reformation. In all these writings there is a large political or religious agenda either on or just below the surface. For example, in his *History of Greater Britain* (the title is a pun;

it could also be translated as *Mair's History of Britain*) Mair argues that an Anglo-Scottish union is preferable to the state of affairs then obtaining, namely two countries with a common border and strong mutual distrust and hostility. The dedicatee of the book, James V, who was the son of a Scottish king, James IV, and grandson of an English king, Henry VII, was a fitting symbol of Mair's agenda. By the time the book, first printed in 1521, was reprinted in 1740, the union for which Mair had argued had come to pass.

Mair's *History* was little read in his own day. Hector Boece's *Scotorum Historiae* (Paris, 1527), on the other hand, which traces the Scots back to the Greek warrior Gathelus (progenitor of the Gaels) and the princess Scota at the court of Pharaoh, had a wide popular readership. Boece was less respectful than Mair of standards of historical evidence that would be acceptable today, and he produced, under the heading 'history', many stories that Mair would have dismissed as frankly incredible. Nevertheless Boece knew how to hold a reader's attention, and his stories were important in enabling the Scots, blessed with such amazing ancestry, to hold their heads proudly among the nations of the world. Mair, with his eye on other histories of the Scots, affirmed in the preface to his *History*: '. . . with those who have given themselves to the pursuit of knowledge, it is of more moment to understand aright, and clearly to lay down the truth on any matter, than to use elegant and highly coloured language'. (p.cxxxv)

One notable feature of my short list of sixteenth-century Scottish historians is that all had had a training in philosophy and theology; two of them indeed had been distinguished teachers in these fields in the University of Paris before returning to major university appointments in Scotland. The parallel with Enlightenment Scotland should hold our attention, for all the leading Scottish historians of the eighteenth century had also had a training in philosophy; among them were Hume, Smith, Kames, George Turnbull and Ferguson, all of whom made major contributions to the philosophical culture of the country, and another of the major historians, William Robertson, was one of the leading churchmen of the age. Matching Boece's achievement with the *Scotorum Historiae*, during the Age of

Enlightenment no academic discipline had a more popular appeal than history and Hume and his friends found within Scotland an avid readership.

There are no doubt special reasons why Scots of the eighteenth century might have found history so absorbing and I shall come to those reasons later, but first we should note Scottish Enlightenment reponses to the question why, aside from local reasons, the study of history might be a valuable exercise. Both Hutcheson and Hume have interesting things to say on this matter.

In the course of his account of beauty, Hutcheson discusses the fact that 'the taste or relish of it [history] is universal in all nations'. He believes that essential to our perception of a thing as beautiful is our recognition of it as having uniformity or unity amidst diversity, and holds that it is this recognition that explains why reading a collection of 'gazettes', which merely describe the external events that occurred, is always found boring compared with the reading of history, where we are presented with 'a character well drawn wherein we find the secret causes of a great diversity of seemingly inconsistent actions' and where we see 'an artful view nicely unfolded, the execution of which influences very different and opposite actions as the circumstances may alter'. (Hutcheson, *Philosophical Writings*, p.35) The point here is that numerous, seemingly disparate and unconnected events are presented by the historian as having a real unity. This unity amidst the diversity of disparate events prompts us to see in the story a beauty that we would never find in a gazette, which simply lists facts. The beauty of the historical narrative ensures that the narrative captures and holds our interest and attention.

Hutcheson here indicates that an important part of the business of the historian is the provision of historical explanations. The good historian says not merely what events occurred, but also why they did; not only what a person did, but also what motivated him. When we know the 'why', we see the agent's actions not just as one thing after another, but instead as playing their role either as expressions of his values, or relatedly as pieces falling into place in the gradual unfolding of his plan. The plan confers unity on those disparate acts, and the plan itself was devised for the sake of a goal the agent was aiming at, some outcome that he *valued*. In Hutcheson's view, exposition of that goal, considered as a principle of unity, is a main part of the business of the historian. Without that exposition the writing lacks beauty. Hutcheson is speaking solely about the quality of the historian's performance, not about the 'character' *simpliciter* of the historical personage but about what Hutcheson terms 'the character *well drawn*'. It is therefore solely the historian's *mode of presentation* that is at issue, his presentation of events, not as 'one fact after another', but as, in Hutcheson's phrase, 'unity amidst diversity'.

The second response I wish to consider to the question why the study of history is such a valuable exercise is that of Hume, whose judgment on this matter has to be treated with particular respect, first because the question of the value of history can fairly be treated as a philosophical question; and Hume always has something interesting to say on philosophical matters, and secondly because his reputation as a historian was hardly surpassed in his own day. As both a philosopher and a historian Hume seems particularly well qualified to answer the question.

In his essay 'Of the study of history' he considers three good reasons for such study. The first is perhaps the most obvious, that it amuses or entertains. It enables us to observe human society in its infancy making its first sorties into the arts and sciences; it show us 'the civility of conversation refining by degrees, and every thing which is ornamental to human life advancing towards its perfection'. (Hume, *Essays*, p.566) We see all humanity, from the beginning of time, pass in review before us in their true colours. We see the virtues which contributed to great empires, and the vices which led to their ruin. And Hume asks: 'What spectacle can be imagined, so magnificent, so various, so interesting?' (p.566) Central to this judgment is the distinction between fact and fiction. Fiction can be amusing and entertaining, but in Hume's view there is no work of fiction that tells a story more extraordinary and enthralling than many stories told by historians, who 'remark the rise, progress, declension, and final extinction of the most flourishing empires'. (p.566)

And history has the great advantage that it is true. Speaking generally, a tale gains an additional dimension of interest when it is revealed as true, and the interest and even entertainment value of a tale related as true diminishes when it is revealed to be fictitious.

This points to a second reason for studying history, the fact that it deals with truth and hence the fact that such study leads to an increase in one's stock of knowledge. Of course knowledge has an intrinsic value – it is better to be knowledgeable than ignorant – and hence the study of history also has a value. Indeed erudition, which is in large measure a deep knowledge of aspects of history, is an intellectual virtue. The study of history, as leading towards erudition, leads therefore to an improvement of the mind. Furthermore, historical knowledge is a precondition of almost all intellectual development. The development of science and the arts would be impossible without it. Knowledge of past experiences and developments means that instead of each generation having to start from scratch it is able to build upon the successes of previous generations. Scientists, knowing what previous scientists have achieved, can take up the challenge where their predecessors left off; builders and engineers likewise, and so also in the fields of arts and humanities. We make improvements today in light of results gifted to us by previous generations. Hume finds a telling way to put the point: 'And indeed, if we consider the shortness of human life, and our limited knowledge, even of what passes in our own time, we must be sensible that we should be for ever children in understanding, were it not for this invention, which extends our experience to all past ages, and to the most distant nations; making them contribute as much to our improvement in wisdom, as if they had actually lain under our observation. A man acquainted with history may, in some respect, be said to have lived from the beginning of the world, and to have been making continual additions to his stock of knowledge in every century.' (pp.566–7)

These two reasons for studying history relate respectively to the mental powers of imagination and intellect. So far as it amuses the fancy it engages the imagination. So far as it improves science it engages the intellect. But, and here we come to the third reason

Hume offers, history has the power to engage the faculty of will in the direction of virtue. If Hume is right about this then the study of history has not only a theoretical but also a practical justification. His position is based upon his observation that historians have been 'almost without exception' friends of virtue, and have painted the virtues in their true colours. In this they are to be contrasted with some poets who have made vice seem attractive. They are to be contrasted also with some philosophers who appear to have denied that there are any moral distinctions in reality. In any case historians have the advantage over philosophers, for the latter operate at a very high level of abstraction, so much so that their descriptions of virtue and vice are likely to leave the mind of the philosopher and also the minds of his readers entirely unmoved.

At the opposite end of the spectrum from the philosopher is the kind of person – Hume is thinking of the unscrupulous businessman – who always sees things through the distorting lens of self-love and self-interest. He does not restrict himself to the high level of abstraction of the philosopher, for he thinks about human beings in their individuality. But his thinking about them is thoroughly unattractive, for his sole concern is with using others for his own ends. If he wrote about people as he thought about them his readership would be repelled by the picture for we are repelled by accounts that fail to acknowledge our right to respectful treatment.

Intermediate between these two positions is that of the historian. Unlike the philosopher who describes people only abstractly and does not attend to us in our uniqueness, the historian writes about real flesh and blood people. Unlike the unscrupulous businessman the historian's perspective is not distorted or corrupted by considerations of self-love or self-interest. He takes a detached but not unkindly view; he wants to portray reality, and reality includes well-intentioned as well as ill-intentioned people. The story that the historian tells should therefore engage the emotions of the reader, who recognises that the historian is writing about real live people, and who approves of some of those people and disapproves of others. These acts of approval and of disapproval are, on Hume's analysis, moral judgments, which therefore have a natural tendency to prompt the will. In so far as the historian paints portraits of virtuous acts in their proper colours, these portraits have a natural tendency to strengthen people in their virtue. History, in short, is good for you in the most practical way possible.

It has been argued that William Robertson's historical writings were taken up as a major resource by members of the cultural élite of America in the late eighteenth century and during the nineteenth, precisely because those writings had the power to direct people's will in the direction of civic virtue. The role call of those who knew Robertson's writings well is impressive; it includes Benjamin Franklin, Thomas Jefferson, John Adams, Alexander Hamilton, Benjamin Rush and Nathaniel Carter. Robertson had been a moderniser in the Church of Scotland, rejecting attitudes of the kind that had found expression in the hanging of Aikenhead. Such attitudes, branded as fanaticism and enthusiasm, were seen by Robertson as dangerous, working against both civic peace and economic progress. In their place was the value of consensus and therefore toleration, which would bring a peaceful society and the consequent possibility of economic progress. Moderate Protestantism was the Enlightenment baptised, and this virtuous stance, call it Christian Enlightenment or enlightened Christianity, was promoted in Robertson's histories. Because of their improving qualities his books were strongly promoted, and no doubt the promotion of them contributed to the fact that in the 1820s Robertson was judged to be the most widely read historian in America. For many years his *History of America* was a school text in America, in a version (with examination questions attached) published by John Frost (1800–59), one of the most prominent educators of his era and a man whose credentials as a highly motivated moral improver are indisputable. (See Aspinwall, 'William Robertson and America', pp.152–5) As regards the international trade in invisibles, the Scottish Enlightenment is one of the most successful commodities that Scotland has ever exported. Whenever it is (if ever) that the Scottish Enlightenment ended in Scotland, there is no doubt that it thrived in America well into the nineteenth century.

In discussions of the impact of the Scottish Enlightenment on America it is common to find pride of place given to the role of the philosophical writings, especially those of the common sense school, which admittedly had a massive influence on the universities. But it may be that their influence was no greater than the historical writings, and in the case of the latter the reason for their influence was entirely in line with Hume's emphasis on the role of the study of history in confirming or strengthening virtue. It should be added that if Robertson could have such an influence as a moral improver in America, the influence on his Scottish readership could have been no less great; if anything it would surely have been greater, given his triply authoritative status as principal of Edinburgh University, Historiographer Royal and for many years leader of the Moderate Party, the reforming wing, in the Kirk. In his *History of Scotland*, a work that went through fourteen editions during his lifetime, Robertson presents a picture of seventeenth-century Scotland going down a religious and moral blind alley when it embraced the Covenanting movement – a movement with origins in 'banditry', according to Robertson. In contrast he portrays the Union of the Parliaments as leading to a strong cultural surge in Scotland: '[A]dopted into a constitution, whose genius and laws were more liberal than their own, they [the Scots] have extended their commerce, refined their manners, made improvements in the elegancies of life, and cultivated the arts and sciences.' (vol.2, p.254) 'And the Scots, after being placed, during a whole century, in a situation no less fatal to the liberty than to the taste and genius of the nation, were at once put in possession of privileges more valuable than those which their ancestors had formerly enjoyed.' (vol.2, p.260) For Robertson the Union and the Kirk, that is, the Presbyterian Church under the moderate leadership of Robertson, provided a context within which the people could extend commerce, refine manners, improve the elegancies of life, and cultivate the arts and sciences, in liberty and according to the genius of the nation. Robertson's *History of Scotland* drives home the message that these are the valuable things, which enhance the life of the individual and of the state. They are therefore things that the people should aim for; and they can be achieved by a combination of civic virtue and native genius. On the one hand the Episcopalian Church, partly on account of its close association with Jacobitism, and on the other the austere, narrow, intolerant wing of the Kirk, are portrayed as working against the virtues of Enlightenment. The readers of the *History* are thus in effect invited to reject these alternatives, the only realistic alternatives to moderate Calvinism, and to throw in their lot with civilised religion and its chief associate, civic virtue.

As regards Hume's description of the work of the historians as strengthening people in virtue, it might be said that he takes a highly charitable view of the matter. For historians can be as prejudiced as anyone else when it comes to portraying an individual or an institution. Historians often write with an agenda, as Robertson assuredly did, and the agenda can seriously distort the truth. And if the story they tell is a serious distortion then it is not a useful tool on behalf of virtue. Against this it should be said that Hume would not be impressed with the suggestion that there was anything wrong with being prejudiced in favour of Enlightenment virtues, the virtues of rationality and toleration. If one's agenda is to promote these, then one's agenda leads not to distortion of the truth but to its promotion.

In any case the vice of which Hume was seeking to absolve historians was not prejudice, but self-love or self-interest. One can be prejudiced without being prejudiced on one's own behalf. The historian, even if in fact prejudiced, can still have as his goal the impartial description of what people were like and what they did. Alternatively we might agree with Hume's account of what historians do, so long as his account is understood to be about the best historians, perceptive historians who write about real people and form impartial judgments about them. Such writers portray accurately the virtues of virtuous people, and the vices of the vicious, and Hume plainly believes that such literature is beneficial, not only as instructing us, but also as fortifying us in our virtue and as leading us to be less tolerant of our vices. Hence history not only addresses the imagination and the intellect but also the will, for through reading history we can be motivated to change ourselves. On this account of the value of studying history, an account which emanates from the heart of the Scottish Enlightenment, there could hardly be a more important academic discipline.

Hume's list of reasons for studying history is ordered according to importance; instruction is more important than entertainment, and strengthening in virtue is more important than instruction. As regards the relation between instruction and the strengthening in virtue, there is a unity here, for the better one has studied history the more one is strengthened in virtue, and the virtuous person is motivated to study history further as a means to refining and deepening his moral sensibility. The unity is a unity of theory and practice. But even if the two things united are mutually dependent, it is the practical side of the unity that has primacy. In short it is better to be a good citizen than a good scholar, though of course in practice the best citizen is the one whose sense of civic virtue has intellectual depth. It is well formed, or well informed, by suitable reading, and as regards what is suitable, Hume and Robertson would say 'history'. No doubt some would reply to the two historians: 'They would say that, wouldn't they?' What I have sought to show is that there are strong theoretical considerations underpinning the position.

The idea that history should engage the imagination, intellect and will, an idea central to Hume's exposition, duly resurfaces in student notes of the lectures that have come down to us from Adam Smith's *Lectures on Rhetoric and Belles Lettres* (*LRBL*). He writes: 'The design of historicall writing is not merely to entertain; (this perhaps is the intention of an epic poem) besides that it has in view the instruction of the reader. It sets before us the more interesting and important events of human life, points out the causes by which these events were brought about and by this means points out to us by what manner and method we may produce similar good effects or avoid Similar bad ones.' (*LRBL*, p.90) Smith is not denying the entertainment value of history. His point is that history offers something in addition.

As regards the entertainment value of human history, Smith thinks (like Hume) that it has at least as much power to entertain as other art forms do. I mention human history to contrast it with natural history, the history of plant life and of other natural phenomena. What is special about human history is that the lives of other people engage our sympathy: 'The accidents . . . which affect the human Species interest us greatly by the Sympatheticall affections they raise in us. We enter into their misfortunes, grieve when they grieve, rejoice when they rejoice, and in a word feel for them in some respect as if we ourselves were in the same condition.' (*LRBL*, p.90) At many points in his historical writings Robertson displays his ability to enter in a Smithian way into the shoes of the person he is describing. Sympathy is to the fore when Robertson describes Mary Queen of Scots being led past an angry crowd after her arrest for Darnley's murder: 'The Queen, worn out with fatigue, covered with dust, and bedewed with tears, was exposed as a spectacle to her own subjects.' (*History of Scotland*, vol.1, p367) Robertson is here using a tactic that Thucydides and other ancient historians used to great effect, a tactic that attracted the attention of Smith: 'The ancients carry us as it were into the very circumstances of the actors, we feel for them as it were for ourselves. They show us the feelings and agitation of Mind in the Actors previous to and during the Event.' (*LRBL*, p.96)

We can of course have these sympathetic reactions even to accidents that befall fictitious characters. What is important about history is that it is about the truth, what really happened; 'important' because the practical value of history depends on our taking the narrative to be true. As Smith puts it: 'The facts must be real, otherwise they will not assist us in our future conduct, by pointing out the means to avoid or produce any event. Feigned Events and the causes contrived for them, as they did not exist, can not inform us of what happened in former times, nor of consequence assist us in a plan of future conduct.' (*LRBL*, p.91)

It should be added that prior to the writings by Hume, Smith and Robertson which I have just commented on, George Turnbull of Aberdeen had already called for history to be given a particularly prominent role in the education curriculum. In 1740 he wrote: "Tis certainly one main End of Education, to form betimes a Taste for reading History with Intelligence and Reflection, and not merely for

Diversion: Now what else is this but teaching or iniuring Youth to make useful Remarks, in reading Histories, upon Men and Manners, Actions, Characters, and Events; the moral Springs and Causes of Moral Appearances; the Beauty of Virtue, and the Difformity of Vice'. (*A Treatise on Ancient Painting*, p.145) Turnbull, thinking particularly about the educative value of the 'Grand Tour' undertaken by the sons of well-to-do families, and thinking more widely about the moral health of the country, saw the teaching of history as an effective means of instilling moral values, particularly civic virtue. Turnbull writes about narrative paintings in which a story of civic virtue is related by the artist: 'The Design of moral Pictures is, therefore, by that Means, to shew us to ourselves; to reflect our Image upon us, in order to attract our Attention the more closely to it, and to engage us in Conversation with ourselves, and an accurate Consideration of our Make and Frame.' (p.147) Historical pictures therefore are seen by Turnbull as able to make a significant difference to our self-perception, to our will and therefore to our way of life. By teaching students of history about the benefits of a virtuous life, about the destructiveness of a vicious life, and by furnishing them with the powerful role models with which histories abound, a generation can be guided down the path of civic virtue. Plainly to Turnbull's mind no subject could have a more noble purpose or more noble outcome. Hume, Smith and Robertson would not disagree with a word of Turnbull's analysis.

Section 2: The dynamic of society

Given that history addresses itself to the imagination, the intellect and the will, I should like to consider briefly the second of these cases – history in its relation to intellect or understanding. We want to understand our circumstances, to know not only what is happening around us but also why it is; so far as we do not know the *why*, we do not understand the *what*. In general, if not always, to ask why something is the case is to ask about its cause, and the Enlightenment was a sustained search for causes. Natural scientists had before them a model of success, for Newton's inverse square law accounts for the position and the motion of all particles of matter;

scientists thereafter knew for example not only that planetary motion is elliptical but also *why* it is. The knowledge won by Newton is plainly universal in scope, for *every* body in the universe is subject to his law. This universality encompasses us humans also, since if every *body* is subject to that law then *everybody* is, that is, all of us. For whatever else we are, we are also bodies, composed of particles of matter. This implies of course that in at least one respect, as bundles of particles of matter, we are appropriate objects of study by natural science. As bodies we can also be investigated by anatomists, physiologists, neurologists, and so on, and they can provide for us explanations of bodily occurrences, saying not only *what* happens to us, physically speaking, but also why *that* happens rather than something else.

But there is more to us than the materials out of which our bodies are formed; we are also thinking, feeling beings, who live in societies and embody moral, political, economic, aesthetic and religious values, values that contribute, no less than our bodies do, to our humanity. These facts about us prompt the question whether there is a sense in which we, in respect of our humanity including our values, are also proper objects of study by natural science. This question is one which can best be answered empirically, that is, by applying the methods of natural science to human beings and seeing whether the application leads to progress in understanding ourselves. Such progress would confirm the view that we are, in respect of our social and cultural dimensions, parts of nature.

The literati wrote a good deal on this topic and sought to demonstrate that we are indeed proper objects of natural science, and in particular that empirical scientific investigation of human beings can yield deeper understanding of human nature, and of our institutions, political, religious, legal, economic, and so on, which form or inform our nature. This understanding, as already hinted, implies a knowledge of causes. The investigations deepen our understanding of our present-day institutions by demonstrating the causes both of their creation and also of the direction of their development. This understanding involves a grasp of the dynamics, the inner principles of change, in our society and its institutions, and as such is practical since it includes knowledge of how society or its institutions would react to possible future contexts, and this implies that in so far as we can control the context we can control the direction of change of society itself. We will be able to manage our society and therefore guide it along desirable pathways. Since the great watchword of the Enlightenment was 'improvement', the understanding of which I am speaking is of the highest importance in relation to the values of the Age.

Plainly the understanding here at issue requires a grasp of history. To discover the inner principles of change in a society or an institution it is necessary to discover patterns of change, and except via the study of history no such discovery is possible. We might try to work it out from first principles but the result will be a conjecture which is worthless unless tested against the empirical evidence, and the conjecture is worthless if the evidence is not available. The large-scale practical agenda of the literati was one reason why they studied history. It is noteworthy that the questionnaire, on the basis of which Sir John Sinclair compiled his *Statistical Account of Scotland*, was designed to yield information about the past with the practical aim of securing improvements for the future. For example, Sinclair asked the parish ministers: 'What was the ancient state of the population of the parish, so far as it can be traced?' and 'Is the population of the parish materially different from what it was 5, 10, or 25 years ago? and to what causes is the alteration attributed?'

Likewise, Adam Ferguson saw the study of history as of great practical value as setting us on our guard against the rise, within the most enlightened segment of society, of forces that work insidiously on behalf of civic corruption (*An Essay on the History of Civil Society* part 6, sect.5). And Adam Smith's historical studies in his *An Inquiry into the Nature and Causes of the Wealth of Nations* were all presented with a view first to uncovering the principles of change in society and then to formulating policies for economic progress. He deployed a vast range of historical information in the course of, for example, his sustained argument in favour of a particular version of a policy of free trade. The practical import of historiography is also explored by Smith in his *Lectures on Rhetoric and Belles Lettres*: 'The design of historicall writing . . . has in view the instruction of the reader. It sets before us the more interesting and important events in human life, points out the causes by which those events were brought about and by this means points out to us by what manner and method we may produce similar good effects or avoid similar bad ones.' (p.90)

This then is a major reason for the study of history. In so far as historical studies disclose the inner dynamic of a society, they disclose the grain of the society, and knowledge of the lie of the grain alerts us to the shape that social policies should have. Those which cut across the grain of society are the more likely to fail. It is plain therefore that a properly slanted study of the history of a society will yield up information of great practical significance. Such a view of the practicality of history underlies the dictum that those who do not study their history are condemned to relive it.

One further reason for the study of history should be mentioned here as relating specifically to eighteenth-century Scotland. With few exceptions among the Scottish historians, the concept of the role of providence in history was taken seriously. There was no suggestion in eighteenth-century Calvinist theology that God created the world and then walked away from it, leaving it to its own devices. This is not to say that God was thought to intervene frequently; but since he set it on a certain path, providence was at work when things worked out according to the divine plan. Thus, for example, Robertson's reference to divine providence working on the side of Protestant England in the destruction of the Spanish Armada in 1588 (*History of Scotland*, vol.2 p.166), does not imply that he believed God to have, so to say, stepped in specially on behalf of England and Protestantism. It points to a more general concept that Robertson had of human history as the gradual unfolding of a divinely ordained plan. Even if the rise of Presbyterianism to a position of pre-eminence in Scottish society in the eighteenth century can be given an explanation in terms of psychological and sociological causation, its rise was according to God's will and in the light of a concept formed in the divine intellect. From this it follows that an investigation of human history is also an investigation into the mind of God. With due humility we must accept that we can know almost nothing of God's mind by such an investigation; but it is more than nothing, by however little, and any theologian would be grateful for advance in that direction, however short the step. This consideration points to a reason, additional to those already mentioned, as to why the theologian William Robertson was preoccupied by history and by questions of historical causation. By the same token we need not be surprised that the need to gain insight into the mind of God was not one of the three reasons Hume gave as to why we should study history.

Section 3: History and national identity

One consequence of the study of history should be mentioned as relating to the experience of eighteenth-century Scotland, and especially to the experience of the Union of the Parliaments. National identity is inseparable from national history. A person who has no idea of his past has no idea who he is, and likewise a nation, to be a nation, must know its past, at least something of it. Scottish national identity after the Union of 1707 had a problematic aspect. Since the Acts of Union in 1707 created a brand new entity, a British parliament, there was no longer a Scottish parliament. Scotland had been absorbed into the new British state and, logically enough, some people called Scotland 'North Britain' and the Scots 'North British'. Of course, by the same token, England also had been absorbed into the new British state. But people did not call England 'South Britain' nor the English 'South British', largely because economically, politically and demographically England was the overwhelmingly dominant partner in the new state. The London parliament could still 'feel' English to the English, for nine tenths of the MPs sat for English constituencies. In that problematic situation the Scottish readership of histories could only be strengthened, never weakened, in their awareness of themselves as Scots. Especially they would learn that, even if the Scottish parliament had ceased to exist in 1707, Scotland remained alive and well, for the great institutions of the Church, the law and the universities, with which and through which they lived after 1707, were, legally and in every other way, the same institutions that had existed in Scotland prior to the Union. And they were therefore just as Scottish as they had always been. This is not to say that post-Union Scots did not identify themselves with Great Britain; many did, and perhaps particularly in consequence of the growth of the British Empire, a development in which Scots played a disproportionately large role. But loyalty to Britain does not exclude identification with Scotland. Concentric loyalties and adjacent loyalties are common enough: loyalty to family, friends, church, country, and so on. My point is that the work of Hume, Robertson, and others writing about the history of Scotland, would always tend to confirm Scots in their identification with Scotland, even when, as no doubt often happened, it also confirmed them in their identification with Britain.

It might indeed seem that England helped some Scots to think of themselves as Scots. In the course of correspondence with Gilbert Elliot of Minto, Hume, in a letter dated 22 September 1764, famously asserted: 'I do not believe there is one Englishman in fifty, who, if he heard that I had broke my Neck to night, woud not be rejoic'd with it. Some hate me because I am not a Tory, some because I am not a Whig, some because I am not a Christian, and all because I am a Scotsman.' (*Letters*, vol.1, p.470) These seem the words of a man confident about his national identity.

Yet Hume's position regarding his relation to Scotland was highly ambiguous, and the ambiguity is worth noting in view of Hume's pre-eminence in the Scottish Enlightenment. In the passage just quoted he is not declaring himself to be a Scot or even implying that he is one; he is speaking about the perception that others, who are English, have of him. I say this because of other parts, less well known, of that same exchange of correspondence. Gilbert Elliot had written to Hume: 'Love the French as much as you will, many of the Individuals are surely the proper objects of affection, but above all continue still an Englishman.' (Hume, *Letters*, p.469, fn.3) To which Hume, writing from Paris, replied: 'Can you seriously talk of my continuing an Englishman? Am I, or are you, an Englishman? Will they allow us to be so? Do they not treat with Derision our Pretensions to that Name, and with Hatred our just Pretensions to surpass & to govern them?' I am a Citizen of the World; but if I were to adopt any Country, it would be that in which I live at present, and from which I am determin'd never to depart, unless a War drive me into Swisserland or Italy.' (*Letters*, vol.1, p.470) It was perhaps with that period in mind that, shortly before he died, Hume wrote in his brief, moving *My Own Life*: 'I thought once of setling there [*sc*. Paris] for life.'

Of course, one should not read too much into a single case. But the case is, after all, that of Hume, who was the literatus *par exellence*, and that makes the exchange especially interesting. This most famous of Edinburgh's citizens sees himself as a 'Citizen of the World' but would choose to be French if he were to make a choice, thus confirming a remark he had made to William Robertson some five years earlier in January 1759: 'I have had some invitations, and some intentions of taking a trip to Paris; but I believe it will be safer for me not to go thither, for I might probably settle there for life.' (*Letters*, vol.1, p.294)

There are further levels of complexity indicated in Hume's letter to Gilbert Elliot where he speaks in the plural of 'our Pretensions to that Name [the name of "Englishman"]', a pretension, or claim, that seems to imply the perception not that Scotland and England had been absorbed into the new British state, but that England, also known as Britain, had absorbed Scotland. Furthermore, reference to the English not 'allowing' the Scots to call themselves English and reference to the Scots' 'pretension' to the name, imply that there were Scots, including Hume, who sought the title 'English'. Yet it was the same Hume who in July 1757 wrote, as quoted earlier, to Gilbert Elliot of Minto: 'Is it not strange that, at a time when we have lost our Princes, our Parliaments, our independent Government, even the Presence of our chief Nobility, are unhappy, in our Accent & Pronunciation, speak a very corrupt Dialect of the Tongue which we make use of; is it not strange, I say, that, in these Circumstances, we shou'd really be the People most distinguish'd for Literature in Europe?' (*Letters*, vol.1, p.255) Hume's pride in being a Scot is here undisguised. Admittedly there is a qualification – we are 'the People *most distinguish'd for Literature in Europe*'. But this hardly detracts from Hume's pride, since he tells us in *My Own Life* that literature was his ruling passion. Nothing of greater value could, in Hume's eyes, entitle any country to the accolade 'the most distinguished country in Europe'. Certainly on this matter Hume thought Scotland streets ahead of England whose literature he was later to describe to William Robertson as 'still in a somewhat barbarous state'. (*Letters*, vol.2, p.194)

Section 4: History and moral philosophy

During the Scottish Enlightenment, philosophy had, and was acknowledged to have, a significant role to play in every academic discipline. It is not surprising therefore to find explicit passages of philosophy in the histories written in Scotland during the Enlightenment and also to find philosophical agendas being more or less explicitly served by the histories. History is amusing, instructive, productive of civic virtue, a basis for national identity and, as we shall now see, it is also essential to at least one area of philosophy, in fact the area that was most in the spotlight during the Enlightenment: the study of human nature.

Hume's declared aim to 'introduce the experimental method of reasoning into moral subjects' (sub-title of *Treatise*) prompts the question of what is to count as the 'experimental method of reasoning' in such a context. In the case of dead matter we can 'carry out experiments' in the sense that we can take given substances or artifacts and subject them to a variety of tests to see how they will react. In a controlled way we burn, boil or freeze substances, and we test artifacts to destruction. If a substance or an artifact of a given kind keeps reacting in the same way to the same action performed upon it, we can reason that this is how it will always react, other things being equal. In many cases we do not have to *do* anything to a substance or artifact to get the desired information; it is sufficient that we observe how the things react if left to themselves in well understood circumstances. We do not need to put them in an appropriate variety of circumstances becauses they are in such circumstances in any case. We therefore need do no more than watch to see what happens to them. The 'experimental method of reasoning' includes observation when the observation is of the sort just described. It is not a mere seeing, but a seeing informed by experience, in particular by experience of previous similar situations. It is just such seeing that characterises the scientist when he is seeking to formulate natural laws, and it contains, as an essential part, a historical dimension, for the scientist formulating laws concerning how things of a given kind always behave, argues on the basis of his knowledge of how, in his experience, such things always have behaved. He relies on 'natural history' in the sense of the 'history of naturally occurring events'.

Everything that has just been said can be applied, with due alteration in details, to 'moral subjects'. The experimental method of reasoning is first and foremost reasoning based on observation. The experiments, so far as it is appropriate to speak of 'experiments', are observational. We do not normally carry out experiments on people. Instead we observe and take note of regularities, and on the basis of such observations we formulate laws concerning human nature. The more observations the better, in the sense that additional observations of the same regularities tend to confirm hypotheses. And the wider the range of observations the better. Observations in widely separated places and at widely separated times are more helpful to the construction of a science of human nature than are observations which are clustered around the here and now. It is for this reason that history is important. History teaches us of the nature of people in the more or less distant past. The study of history is a way of, so to say, extending our powers of observation, so that we see not only present events here through our own eyes, but also distantly past events through the eyes of the distantly past reporters who were eyewitnesses to those events. We thus discover that, just like us, distantly past people, as distantly past as reports of people go, were moved by ambition, jealousy, hate, avarice, self-love, vanity, friendship, generosity, public spirit. History, even the most ancient history available to us, is replete with descriptions of people who are just like ourselves in their emotions, motives and actions.

Histories thus contribute to the scientific account of human nature by massively extending our otherwise very limited observational data base. Hume writes:

> Mankind are so much the same, in all times and places, that history informs us of nothing new or strange in this particular. Its chief use is only to discover the constant and universal principles of human nature, by showing men in all varieties of circumstances and situations, and furnishing us with materials from which we may form our observations and become acquainted with the regular springs of human action and behaviour. These records of wars, intrigues, factions, and revolutions, are so many collections of experiments, by which the politician or moral philosopher fixes the principles of his science, in the same manner as the physician or natural philosopher becomes acquainted with the nature of plants, minerals, and other external objects, by the experiments which he forms concerning them. (Hume, *Enquiry Concerning Human Understanding*, pp.83–4)

On this account of history, it is perhaps the single most important resource for the philosopher seeking to construct a scientific account of human nature.

History teaches us about people, not just about this person and that, but about people as human beings, about what we share, our common humanity. When our knowledge rises to that level of generality, it merits the title 'science'. It was a common perception of the Scottish Enlightenment that it is only in virtue of our historical knowledge that our knowledge of human beings merits that title. This is surely just the sort of role for history that Hume has in mind when he speaks in his essay 'Of the study of history' of our using historical knowledge as a means to 'our improvement in wisdom' and of our remaining otherwise 'for ever children in understanding'. We do not increase our understanding merely in the acquisition of singular facts. We do not understand things, for example human acts and human character, except by bringing general or universal truths to bear on the singular facts.

Furthermore individual past events are better understood to the extent that we grasp the contour of their historical environment. Historians are therefore concerned with delineating the shape of the past, and of course if an event is seen as part of a shape it is seen not merely as a discrete event but also as causally related to other events, whether as their cause or their effect. But one event cannot be identified as the cause of another except on the basis of some general truth relating such events. Again, therefore, it is not just the singular that interests the historian, but the general or universal.

Section 5: Conjectural history

The origin of the British state in 1707 was well documented. Many participants in the action took the trouble to write their accounts and their opinions, and later historians have therefore a great wealth of high-class material to sift through. Other origins however are not so easily dealt with though they also attracted the attention of many writers. The eighteenth century was an age for the scrutiny of origins of all sorts, especially of origins which lie in the very distant past, such as the origin of language, society, government, religion and painting. In Chapter 2 we noted Hector Boece's account of the origin of the Scottish nation, an account that could not be expected to satisfy any of the literati since there is not a shred of evidence for it. It was for this reason that William Robertson declared that Scottish history prior to Kenneth II should be 'totally neglected or abandoned to the industry and credulity of antiquaries'. (*History of Scotland*, p.4) The only reason for accepting the stories of the early kings of Scotland is that previous historians had told the stories. But we are entitled to ask for the sources used by those historians. If we do not, but instead simply accept their word for it, then this would be to rely on authorities in a way which is not scientifically respectable, and is certainly contrary to the ideals of the Enlightenment.

A further source of information of an early state of society, in Gaeldom if not more widely in Britain, was a set of Gaelic epics translated by James Macpherson (1736–96). *The Poems of Ossian* (1763) were a huge literary success, in Europe generally and not only in Britain, despite (or even with the help of) the large controversy regarding the authenticity of the work. Major figures opposed each other in the dispute. Many editions of the *Poems* included *A Critical Dissertation on the Poems of Ossian*, by Hugh Blair, who believed in the authenticity of Macpherson's *Ossian*, in contrast to Hume, who suspected that *Ossian* was a fraud and who sought to cool Blair's enthusiasm. I mention the *Poems* here because they gave Blair an opportunity to do a good deal of conjecturing about the distant past on the basis of the translations:

> In the infancy of societies, men live scattered and dispersed, in the midst of solitary rural scenes, where the beauties of nature are their chief entertainment. They meet with many objects, to them new and strange; their wonder and surprize are frequently excited; and by the sudden changes of fortunes occurring in their unsettled state of life, their passions are raised to the utmost. Their passions have nothing to restrain them: their imagination has nothing to check it. They display themselves to one another without disguise; and converse and act in the uncovered simplicity of nature. As their feelings are strong, so their language, of itself, assumes a poetical turn. Prone to exaggerate, they describe every thing in the strongest colours; which of course renders their speech picturesque and figurative. (Blair, *Critical Dissertation*, p.2)

How did Blair know all this? If he simply deduced it all from the *Poems* then his methodology is unsatisfactory since the deduction immediately prompts the question how he knows that the *Poems* are a true portrait of people, society and linguistic practice in ancient Gaeldom. Blair might have replied that he was being, in a real sense of the term, scientific, for on the basis of long observation of his fellow humans he had worked out a conception of human nature, and on the basis of that conception he could deduce how people must have lived and spoken in primitive times. In that case if an epic emerges in which people are portrayed in primitive society just as he would expect on the basis of his antecedent conception, this measure of agreement between his conception and the epic would have some tendency to confirm the authenticity of the epic. If that was indeed

Blair's approach then, as we shall now see, he was not so far in spirit from those who wished to write genuinely scientific history.

The literati wished to write history that would survive scientific scrutiny. The attempt was made to 'introduce the experimental method of reasoning' into human history by requiring a suitably stringent use of evidence. But what evidence is there for, say, the origin of language? We cannot suppose that the first language users, if they existed, would have written an account of the origins of language. Yet literati wrote accounts of the origin of language. On the basis of what evidence? Likewise, we have no account of the origin of religion that is contemporaneous with that origin. On the basis of what evidence, then, could literati construct their confident accounts of its origin?

In his *Account of the Life and Writings of Adam Smith LL.D.* Dugald Stewart says of Smith's *Dissertation on the Origin of Languages* that 'it deserves our attention less, on account of the opinions it contains, than as a specimen of a particular sort of inquiry, which, so far as I know, is entirely of modern origin'. (Smith, *Essays on Philosophical Subjects*, p.292) Stewart then spells out, in a famous passage, the 'particular sort of inquiry' that he has in mind. He notes the lack of direct evidence for the origin of language, of the arts and the sciences, of political union, and so on, and affirms: 'In this want of direct evidence, we are under a necessity of supplying the place of fact by conjecture; and when we are unable to ascertain how men have actually conducted themselves upon particular occasions, of considering in what manner they are likely to have proceeded, from the principles of their nature, and the circumstances of their external situation.' (p.293) Nor are such inquiries of merely theoretical interest. For Stewart they are of practical importance, for by them 'a check is given to that indolent philosophy, which refers to a miracle, whatever appearances, both in the natural and moral worlds, it is unable to explain'. (Smith, *Essays*, p.293) Stewart uses the term 'conjectural history' for the sort of history exemplified by Smith's account of the origin of language. Conjectural history is a bulwark against the illegitimate encroachment of religion into the lives of people who are much too quick to reach for God as the solution to a problem when careful extrapolation from scientifically established principles of human nature will provide a solution that speaks confidently to our intellect.

It might be thought that there is a surprising element in conjectural history. The scientific spirit of the Enlightenment was defined by the experimental method – the scientist relies on observation and experiment. Yet the ancient origins of the great institutions of civilisation are not available to us – we can neither observe them nor experiment on them. Neither of course can we remember them. How then does conjectural history accord with the scientific spirit of the Enlightenment? The answer is that on the basis of our experience we formulate laws, empirical laws; and on the basis of those laws we can perform experiments in our imagination. Knowing what we do about human nature, about our intellect and will, our emotions and fundamental beliefs, we ask how people would have behaved in given circumstances. Love and hate, anger and jealousy, joy and fear, do not change much through the generations. Much the same things have much the same effect first on the emotions and then on behaviour. In his *Dissertation: Exhibiting the Progress of Metaphysical, Ethical, and Political Philosophy, since the Revival of Letters in Europe*, Dugald Stewart formulates the principle underlying the development of conjectural history: it has 'long been received as an incontrovertible logical maxim that the capacities of the human mind have been in all ages the same, and that the diversity of phenomena exhibited by our species is the result merely of the different circumstances in which men are placed'. (*Collected Works*, vol.1, p.69)

However, since a good deal of conjectural history was written by Scots during the Enlightenment, it is worth enquiring into the credentials of Stewart's 'incontrovertible logical maxim'. If the claim that human nature is invariant is an empirical claim, it must be based on observation of our contemporaries and on evidence of people's lives in other places and at other times. Such evidence needs, however, to be handled with care. The further back we go the more meagre it is, and so the more we need to conjecture to supplement the few facts available to us. Indeed we can go back so far that we have no facts beyond the generalities that we have worked out in the light of our experience. But to rely on conjecture in order to support the very principle that forms the first premiss in any exercise in conjectural history is to come suspiciously close to a circular argument.

Let us say that Stewart's incontrovertible logical maxim has the status of a well-founded empirical law. That is to say, as far as evidence is available, and a good deal of evidence *is* available, the maxim holds good. One problem faced by historians writing about the distant past is precisely that of assessing the evidence. Lord Kames shows himself alive to the problem in his *Historical Law-Tracts*. Admittedly Hume did not much like the book. He told Smith: 'I am afraid of Lord Kaims's Law Tracts. A man might as well think of making a fine Sauce by a Mixture of Wormwood and Aloes as an agreeable Composition by joining metaphysics and Scotch Law. However, the Book, I believe, has Merit; tho' few People will take the Pains of diving into it.' (Smith, *Correspondence*, p.34) However, one significant merit of the book is that Kames shows himself sensitive to the methodological difficulties of writing a history of law when the hard evidence is in short supply. He writes:

> In tracing the history of law through dark ages, unproved with records, or so slenderly provided as not to afford any regular historical chain, we must endeavour to supply the broken links, hints from poets and historians, by collateral facts, and by cautious conjectures drawn from the nature of the government, of the people, and of the times. If we use all the light that is afforded, and if the conjectural facts correspond with the few facts that are distinctly vouched, and join all in one regular chain, more cannot be expected from human endeavours. (Kames, *Historical Law-Tracts*, p.25)

But all of this supposes that we are entitled to place trust in some of the ancient evidence, such as ancient reports of 'the nature of the government, the people and the times'. What entitles us to do this? It is true that we can and perhaps always do bring our concept of human nature to bear, and in the light of that concept we judge some evidence credible and other evidence incredible. But judgments of credibility or incredibility are not always easily made. I shall turn briefly to a method employed to aid our judgment on these matters.

William Robertson made much of the principle: 'our human mind, whenever it is placed in the same situation, will, in ages the most distant, and in countries the most remote, assume the same form, and be distinguished by the same manners'. This principle, which is a close relative of Stewart's incontrovertible logical maxim, is deployed by Robertson to underpin a variety of historical writing, so-called 'comparative history', that was common during the Enlightenment. Ancient historians had a good deal to say about people and societies whom they knew by observation or report. Why believe those historians? We can of course decide in the light of our knowledge of human nature whether those ancient accounts are credible or not. But we can do better than that, for there were during the eighteenth century numerous reports of 'primitive' or 'rude' societies and such reports invited comparison with those of the ancient historians. As Adam Ferguson, who endorsed this methodology, puts the point: 'If, in advanced years, we would form a just notion of our progress from the cradle, we must have recourse to the nursery, and from the example of those who are still in the period of life we mean to describe, take our representation of past manners, that cannot, in any other way, be recalled.' (*Essay*, p.80)

One of the most famous comparisons is in *Moeurs des sauvages ameriquains, comparées aux moeurs des premiers temps* (1724) by the Jesuit father Joseph-François Lafitau. Another, likewise based on close personal observation of native tribes of North America, is in Cadwallader Colden's *History of the Five Nations of Canada* (1727). Adam Smith, who speaks in the *Theory of Moral Sentiments* about the toughmindedness of North American tribes, might have read these books or alternatively one known to have been owned by him, *Histoire et description général de la Nouvelle France* (1744) by the Jesuit father Pierre-François de Charlevoix. Reports were also coming onstream from Asia and Polynesia, most spectacularly from Captain James Cook, who discovered Tasmania and plotted the outline of New Zealand during his expedition of 1768–71 in the *Endeavour*. Cook's edited log books, which became best sellers, provided a vast quantity of information about the peoples of newly discovered territories.

All this has an immediate bearing on the methodology for weighing historical evidence. Robertson, following in the footsteps of Lafitau, compared the native tribes of North America with the tribes of Germany which had been described by Caesar and Tacitus. In line with his principle quoted above, 'our human mind, whenever it is placed in the same situation, will, in ages the most distant, and in countries the most remote, assume the same form, and be distinguished by the same manners', Robertson reasoned that we know how modern primitives live, since we have detailed reports by Lafitau and others. Since modern primitives and ancient primitives have the same nature, we would expect the ancient primitives to live in much the same way as their modern equivalents. Robertson demonstrates that there is indeed a close correspondence between the descriptions of the modern reporters and the ancient historians. This correspondence can be interpreted as a demonstration of the accuracy of the ancient reports. But a question remains as to how far these few reports permit extrapolation to other times and places. Must all ancient primitives have been like modern primitives? Are there not many forms that primitive life can take, and can we be sure that the similarity between the institutions of the American and of the ancient Germanic tribes is more than a coincidence?

In all such work there is an element of conjecture, but the conjecture is not pure guesswork. We argue on the basis of observed uniformities. And the more experience we have of given uniformities the greater credence we will give to reports that speak of the occurrence of the uniformities, whether they concern dead matter or living people and their institutions. In a famous passage Hume writes:

Whether we consider mankind according to the difference
of sexes, ages, governments, conditions, or methods of
education; the same uniformity and regular operation of
natural principles are discernible. Like causes still produce
like effects; in the same manner as in the mutual action
of the elements and powers of nature ... Men cannot
live without society, and cannot be associated without
government. Government makes a distinction of property,
and establishes the different ranks of men. This produces
industry, traffic, manufactures, law-suits, wars, leagues,
alliances, voyages, travels, cities, fleets, ports, and all those
other actions and objects, which cause such a diversity, and
at the same time maintain such a uniformity in human life.
(Hume, *Treatise*, pp.401–2)

Hume speaks with great confidence on these matters, and so
would most of us, and in general the practitioners of conjectural
history were not notably diffident about their conjectures. They
were confident about their insights into human nature, and confident
also about the implications of those insights for the way people
behaved at the beginnings of things, of society, religion and so on.
So long as conjectural history stayed at a high level of generality
we could (perhaps) be almost as confident as we could of a very
precise and detailed event in recent history, such as a speech or
a battle. There is a sliding scale here. Conjectural history is not
really different in kind from the kind of history ordinarily practised,
which we may call 'scientific' history; it is different in respect of the
level of generality of the evidence which is utilised. It argues from
general facts about human nature, and speaks of the likelihood of
an institution arising in a given manner among beings with such
a nature.

It seems appropriate to call such exercises 'history', but all the
same there is enough here to give us pause. Is it really entitled
to the honoured title 'history' if it deals only in likelihoods and
stays at such a high level of generality? It is Dugald Stewart

himself who brings this issue to a head in a famous passage, which some commentators have read as pointing to an anti-historical streak in Stewart's thinking about the past. In the same essay, the *Life and Writings of Adam Smith*, in which he introduces the concept of conjectural history, Stewart writes: 'In most cases, it is of more importance to ascertain the progress that is most simple, than the progress that is most agreeable to fact; for, paradoxical as the proposition may appear, it is certainly true, that the real progress is not always the most natural. It may have been determined by particular accidents, which are not likely again to occur, and which cannot be considered as forming any part of that general provision which nature has made for the improvement of the race.' (Smith, *Essays on Philosophical Subjects*, p.296)

Stewart's talk of a preference for simplicity over that which is 'most agreeable to fact' is likely to send alarm bells ringing in the head of a historian. What, after all, is wrong with 'the progress that is most agreeable to fact'? The answer is that nothing is, but that it accounts for only a small part of the historian's job. His job is not only to discover and record facts but to make sense of them. A bare fact, that X happened, is of little or no interest except as rendered intelligible by its relations to other facts. In the course of a great event something might happen, some detail, that was really incidental, in the sense that it made no significant contribution to the event. But to identify something as an incidental detail is already to have a conception of the event, a broad picture of the significance of the overall event and of what contributed to its being significant. This broad picture is a simplification in the sense that it is not simply a list of facts, but instead an orderly story so told as to permit the reader to understand or make sense of what actually happened. The list is 'agreeable to fact'; but if there were no structuring principle conferring sense on the event, that would be a failing from the point of view of the historian. This, then, is at least part of what Stewart has in mind when he praises simplicity as against agreeableness to fact. I think that Stewart's concept of 'progress that is most simple' is also in

Kames's mind when he writes: 'We must be satisfied with collecting the facts and circumstances as they may be gathered from the laws of different countries: and if these put together make a regular chain of causes and effects, we may rationally conclude, that the progress has been the same among all nations, in the capital circumstances at least; for accidents, or the singular nature of a people, or of a government, will always produce some pecularities.' (*Historical Law-Tracts*, p.26)

In light of these considerations it might well seem that the difference between conjectural history and scientific is the difference in respect of the quantity of significant detail in the two sorts of history. But they do not apparently differ in respect of the rational input. Conjectural history is no more a fairy tale or myth than is scientific history. The conjectural historian cannot write just whatever he wants. The conjecture is tightly controlled by the account of human nature that is deployed, an account that has a scientific basis, in the sense that it is the product of the toughminded and systematic application of a scientific methodology, and is tightly controlled also by the rules that permit the historian to reach his conclusions about what happened. Hume was as well qualified as anyone has ever been to write the many passages of conjectural history that occur in his writings. Chief among his qualifications is the fact that he wrote a treatise containing a profound exposition of a scientifically grounded theory of human nature. It was on the basis of that exposition that he went on to consider such things as the origin of religion, of society, of government, of justice, and so on. In so far as the account of human nature deployed by the conjectural historian is scientifically respectable, to that extent conjectural history is not the less scientific for being conjectural.

But there remains a large methodological problem, one which set Adam Ferguson against many of his fellow literati. Conjectural history is based on an account of how human beings in a supposed original state, and therefore lacking the kind of education available to the literati, would have reacted to certain conditions. But how well placed were the literati, or anyone else, to say what people in some original state were like? Ferguson writes:

> Our method, notwithstanding, too frequently, is to rest the
> whole on conjecture; to impute every advantage of our
> nature to those arts which we ourselves possess; and to
> imagine, that a mere negation of all our virtues is a sufficient
> description of man in his original state. We are ourselves the
> supposed standards of politeness and civilization; and where
> our own features do not appear, we apprehend, that there
> is nothing which deserves to be known. But it is probable
> that here, as in many other cases, we are ill qualified, from
> our supposed knowledge of causes, to prognosticate effects,
> or to determine what must have been the properties and
> operations, even of our own nature, in the absence of those
> circumstances in which we have seen it engaged. (Ferguson,
> *Essay*, p.75)

This, however, is not to imply criticism of the methodology of
comparative history. For, as that methodology was applied in the
eighteenth century, it dealt with facts sufficiently well attested, on
the one hand facts reported by ancient historians regarding the way
of life of tribes that were contemporaneous with the historians, and
on the other hand facts regarding the way of life of present-day
primitive tribes.

Conjectural history was not solely in the hands of the historians.
The painters also made a contribution in their portrayals of the
ancient legend, related by Pliny, of the origin of painting. A young
Corinthian woman, the daughter of Debutades, drew on a wall the
outline of the shadow cast by her lover's face. He was about to
go to war, and this outline would remain to her when he left.
Alexander Runciman (1736–85) and David Allan (1744–96) both
depicted this scene, though in very different ways. Runciman's,
painted in Edinburgh in 1773, is the more complex work in so far
as it contains a third person, Cupid the god of love, who guides the
maiden's hand as she traces the outline on the wall. But in Allan's
painting also (painted in Rome in 1775 – see Plate 2) it is made clear,
from the warrior's arm placed affectionately round the maiden's

waist, that the first portrait was painted as an act of love. Given that philosophers of the Scottish Enlightenment were interested in the extent to which aesthetic judgment is an expression of feeling or sentiment, many of them would have thought it peculiarly fitting that love begat the art of painting.

Section 6: The course of history

The Enlightenment emphasis on the scientific nature of historical studies, on the need to give due weight to evidence and especially to give due weight to the common facts of human nature, prompts a disturbing question which needs to be acknowledged. Given that the scientist who served most conspicuously as the model for the literati was Newton, the fact that his law of gravity made a universal claim must have given the literati pause. Since it was such a truth that his methodology yielded up and since many literati applied that same methodology to their study of human beings, does this mean that history is as much the story of necessary happenings in the lives of people as the story Newton tells is of necessary happenings in the physical world? Accounts of human nature, when they are conducted at the level of abstraction at which Hutcheson, Hume, Smith and Reid conducted theirs, are universal in the sense that they are intended to be true of all human beings no matter when or where they live. It is because of this universality that conjectural historians, deploying these accounts, speak with confidence about what human beings did at the very beginning of the great institutions, this despite the fact that there are no written records, or other tangible or visible traces of those beginnings.

The fact that the fundamental truths about human nature are universally true means that necessarily people conform to them, for if they did not then of course the truths would not always be true. There appears to be a clear indication of history as embodying universal and necessary laws in Adam Smith's 'stadial theory' of human development, a development through four stages from the hunter-gatherer, to the pastoral, to the agricultural, to the commercial stage. In the first stage the hunter-gatherers possess almost no property. They own the animals they capture and the fruit they pluck, but this food is not wealth that people are able to accumulate, for having captured or plucked they then eat what they have. In the second, less mobile though still nomadic stage, shepherds can accumulate wealth by increasing their herds. In the third stage, which is even less mobile, since farmers live in permanent housing, there are more ways to accumulate wealth, and the possibility of greater inequality of wealth. In the fourth stage, property ownership, and laws governing property, are yet more complex than in the previous stage. Smith developed his theory of the four stages of society in the context of the lectures that he delivered on jurisprudence, where the chief purpose was to expound the development of property law, in particular to expound the way in which the development of the legal framework governing property has been a function of changes in the forms of production. But the stadial theory is also a contribution to conjectural history, expounded on the basis of Smith's understanding of human nature and of his conjectures about the different kinds of physical circumstances in which people would have found themselves in most primitive, and then progressively less primitive, conditions.

There is no doubt that Smith believed that the four stages were stages in progress or improvement in the lives of people, where what is at issue is not just material progress but also progress in terms of the cultural values that are embodied in our lives. In the present context what needs to be emphasised is that Smith did not believe progress to be linear or inevitable. Two steps forward may be followed by one step back, or even three, as witness the cultural impoverishment in western Europe precipitated by the collapse of the Roman Empire. Furthermore, a society can get stuck at a given stage, or can even display simultaneously characteristics of different stages. The necessity Smith sees lies not in the move from one stage to the next but in the correlation between on the one hand the given stage of society and on the other the regulations concerning the method by which property is acquired at that stage. In that sense, the stadial theory does not imply historical determinism. It might represent what is in some sense a 'natural' sequence, but the question whether history conforms to it is a substantive question to which the answer may be 'no'.

This is an appropriate point at which to remind ourselves of a passage by Dugald Stewart that was quoted earlier: 'In most cases, it is of more importance to ascertain the progress that is most simple, than the progress that is most agreeable to fact; for, paradoxical as the proposition may appear, it is certainly true, that the real progress is not always the most natural.' The stadial theory, in Smith's view, describes a progress that is 'most simple' and 'most natural', even if the description is not necessarily 'most agreeable to fact'. It should be added that in the case of this theory it is more important for Smith to know what is most simple rather than most agreeable to fact because his task is to trace the development of property law, and he believes that knowledge of the natural sequence by which property law acquired the form it now has in the commercial stage of society aids us in our understanding of the present state of the law. However the chief point in the present context is that Smith acknowledges, as does Stewart after him, that what actually happens may have been the result of accidents which might never recur and which, in Stewart's interesting phrase, 'cannot be considered as forming any part of that general provision which nature has made for the improvement of the race'. There is absolutely no hint of historical determinism in this position.

FOUR

Morality and Civil Society

Section 1: Some key concepts

The Enlightenment was a social phenomenon in two ways. It involved an international Republic of Letters whose citizens acknowledged that progress in intellectual matters could be achieved only by communal thinking, thinking with and through others. It also involved a general acknowledgement of our right to put our ideas into the public domain. At the practical level such acknowledgement had an essentially moral dimension in so far as it involved a toleration of the publication of disagreeable or discomforting ideas, for such toleration is a moral virtue. In that sense the Enlightenment was a cooperative enterprise within which not only the literati but also those who tolerated them made a contribution.

The literati knew just how lucky they were. They saw themselves as a living proof of the possibility of social and moral progress, for their self-image involved essentially a contrast with the Middle Ages in the Christian west; a contrast out of which the Middle Ages emerged with little or no credit, for it was seen as an Age of Intolerance, whether it was the secular or the ecclesiastical leadership that was at issue. Of course there are some things that ought not to be tolerated, and there is therefore no suggestion here that all intolerance is a bad thing. But intolerance in the name of a religious or political system which is unable to withstand cross-examination before the tribunal of reason cannot be accounted on the side of the good. And it was a common perception among the literati that the intolerance that characterised the Middle Ages was rationally and therefore morally unjustified.

For good reason therefore the literati saw themselves as lucky. 'Lucky' is an appropriate word here, for even among the literati who thought that there was something natural about moral progress it was recognised that reality did not always accord with what was most natural, and that, on the contrary, accidental or incidental things could happen that would block progress or even send society into reverse. Furthermore, as well as sheer bad luck, a society is always prey to individuals, free riders, who have insufficient respect for civilised values, and who are prepared to do uncivilised things while believing that enough people will continue to do the civilised thing to prevent the heavens falling. In light of such considerations the literati tended to think both that the progress that had undoubtedly been made was not necessarily secure, and also that nothing could be done to make it secure. There were certain things that could be done to increase the chances that progress would be maintained, but progress was a fragile thing. At no stage could society safely rest on its laurels. According to this perception, civilisation is a rather thin veneer, and the best thing a society can do is to rear a citizenry dedicated to protecting that veneer. If morality is about anything it is about that – protecting the civilised values vested in society.

Several concepts are here displayed which were at the heart of Enlightenment concerns, namely, society, its progress and the obstacles to progress, and moral values. Scottish thinkers were very much to the fore in the development of these concepts; three Scots at least, Hutcheson, Hume and Smith, were among the most influential moral philosophers in Europe. Adam Ferguson and John Millar were two of the founders of modern sociology, a field to which Smith and Kames, among many other Scots, also made significant contributions. Scottish Enlightenment discussions of the concepts here at issue are full of good things, and in this chapter I shall take a small group of these good things, which are systematically related at several levels, and shall comment briefly on them. Adam Ferguson will be my guide, at least for the opening steps.

Section 2: Nature and society

A distinction was commonly made between society and the state of nature which was thought of as antecedent to society. The literati were, as we have seen, interested in origins, believing that an insight into the origin would yield insight into what was thus originated. The question of the origin of society had been discussed by philosophers of classical Greece and had been on the agenda ever after. The literati had before them two particularly prominent models, one by Thomas Hobbes (1588–1679) and the other by Jean-Jacques Rousseau (1712–78). At the start of his *Essay on the History of Civil Society* Ferguson presents in briefest outline the position of these two philosophers though he does not there name them. He represents Rousseau as holding that men antecedent to society do not exercise those of their faculties that render them superior to brute animals, and are 'without any means of explaining their sentiments, and even without possessing any of the apprehensions and passions which the voice and the gesture are so well fitted to express'. (*Essay*, p.8) Ferguson continues: 'Others [he has in mind Hobbes in particular] have made the state of nature to consist in perpetual wars, kindled by competition for dominion and interest, where every individual had a separate quarrel with his kind, and where the presence of a fellow-creature was the signal of battle.'

In a certain respect these two models can be thought of as contraries. Hobbes represents the state of nature as the worst of all possible states, one in which the life of man is 'solitary, poor, nasty, brutish and short' (*Leviathan*, ch.13), in which conditions are so bad that any state of society, however bad, is better. Rousseau on the other hand represents the savage in the state of nature as an innocent who then becomes corrupted by the encroachment of society. In specifiable ways, therefore, his life becomes worse. According to Hobbes, society is created by a contract seen by people as desirable because through it the risk, ever present in the state of nature, of an early and violent death is reduced. On the Hobbesian analysis therefore the social state, far from being a principle of corruption for its members, provides their best (indeed their only) chance of longevity.

Although it seems that Hobbes and Rousseau give opposite accounts of the state of nature, Ferguson argues that on the most important matter they say the same thing, and on that matter they are both wrong. His starting point concerns the methodology that has to be deployed if the issue between Hobbes and Rousseau is to be resolved. Ferguson applies the experimental method of reasoning to moral subjects. Though accepting that there is a place for conjectures or hypotheses, they have to be confirmed if they are to be used as premisses in a scientific argument. Hobbes and Rousseau may, of course, without rejecting sound scientific methodology, conjecture that there was a state of nature, but at some stage in their argument they need to demonstrate that there was such a state. Ferguson's chief point is that there is no proof, and that what Hobbes and Rouseau offer as proof is hopelessly inadequate. In each case the philosopher 'substitutes hypothesis instead of reality, and confounds the provinces of imagination and reason, of poetry and science'. (*Essay*, p.9)

The introduction of the experimental method of reasoning into moral subjects requires us to give priority to hard evidence when it conflicts with conjectures and hypotheses. Ferguson's point is that there is ample evidence to hand, evidence which must be duly noted in our inferences about human nature: 'If both the earliest and latest accounts collected from every quarter of the earth, represent mankind as assembled in troops and companies; and the individual always joined by affection to one party, while he is possibly opposed to another; employed in the exercise of recollection and foresight; inclined to communicate his own sentiments, and to be made acquainted with those of others; these facts must be admitted as the foundation of all our reasoning relative to man.' (*Essay*, p.9)

The reference in this prescription to mankind in 'troops' and 'companies' is of some biographical interest in view of its overtones of military organisation; it is an oblique reminder of the fact that Ferguson had been a chaplain for nine years in the Black Watch, a highland regiment in which he had seen service, even though there is reason to doubt the claim, commonly made, that he had wielded a sword at the Battle of Fontenoy. However the main point of the passage just quoted is clear, that all available hard evidence points to human beings as living in society, and the hard evidence has to be the bottom line for any scientific investigation of our nature; whoever oversteps that line is indulging in 'poetry' or 'fancy'. So, application of the experimental method of reasoning leads us to this: '[Man's] mixed disposition to friendship or enmity, his reason, his use of language and articulate sounds, like the shape and erect position of his body, are to be considered as so many attributes of his nature: they are to be retained in his description, as the wing and the paw are in that of the eagle and the lion, and as different degrees of fierceness, vigilance, timidity, or speed, are made to occupy a place in the natural history of different animals.' (*Essay*, p.9)

A distinction has to be made between people and other animals in this sense, that generally speaking the perfections that an animal is able to develop it do in fact develop in the course of its lifetime. The species of cats does not progress over the generations. The sorts of things they did millennia ago are the same sorts of things they still do. People are related otherwise to their perfections. Successive generations add to knowledge and this accumulation means that people, supported by our science, technology, arts and humanities, are now able to master skills undreamed of by our forebears. In this sense the life of the species has been one of development. This is a main reason why the history of human beings is so much more interesting than the history of dogs and cats. *We* are developing; they are not. *We* have a concept of progress and seek to give it concrete form. This progress naturally prompts a question of how we arrived at our present state of civilisation, and for Ferguson the question is reasonable and he himself points to possible answers. What he finds unacceptable is the idea that we have an origin which is utterly unlike our present state. Rousseau held that in the state of nature the savage had not mastered any arts, but Ferguson argues that the contrast between art and nature is bogus. As he puts it: 'art itself is natural to man.' (*Essay*, p.12)

It might seem, in light of this doctrine, that since people are naturally social animals people have always lived in society and therefore have never lived in a state of nature. But Ferguson would reject this inference. His hugely influential teaching is that for people the social state *is* a state of nature. For of course, if to be in a state of nature is to live according to nature, and if it is our nature to be social, then for people the social state *is* the natural state; the relation between these supposedly two sorts of state is one of identity. A human being living entirely outwith society is in an unnatural state, and although Hobbes and Rousseau believed that a great deal could be learned about us by considering a person entirely outwith society, Ferguson believed that a study of such a person would yield up very little useful information, if any. One or two such people were found in the forests of Europe during the eighteenth century and were closely studied, particularly in respect of their language skills. But in Ferguson's view we could learn from them almost nothing that was not obvious. The savage would lack a language, and would have no moral, social, political or religious values. This is not a way of being a person, but rather a way of being deprived of personhood.

In the case of real primitives, the primitives who are known from observation or reports, they display mastery of a considerable array of arts, such as building, weaving, tool manufacture, animal husbandry, hunting skills, and so on. And our efforts at enriching our culture are continuous with their efforts: 'What the savage projects, or observes, in the forest, are the steps which led nations, more advanced, from the architecture of the cottage to that of the palace, and conducted the human mind from the perceptions of sense, to the general conclusions of science.' (*Essay*, p.14)

The advances thus made are, to speak generally, not from the less to the more social, but from the less to the more civilised. The literati distinguished between 'rude' and 'polite' societies, but there is no suggestion in this distinction that the rude societies are somehow the less social. Indeed this distinction between the rude and the polite permits the development of the doctrine that in some respects there is a tendency for societal development to be in the direction of fragmentation, so that in certain specifiable ways individuals come to be cut off from each other. I should like to consider this point briefly from a Fergusonian perspective.

There are societies because there are principles of union in human nature. We have a natural love or affection for people, a natural sympathy for them, and in any case a natural desire to be with people, whether we love them or not. Our being is incomplete outwith society. These are evident truths and can be seen exemplified in all societies, rude or polite. They are perhaps best investigated in rude societies. This at any rate seems the implication of a methodological principle formulated by Ferguson in this way: 'Whatever proofs we may have of the disposition of man in familiar and contiguous scenes, it is possibly of importance, to draw our observations from the examples of men who live in the simplest condition, and who have not learned to affect what they do not actually feel.' (*Essay*, p.23) Of course, by the same token the investigator must turn to more advanced societies to find suitable examples of deception or dissimulation of people's real feelings or thoughts. It is as if the savages live closer to the surface than do citizens in more polite societies. But in all societies we find principles of union. Ferguson's fine rhetoric about the native of North America applies to all of us: 'Send him to the desert alone, he is a plant torn from its roots: the form indeed may remain, but every faculty droops and withers; the human personage and the human character cease to exist.' (*Essay*, p.23)

But a difference between the polite and the rude forms of society has to be noted. The stadial theory, widely accepted, as we have seen, in the Scottish Enlightenment, portrayed a kind of progress, at least so far as measured in terms of the diversity and the efficiency of the economy. Nevertheless, as well as gains there can also be losses when the fourth, commercial stage is reached; and the losses are real enough even if they are not of an easily quantifiable sort. That we have a natural affection for people is not in doubt. Our affection is not based on a calculation about the extent to which others can be helpful to us. On the contrary, it is often when others are least able to help us or even to help themselves that the feeling of affection is strongest – as for example the parent's affection for a sick child, or a person's affection for a friend who is the victim of some gross injustice. These thoughts were quite common currency in the Scottish Enlightenment. Hume, Smith, Kames and Millar, for example, would all have endorsed them strongly. Ferguson, particularly interested in the psychology or psychopathology of commercial society, adds to the picture a warning that these natural feelings can suffer interference in the commercial stage of society. Writing of the commercial state Ferguson affirms: 'It is here, indeed, if ever, that man is sometimes found a detached and a solitary being: he has found an object which sets him in competition with his fellow-creatures, and he deals with them as he does with his cattle and his soil, for the sake of the profits they bring. The mighty engine which we suppose to have formed society, only tends to set its members at variance, or to continue their intercourse after the bands of affection are broken.' (*Essay*, p.24)

This point should not be permitted an exaggerated importance. Ferguson does not suppose that there is a great tendency to fragmentation in the commercial society, over and above such tendencies in earlier social states. His point is the more limited one, that a person's response to pressures to think in commercial terms might cut across feelings that he would otherwise have for people with whom he has commercial dealings, so that he becomes comparatively detached or isolated from them. Such detachment would be widespread in the commercial stage if economic value was given priority over all other values. But it is not, nor even nearly. Other values, moral, religious, aesthetic, and so on, assert themselves often enough to ensure that society in the commercial stage of development continues to look thoroughly human. It is bound to do so because, as Ferguson insists, it is after all manned by human beings, and our natural love, affection and sympathy, precisely because they are part of our nature, cannot in the end be suppressed but will instead naturally well up and shape our actions, attitudes and lives.

Section 3: The fragility of freedom

As one stage of society succeeds another, an ever richer culture develops, richer in the sense that an ever wider range of acts and activities becomes available enabling the expression of an ever wider range of values. Our right to express them is enshrined in law. It is easy to think of the law as encroaching on our freedom in the sense that it prohibits given types of act which therefore we are not free to perform and it requires given types of act which therefore we are not free *not* to perform. But none of the literati thought of law in such terms. For all of them, on the contrary, law provided the conditions under which freedom is possible, enabling the citizens to give concrete form to their civilised values, whether by publicly disagreeing with political or religious leaders, or by attending the theatrical or musical performance they want to attend, or worshipping as they wish, or by writing poems or playing the composers they wish to play, and so on, in general performing the kinds of act that help to identify our society as civilised. Within a polite or civilised society the right to engage in such acts is protected by law. An infringement of such a right is therefore an act of injustice. The law thus ensures our liberty to live civilised, cultured lives.

I have just described a society that embodies Enlightenment values and should like now to consider the question of the stability of such a society, and to do so from a Fergusonian perspective. He writes: 'Liberty results, we say, from the government of laws; and we are apt to consider statutes, not merely as the resolutions and maxims of a people determined to be free, not as the writings by which their rights are kept on record; but as a power erected to guard them, and as a barrier which the caprice of man cannot transgress.' (*Essay*, p.249) The point is of the greatest significance for the concept of Enlightenment, which has at its heart the idea of a tolerant society, a society in which the right of free speech is not merely enshrined in law but is also respected in practice. Exploration of this concept reveals the very highly qualified nature of Ferguson's optimism for the continuation of a polite society such as had developed in eighteenth-century Scotland.

We live under a system of written law which is designed to protect the freedoms proper to a civil society. The question Ferguson addresses is: How effective is this law at securing the end for which it was designed? Are the rights of the citizens of Edinburgh, who are judged by a judge interpreting a complex system of written law, better protected than the rights of the citizens of Turkey, who are judged by a pasha who decides each case in light of his rational consideration of the rules of natural equity. Perhaps surprisingly Ferguson does not answer this question with an unqualified 'yes'. But he is supported by a formidable argument which takes its starting point from the fact that it is one thing for a legislative body to pass a law which is designed to protect the rights of the citizens, and it is another thing for that law to be properly enforced. It is well said that the intentions of the legislator do not make the law, for the law is according to the actual formulation, not according to the legislator's intention. In that case the judge must consult not what the legislator meant but what he wrote. And what he wrote has to be interpreted in relation to each case. Nobody supposes that this process is always purely mechanical; perhaps it never is. But at any rate the fact that the law has to be interpreted means that a judge can adjudicate according to the letter of the law while going totally against its spirit. This can be dangerous to the freedoms enjoyed by the citizens.

Ferguson opens up this line of thought with a statement which I quote in full in view of its significance for our understanding of the Scottish Enlightenment:

> If forms of proceeding, written statutes, or other constituents of law, ceased to be enforced by the very spirit from which they arose; they serve only to cover, not to restrain, the iniquities of power: they are possibly respected even by the corrupt magistrate, when they favour his purpose; but they are contemned or evaded, when they stand in his way: And the influence of laws, where they have any real effect in the preservation of liberty, is not any magic power descending from shelves that are loaded with books, but is, in reality, the influence of men resolved to be free; of men, who, having adjusted in writing the terms on which they are to live with the state, and with their fellow-subjects, are determined by their vigilance and spirit, to make these terms be observed. (Ferguson, *Essay*, p.249)

Ferguson was particularly interested in the phenomenon of political corruption. He believed that the possession of Enlightenment values is not an effective barrier to corruption. Even a benevolent leader, one solicitous of the well-being of the citizens, will tend to seek to adjust the existing structures to ensure as far as possible that he stays on top. He will think that this is not unreasonable of him, for since he has an exceptionally clear insight into what is best for the people it makes sense that he should guide them for as long as possible. A political leader is not the less dangerous for being well-meaning. What is required therefore is a system of checks and balances in the body politic to prevent a well-meaning leader, one with a natural regard for justice and a belief in liberty of the citizens, from posing a threat to the system of justice and the liberty of the citizens. Ferguson has a good deal to say, as important today as it was when he wrote, about the ways in which a political leader will seek to adjust the system of checks and balances to ensure that he is not himself checked and balanced while engaged in his noble task. Above all, therefore, the system of checks and balances has to be maintained. Such a system ensures the continued existence within the political state of what especially characterises the Republic of Letters, namely robust public debate. Any projected adjustment to the system must itself first be subject to robust public debate.

From a Fergusonian perspective the Enlightenment has a self-destruct button, and not even the literati can be trusted not to press it. The danger is described succinctly:

> We have reason to dread the political refinement of ordinary men, when we consider, that repose, or inaction itself, is in a great measure their object; and that they would frequently model their governments, not merely to prevent injustice and error, but to prevent agitation and bustle; and by the barriers they raise against the evil actions of men, would prevent them from acting at all. Every dispute of a free people, in the opinion of such politicians, amounts to disorder, and a breach of the national peace ... Men of superior genius sometimes seem to imagine, that the vulgar have no title to act, or to think. (Ferguson, *Essay*, p.209)

Ferguson is here targeting the literati, the polite society. These 'superior geniuses' might well regard civic disorder with fear, and would think ill of any group that engaged in serious civil commotion and thereby risked destabilising the existing structures, for those are the very structures that support polite society, the crowning glory of the state. Hence the imposition of laws limiting freedom to act in a seriously uncivil way is likely to be supported by polite society. Yet they would thereby be condoning an intrusion into civil liberties, even though they would of course consider the intrusion to be a means of defending Enlightenment values.

Ferguson, on the contrary, would say that in so acting the polite folk would be aiding and abetting a real or potential despotism. The political leader himself might, in the situation Ferguson is envisaging, congratulate himself on the way he has brought enlightened values to bear on a tricky situation to bring some less than civil members of the society under proper civic control. But the civic commotion might have been the demonstration of a vigorous and independent spirit provoked by a perceived injustice on the part of the civic authorities, and the demonstration would therefore have been a manifestation of the values and spirit to which the polite society was supposedly dedicated. In this obvious sense, polite society will have betrayed its own values, while those it is acting against are in effect seeking to defend the very values that the polite society claims to live by. Public demonstration as a means of drawing attention to and protesting against perceived injustice is, or should be, part of the system of checks and balances in a free society. Such commotion is a price well worth paying. Ferguson writes:

> . . . if a rigorous policy, applied to enslave, not to restrain from crimes, has an actual tendency to corrupt the manners, and to extinguish the spirit of nations; if its severities be applied to terminate the agitations of a free people, not to remedy their corruptions; if forms be often applauded as salutary, because they tend merely to silence the voice of mankind, or be condemned as pernicious, because they allow this voice to be heard; we may expect that many of the boasted improvements of civil society, will be mere devices to lay the political spirit at rest, and will chain up the active virtues more than the restless disorders of men. (*Essay*, p.210)

Ferguson repeatedly warns against the passivity of the citizenry, against its failure to participate in public affairs, against its willingness to 'chain up' by default its active virtues. It would be fatal to civil liberties if the citizens dedicated themselves to commercial activities to the exclusion of political activity. If the politicians get on with politics while everyone else gets on with economic activity the politicians will use the opportunity, made available by default, to strengthen their own position. Which is to say that it is dangerous for a state to permit the development of a political class. Ferguson is thus arguing for a form of republicanism; citizens should see themselves as the guardians of civic virtues and civic liberties. They should therefore be attentive to the activities of the political leaders, and be ready to enter into vigorous public debate to ensure that at no point do the political leaders have a free hand on any matter. Politics is much too important to be left to the politicians. Or, put alternatively, every citizen should see himself as a politician. Only in this way can our civil liberties be protected.

It should be noted that from Ferguson's point of view one thing here at issue is the limit to the benefits of the division of labour. The danger of the division of labour is that 'society is made to consist of parts, of which none is animated with the spirit of society itself'. (*Essay*, p.207) A professional political class will be animated not with the spirit of society but with the spirit of the political class. Separation of the arts of the clothier and the tanner means that we are better supplied with shoes and clothes: 'But to separate the arts which form the citizen and the statesman, the arts of policy and war, is to attempt to dismember the human character, and to destroy those very arts we mean to improve.' (*Essay*, p.218) The fact that Ferguson here links the arts of policy and of war is significant. He no more approves of the idea of a professional military class than of a professional political class. For in the case of the military art, as with the political, the division of labour is a bad thing, working against and not in favour of the defence of the state. Ferguson is here arguing against a standing army and in favour of a militia, a citizens' army. Such an army will be 'animated with the spirit of society', and will contribute also to the integration, not the 'dismemberment', of the characters of the citizens.

Some eleven years before the *Essay on the History of Civil Society*

Ferguson was already expressing concern both about the lack of a militia in Scotland and also about the difficulties that would be experienced in any attempt to establish one:

> ... self defence is the business of all: and we have already gone too far in the opinion that trade and manufactures are the only requisites in our country. In pursuit of such an idea, we labour to acquire wealth; but neglect the means of defending it. We would turn this nation into a company of manufacturers, where each is confined to a particular branch, and sunk into the habits and peculiarities of his trade. In this we consult the success of manufacture, but slight the honours of human nature: we furnish good work, but educate men gross, sordid, void of sentiment and manners, who may be pillaged, insulted, trod upon by the enemies of their country. (*Reflections previous to the Establishment of a Militia*, p.12)

What was required was a citizen army.

The point was being made at about the same time on the Scottish stage, in John Home's play *Agis*, produced shortly after his successful *Douglas* (though written before it). In the Prologue the civic virtue of Sparta was celebrated: 'Then citizens and soldiers were the same: / And soldiers heroes; for their wealth was fame.' (Home, *Works*, vol.1, p.191) Home is here tapping a rich seam of hurt national pride. By the Militia Act of 1757 England and Wales had a militia, but the Scotch Militia Bill was defeated. The reason for the disparity was almost certainly that English distrust of Scotland was still strong a decade after the Jacobite rebellion of 1745–6. But this distrust was perceived in Scotland as misplaced and unworthy, and Ferguson's contributions on the subject were part of a wide debate among the literati, many of whom were both anti-Jacobite and pro-militia. A club was founded, named the Poker Club by Ferguson, who intended that it should have the job of a poker, as a stirrer up, in this case stirring up support for a Scottish militia. Alexander Carlyle, a leading light among the literati, described the club membership as 'zealous friends to a Scotch Militia, and warm in their resentment in its being refused to us, and an invidious line drawn between Scotland and England'. (*Anecdotes and Characters of the Times*, p.214) Many of the intellectual giants of the Scottish Enlightenment were members, including Hume, Smith, Blair, John Home, Joseph Black, William Robertson and of course Ferguson. Which is not to say that they were all in agreement with each other on this topic. Indeed in a letter to Smith that was otherwise highly complimentary of the *Wealth of Nations* ('You are surely to reign alone on these subjects, to form the opinions, and I hope to govern at least the coming generations.') Adam Ferguson expressed reservations about just one issue: 'You have provoked, it is true, the church, the universities, and the merchants, against all of whom I am willing to take your part; but you have likewise provoked the militia, and there I must be against you.' (Smith, *Correspondence*, p.194)

Smith is not in fact totally opposed to militias, but equally he is not committed to the Fergusonian perception that the establishment of a standing army in place of a militia would lead to the undermining of civic virtue generally and would, specifically, pose a threat to civil liberty. On the contrary he argues that in many kinds of case a standing army is favourable to liberty (*Wealth of Nations*, pp.706–7) Not surprisingly, Smith is inclined to see the army in terms of the category of 'division of labour'. Of course he has a wider view than that; as with all large, publicly financed structures, he asks the three questions about the army: why is it necessary? how is it organised? and how is it paid for? But he was bound to seek to apply the principle of division of labour to the military arts, and he concludes that a full-time professional army has a more secure mastery of its job than a militia could. Evidently, therefore, in Smith's view whatever virtues a militia can bring to bear they are bound to be trumped by the sheer professionalism of the professionals.

It has to be noted that Smith produces an apparent counter-example to this position, but it is no more than apparent. He writes prophetically about the war in the American colonies: 'Should the war in America drag out through another campaign, the American militia may become in every respect a match for that standing army, of which the valour appeared, in the last war [the Seven Years War, 1756–63], at least not inferior to that of the hardiest veterans of France and Spain.' (*Wealth of Nations*, p.701) But there is no contradiction here because if a militia has served through several campaigns, as the American militia looked likely to, it has become in effect a standing army, for the soldiers will be as well practised in obedience, and in the use of their weapons, as are full-time professionals. The Americans would therefore, as Smith foresaw, have the advantage over the British army, for they would have a large well-trained citizens' army operating within a highly supportive general population and would also have short supply lines, as contrasted with the British who had to maintain large expeditionary forces several thousand miles from home, with correspondingly stretched supply lines, and facing a strongly hostile general population.

Kames was more on the side of Ferguson than of Smith in the militia dispute, but he saw a problem with militias no less than with standing armies, though it was a different problem in the two cases: 'A standing army in its present form is dangerous to liberty; and but a feeble bulwark against superior force. On the other hand, a nation in which every subject is a soldier must not indulge any hopes of becoming powerful by manufactures and commerce: it is indeed vigorously defended, but is scarce worthy of being defended.' (*Sketches of the History of Man*, vol.1, p.444) Kames's solution was a system of rotation, with every man doing five to seven years service, with no system for exemption. To ensure that the private soldier was properly habituated to work, as well as to the service of his country, he would spend three-quarters of each year on public works. While details of Kames's proposal were novel, this last point was not far removed from what in any case tended to take place. One need look no further than the system of roads built by General Wade. The primary purpose of the system was military, but in the nature of the case, once the roads had been built by the army, they were there as much for the use of the general public as of the army. Wade's road system was therefore in effect a massive exercise in public works. As regards Kames's proposal of compulsory military service, one conspicuous aspect of it is puzzling. For, as has been pointed out by John Robertson (*The Scottish Enlightenment and the Militia Issue*, p.211), Kames thought that civil liberties were better protected by a militia than by a standing army, and that indeed a standing army was a permanent threat to civil liberties; and yet compulsory military service, such as advocated by Kames, was, in an obvious way, totally incompatible with the liberty of the individual citizen.

In this debate regarding the merits of a militia, and particularly concerning whether a militia is best able to protect the burgeoning commercial state, some of the disputants were better informed than others on military matter. Among them Ferguson holds perhaps a special place, partly because of the sheer depth of his thinking on this matter, but also for the very human reason that, unlike most of the people he was arguing with, he had spent many years in a regiment, the Black Watch, and therefore knew what he was talking about on the basis of extensive first-hand experience. It should be added that, for all the English worries about Scottish Jacobites posing a threat to England if Scotland were granted a militia, Ferguson's own pro-Hanoverian credentials were excellent; he would not otherwise have been appointed chaplain to a Highland regiment. Despite the depth of his thinking on these matters, however, he failed to persuade the people who mattered – Scotland never did get a militia. Gradually the agenda moved on to other things, from national defence to defence of the British Empire, for which a professional army was requisite. Few people, if any, thought that it made sense to have a professional army abroad and a militia at home.

Section 4: Patriotism as a passion

Patriotism was a common topic in Scotland during the Age of Enlightenment. No doubt part of the reason for this was the fact that Scots had to define their position in relation to Scotland and to Britain. For patriotic Scots was the *patria* Scotland or Britain? Were these two things mutually exclusive or was it possible to have patriotic feelings for both Scotland and Britain? For the literati, and indeed for Scots generally, these could not have seemed trivial questions either intellectually or psychologically. I mention them here to give some indication why the topic was on the agenda. It was obvious to the literati that several large questions came in the train of the concept of patriotism. The overarching one asked what patriotism is, and I shall discuss an important answer given by a leading literatus, Lord Kames. In addition patriotism stands in interesting relation to several of the largest ideas that engaged the attention of the literati, in particular the ideas of Enlightenment, of civil liberty and of the commercial stage of society, and I shall explore some of these relations, beginning with the idea of Enlightenment and with the seeming tension between it and patriotism.

The idea of universality has to be to the fore in accounts of the Enlightenment, one reason for this being the fact that the enlightened ones saw themselves as citizens in a Republic of Letters, a Republic which transcends national frontiers, and whose citizens belong in virtue of their active participation in discussions and debates conducted in the public arena. We are speaking therefore of people of ideas, men and women of letters, who were, for the purposes of their debates, cosmopolitans, citizens not of Scotland or France or Germany, but of the world. They relied for persuasiveness not at all on a shared nationality but solely on the sheer strength of their arguments. They saw their cosmopolitanism as a virtue, raising them, by means of their intellectual activities, above the particularities and irrational divisiveness of nationalism. We recall that Hume declared with pride: 'I am a Citizen of the World.' (*Letters*, vol.1, p.470) Yet patriotism was regarded as a virtue; to be unpatriotic was a vice that in many eyes would bespeak untrustworthiness, a preparedness even to betray one's country. There is an apparent tension here, for how can patriotism, rooted in the particularity of a country, be a virtue if the cosmopolitanism of the literati, rooted in the universality of reason, is a virtue?

I believe that the short answer to this is that these two sorts of citizenship are not incompatible, but that on the contrary each can support and enrich the other. In effect cosmopolitanism, considered as a moral stance, is respect for certain universal values, those of rationality and of civil liberty. A person who respects these can, without contradiction, also love his country and attach to it a value that he does not ascribe to any other country; a value based upon the fact that the country is *his*. Indeed citizens who embrace cosmopolitanism can only bring benefit to a country. How can a country not be strengthened morally by the presence in it of citizens who attach a high value to rationality and civil liberty?

To take but one example, one of great significance in the eighteenth century, enlightened citizens worked to eradicate slavery. The hostility of the literati to slavery was palpable. It is instructive to realise that some of Smith's most powerful words deal with this issue: 'There is not a negro from the coast of Africa who does not ... possess a degree of magnanimity which the soul of his sordid master is too often scarce capable of conceiving. Fortune never exerted more cruelly her empire over mankind, than when she subjected those nations of heroes to the refuse of the jails of Europe, to wretches who possess the virtues neither of the country which they come from, nor of those which they go to, and whose levity, brutality, and baseness, so justly expose them to the contempt of the vanquished.' (*Theory of Moral Sentiments*, pp.206–7) Smith's abolitionist credentials were impeccable. Hume, who notoriously stated: 'I am apt to suspect the negroes to be naturally inferior to the whites' (*Essays*, p.208), nevertheless wrote unequivocally against slavery, describing domestic slavery as 'more cruel and oppressive than any civil subjection whatsoever' (*Essays*, p.383), and in that context refers immediately to slavery in the American colonies. Likewise James Dunbar and Gilbert Gerard (son of the more famous Alexander) declared that 'they conceive that the maxims of policy in every well regulated government ought to be consonant to those of morality and consider the slave-trade as equally repugnant to both, as dishonourable to the British name, degrading the Human Nature and diametrically opposite to the genius of the Christian religion.' (King's College Minutes, 3 March 1792, quoted in Berry, 'James Dunbar', p.264) Much the same stand was taken by Hutcheson, Reid, Ferguson and many others. Civil liberty was demonstrably high on their agenda, and it was a practical, not just a theoretical agenda. In just such ways enlightened ones, through their attachment to a cosmopolitan ideal, could morally enhance the countries in which they lived.

I shall now address the opposite kind of case and consider,

not universalism in relation to the particularism of patriotism, but instead the particularism of patriotism in relation to the extreme particularism of *homo economicus*. There seems to be a tension between these two sorts of particularism in the light of Ferguson's discussion of the commercial stage of society and especially of the natural tendency of the commercial life to lead to a fragmented society and to fragmented individuals. It is useful to remind ourselves here of Ferguson's account, quoted earlier, of the psychopathology of the commercial society: 'It is here, indeed, if ever, that man is sometimes found a detached and a solitary being: he has found an object which sets him in competition with his fellow-creatures, and he deals with them as he does with his cattle and his soil, for the sake of the profits they bring.' (*Essay*, p.24) In the commercial stage people's self-interest is primary, and the interest that anything else has for us is derived from our self-interest. There is evidently a clash here between the self-love of *homo economicus* and the well-integrated citizen's patriotism, his love of his country. If love of your country is truly *of your country* then it is not just a form of love of yourself. This seemed to Ferguson and to many of his friends in the Poker Club to be a real and dangerous problem. The socio-economic form of the problem is: how is commercial life to be squared with civil liberties? It was of course with just this problem in mind that Ferguson called for the introduction of a militia. We have also observed that Kames, alive to the same problem, suggested a similar solution. I shall turn now to Kames's comments on patriotism and the commercial life. What he has to say is full of interest. He offers a kind of natural history of patriotism and also considers the prospects for patriotism. He is pessimistic, and his pessimism is supported by strong arguments.

As regards patriotism, as with much else, the stadial theory of history provides the broad context of discussion; for, given the progress from the hunter-gatherer stage to the pastoral to the agricultural to the commercial, a question arises as to whether or not patriotism is possible at all four stages. The brief answer is 'no'; it is impossible until people have land that they call their own, and that does not happen until the third stage, when people have ceased their wandering and established agricultural settlements. At that point there arises, as if by nature, a new sentiment or passion: love of one's country for its own sake. This is the passion of patriotism. It can be fitted immediately into a moral framework because it stands in opposition to the vice of self-love, that is, self-love as a governing character trait. To have the vice of self-love is to see every practical question primarily in terms of benefit to the dear self, and if you love your country for its sake and not for your own then self-love, by definition, is not your ruling passion. Kames says of patriotism: 'it triumphs over every selfish motive, and is a firm support to every virtue'. (*Sketches of the History of Man*, vol.1, p.440) And if he has overstepped the mark in his next comment: 'In fact, wherever it prevails, the morals of the people are found to be pure and correct,' there is something to be said for the position. For first, as noted, there is the fact that patriotism is contrary to the spirit of selfishness in which vices naturally take root.

Secondly, Kames sees patriotism as a virtue standing between mutually opposed vices, of despotism on the one side and licentiousness on the other. For despotic rule tends to work against people's love of their country – it is not easy to love a country in which you are oppressed, and not even the despot could easily love a country while most of the citizens are his enemies. Likewise licentiousness, clearly on the side of gross self-indulgence, is about self-love, and when that governs the soul it excludes love of one's country for its own sake. Furthermore each of these opposed vices, of despotism and licentiousness, works against civil liberties. That despotism does so is self-evident. Licentiousness works against civil liberties because licentious acts naturally encroach on other people in all sorts of unwelcome ways, intruding on them and limiting their freedoms. Hence patriotism, by holding these vices at bay, works on the side of civil liberty and virtue.

Patriotism is like all other virtues, in that one cannot afford to relax, smugly, safe in the knowledge that having achieved it one has it for life. Any virtue, and therefore patriotism also, once achieved, has to be maintained. It is always under threat. Kames is clear as regards the chief source of danger: 'Successful commerce is not more advantageous by the wealth and power it immediately bestows, than it is hurtful ultimately by introducing luxury and voluptuousness, which eradicates patriotism.' (*Sketches*, vol.1, p.446) Why it eradicates patriotism is plain: 'No cause hitherto mentioned hath such influence in depressing patriotism, as inequality of rank and riches in an opulent monarchy. A continual influx of wealth into the capital, generates show, luxury, avarice, which are all selfish vices; and selfishness, enslaving the mind, eradicates every fibre of patriotism.' (*Sketches*, vol.1, p.445) The problem for a country is how to achieve commercial success without thereafter being destroyed by it. Kames, as we know, thinks that an education in civic virtue is essential and that that is best achieved through the mechanism of a militia. But he sees no grounds for optimism on this matter. In his *Sketches of the History of Man* he produces numerous examples of countries which, following commercial success gained and for some time maintained by a highly patriotic citizenship, succumbed to riches and luxury, and grew soft and weak. Kames shows how, at least in theory, there can be a cycle here, with a commercially successful country going into decline, and later rising to a renewed success. But he adds: 'The first part of the progress is verified in a thousand instances; but the world has not subsisted long enough to afford any clear instance of the other.' (*Sketches*, vol.1, p.452)

It is in the light of analyses such as these that we should consider Enlightenment ideas about progress and improvement. There have been countless cases of national progress and improvement, but there was a rather common Scottish view, that any such progress requires a holding operation if it is to be maintained, and in the longer run the operation is likely, perhaps even certain, to fail. The literati, all of them educated in Greek and Roman literature, were quick to point to Athens and Rome, which had each had their day in the sun, and did not seem likely to have another such in the foreseeable future.

Ferguson adds a caveat as regards our ways of measuring progress. The caveat accords well with his critique of the methodology of conjectural history. We might think that progress has been made over the millennia and even over the past century, at least as far as the distribution of human happiness is concerned, and we might support this belief by the imaginative experiment of forming an idea of ourselves living in some previous age. In all probability we would find the idea disagreeable for, after all, an age which did not have hot and cold running water on tap must seem worse to us than the present day, in which we can enjoy modern conveniences. And we might reasonably conclude that we must be happier with our lot than past generations, lacking mod cons, could possibly have been with theirs.

Ferguson dismisses this argument on the grounds that it is based upon an irrelevant exercise of imagination. To get at the truth of the matter, we should not seek to imagine ourselves into a past age while imaginatively taking into that age our knowledge of, and fondness for, modern conveniences; instead we should imagine how that past age must have seemed to the inhabitants of that time who had no knowledge of the comforts that were going to be available to subsequent generations. Ferguson conjectures that those past generations would in general have been about as happy with their lot as we are with ours. Each generation makes its own accommodation with what is available to it, for what else can it do? No doubt a future generation will look back on the way of life of the inhabitants of Scotland in the early twenty-first century, and will marvel that we survived the pain and discomfort consequent on the lack of certain items of state-of-the-art technology considered requisite for comfortable living in the twenty-second century. If Ferguson is right, then broadly speaking there is no great progress nor great regress as regards the distribution of happiness.

Section 5: Sympathy and education

The process of corruption which Ferguson discusses takes its start from the partiality of those who administer justice. If it is administered in light of a private agenda then no amount of clever drafting of the law will protect the citizen from encroachment on his civil liberties. What is required in addition to just law is rigorous impartiality in its administration. Now, the concept of impartiality is central to the moral theory of the Scottish Enlightenment and I should like to explore it here. It is especially associated with Adam

Smith, whose 'impartial spectator' is a hero of the Enlightenment. A just magistrate will pass judgment from his standpoint as an impartial spectator. This point can be generalised, for since impartial judgment lies at the heart of justice we ordinary citizens must also be impartial spectators if we are to embody the virtue of justice. Famously Smith built his entire moral theory on the concept of sympathy, and for him the concept is inseparable from spectatorship, for it is spectators who sympathise. I shall begin with the concept of sympathy, and this will lead us directly into a consideration of spectatorship. From there I move to one of the many practical implications of Smith's theory, concerning the public funding of education, a major practical doctrine of the *Wealth of Nations*. The moral basis of it is best understood in terms of Smith's account of sympathy in the *Theory of Moral Sentiments* (hereafter *TMS*).

In that account it is our imagination that does most of the work. As spectators of an agent's suffering, we 'form some idea of his sensations' and even feel something 'which, though weaker in degree, is not altogether unlike them', and we do this by means of the imaginative experiment of placing ourselves in the agent's situation: 'we enter as it were into his body, and become in some measure the same person with him'. (*TMS*, p.9).

The feeling that the spectator comes to have by these means is not necessarily one of pity or compassion; it may instead be of delight or happiness, or any passion whatever. Thus in the *Lectures on Rhetoric and Belles Lettres* (*LRBL*) Smith deals explicitly with the power that a historian has to produce a wide range of sympathetic responses in the reader: 'We enter into [other human beings'] misfortunes, grieve when they grieve, rejoice when they rejoice, and in a word feel for them in some respect as if we ourselves were in the same condition.' (*LRBL*, p.90) Smith reserves the term 'sympathy' for 'our fellow-feeling for any passion whatever', and stresses the fact that he is extending the scope of the term. 'Sympathy' is therefore introduced into Smith's system as a technical term, and has to be understood on that basis.

If a spectator is in sympathy with the agent's emotion or passion, then he approves of that passion and judges it 'proper' or 'appropriate'. If he is out of sympathy with it, he disapproves of it and judges it improper or inappropriate. A good deal might go on meantime. In particular, Smith believes that we find disagreeable any disagreement in sentiment between ourselves and others and are therefore motivated to see whether such disagreement can be smoothed out. The efforts a spectator makes to see whether he should modify his sentiments so that they agree with those of the agent may be hard work; he must 'endeavour, as much as he can, to put himself in the situation of the other'; he must 'strive to render as perfect as possible, that imaginary change of situation upon which his sympathy is founded'. (*TMS*, p.21) Whatever love of our neighbour consists in, for Smith it at least includes our willingness to make the effort to see things from our neighbour's point of view. Smith thinks that this is a Christian stance. If adopted it greatly adds to the moral authority of our judgments regarding the propriety or impropriety of other people's actions and passions.

Let us now turn from the bilateral relation between spectator and agent to the trilateral relation, between a spectator, an agent who acts upon someone, and the person who is acted upon, whom I shall call the 'recipient'. The recipient's response to the agent's act may be any one of several kinds. Smith focuses upon two, first a grateful response and secondly a resentful one.

Suppose the agent behaves in a certain way to the recipient, and the recipient is grateful. (Perhaps the agent had acted in a kindly or generous way.) If the spectator judges the recipient's gratitude is proper he sympathises with the recipient, and he therefore approves of the agent's act and judges it meritorious or worthy of reward. Suppose instead that the recipient's reaction is one of resentment. (Perhaps the agent had carried out a gratuitous assault.) If the spectator judges the recipient's resentment proper or appropriate then again he sympathises with the recipient, and he therefore disapproves of the agent's act and judges it demeritorious or worthy of punishment. Judgments of merit or demerit concerning a person's act are therefore made on the basis of an antecedent judgment concerning the propriety or impropriety of another person's reaction to that act. And all four types of judgment, regarding propriety, impropriety, merit and demerit, are based on an antecedent act of sympathy.

As with regard to judgments of propriety and impropriety so also with regard to judgments of merit and demerit, there is a real person into whose shoes the spectator imaginatively places himself. But in the case to which I now turn there seems not to be. In the two-person and three-person models I have been discussing, one person judges another, but how are we to judge our own acts? To speak generally, in the case of our judgment of other people we have a reasonable hope of judging in a disinterested way but may lack requisite information about them. In judging ourselves the situation is the reverse; generally we have the requisite information but need to overcome distortions caused by self-love or self-interest. How do we overcome the distorting effects of self-love when we come to pass moral judgment on our own behaviour? We manage it, argues Smith, by turning for help to a creature of our own imagination, an 'impartial spectator', whose impartiality underpins the agent's disinterested judgments about himself. But how is disinterest achieved when the impartial spectator is a product of the agent's own imagination?

I shall approach this question obliquely by determining first who or what it is that is thus imagined into existence? Is it the voice of society, representing established social attitudes? At times in the first edition of *TMS* Smith comes close to saying this and, in a letter to Smith, Sir Gilbert Elliot seems to have interpreted him in that way. In the second edition, and evidently at least partly in response to Elliot, Smith is rather clearer that this is not the role of the impartial spectator for the latter can, and occasionally does, speak against established social attitudes; or, as Smith puts the matter in his reply to Elliot: 'real magnanimity and conscious virtue can support itselfe under the disapprobation of all mankind.' (*Correspondence*, letter 40) Hence the impartial spectator cannot simply be a repository of the actual opinions of society. Nevertheless the impartial spectator owes its existence to the real spectators. Were it not for our discovery that, while we are watching and judging other people, we are being watched and judged by them, we would not form the idea of a spectator judging us impartially.

The impartial spectator, as a creature of a person's imagination, has no more (nor less) information about what is to be judged than has the agent, for the creature, the impartial spectator, cannot be better informed than is its creator, the agent. In so far as the agent has information about his own situation that is not possessed by the external spectators, 'the great demigod within the breast' is better placed than are external spectators to make a judgment about the propriety of his behaviour. So the agent asks himself what the judgment of the external spectators would be if they knew what he knows. In seeking to answer this question, the agent tries to see his own situation in a disinterested way, that is, through the eyes of others, while at the same time benefiting from the level of information that the agent himself has.

Of course, even if the agent is better informed than the spectators, he may still not be sufficiently well informed. He may be failing, perhaps culpably, to note features in his situation that would make all the difference to his judgment about his own acts and attitudes. But the information he has is all that is available to the impartial spectator, whose judgment therefore is not indefeasible. Hence we can never say categorically that the impartial spectator's judgment is true; it is always provisional even if it is becoming more trustworthy: 'There exists in the mind of every man an idea of this kind, gradually formed from his observations upon the character and conduct both of himself and of other people. It is the slow, gradual, and progressive work of the great demigod within the breast, the great judge and arbiter of conduct . . . Every day some feature is improved; every day some blemish is corrected.' (*TMS*, p.247) Enlightenment is not a state, but an activity, an attempt to access the truth by the use of one's own mental powers, without reliance on an authority to tell one what the truth is. It is just such activity that Smith describes in his account of the impartial spectator, and it is that same activity that provides, in Smith's view, the only defence we can ever build against moral corruption. Without the constant work of the great demigod within the breast we stand no chance in the fight to defend civil liberties, nor perhaps will even realise that they are worth defending.

The points just made have to be set in the context of Smith's teachings in the *Wealth of Nations* regarding the principle of division of labour and the damaging consequences of the systematic application of the principle. We noted in Chapter 2 that Smith spoke of the workers as each engaged in a task 'so simple and uniform as to give little exercise to the understanding; while, at the same time, their labour is so constant and so severe, that it leaves them little leisure and less inclination to apply to, or even think of anything else'. (*Wealth of Nations*, p.785) This consequence of the division of labour destroys the worker: 'The torpor of his mind renders him, not only incapable of relishing or bearing a part in any rational conversation, but of conceiving any generous, noble, or tender sentiment, and consequently of forming any just judgment concerning many even of the ordinary duties of private life.' (*Wealth of Nations*, p.782) Smith is here describing a person who has been rendered utterly incapable of engaging in the kind of imaginative exercise that produces a judgment of the impartial spectator, that is, the kind of exercise that has to be performed by the citizenry if it is to recognise a threat to, or even the value of, civil liberties. Smith's solution, a system of state-funded education, will counteract the mind-numbing effects and thereby increase the health of the body politic. In particular the mind-numbing effects of labour in a commercially advanced society will be counteracted, he thinks, if the labouring poor are taught 'the most essential parts of education . . . to read, write, and account' plus the 'elementary parts of geometry and mechanicks'. (*Wealth of Nations*, p.785)

These points have to made with particular force in light of an account of Smith's 'inhumanity' presented in a popular work on the Enlightenment. We are told: 'Smith himself was frank enough to admit that the extreme division of labour required by modern manufacturing – his prime example was pin-making – reduced the worker to a "hand", a mentally stunted, slave-like machine. But he was not "humane" enough to suggest a remedy . . . *Laissez-faire* economics thus endorsed an *inhumane* system in the name of the "natural laws" of market forces.' (Porter, *The Enlightenment*, p.22) We have seen, however, that Smith, ever responsive to the essential grandeur of human beings, was loudly and clearly on the side of humanity in this matter. He spelled out the problem and spelled out a highly plausible solution. No doubt there were and are inhumane people among *laissez-faire* economists, but Smith is assuredly not of their number. He saw as clearly as anyone could that economic policies must respect moral imperatives and this insight is articulated with the utmost vigour in the *Wealth of Nations*.

It may be added that, given Smith's strongly libertarian stance, it is impressive testimony to his appreciation of the importance of education that he thinks that education deserves to win against certain claims on behalf of civil liberty. He approves of the idea that the 'publick can impose upon almost the whole body of the people the necessity of acquiring those most essential parts of education, by obliging every man to undergo an examination or probation in them before he can obtain the freedom in any corporation, or be allowed to set up any trade either in a village or town corporate'. (*Wealth of Nations*, p.786)

Smith is clear that it is better for the private citizen that he be educated; to lack properly functioning intellectual faculties is like suffering from a mutilation or physical deformity. But he is also clear that the state is so much aided by a reasonably well-educated citizenry that even if the individual citizen were not morally a better person for a good education there would still be a powerful case for providing education for the lowest in society:

> The more they are instructed, the less liable they are to the delusions of enthusiasm and superstition, which, among ignorant nations, frequently occasion the most dreadful disorders. An instructed and intelligent people besides are always more decent and orderly than an ignorant and stupid one ... In free countries, where the safety of government depends very much upon the favourable judgment which the people may form of its conduct, it must surely be of the highest importance that they should not be disposed to judge rashly or capriciously concerning it. (*Wealth of Nations*, p.788)

Earlier we noted that Smith asked three questions about the

army, and it should now be added that he asked the same questions about the provision of education: why is it necessary? how is it organised? and how is it paid for? He explains how it must be paid for, namely out of public monies, describes in detail how it should be organised, even going into some detail about course contents and finally, as we now see, he has a two-pronged approach to the question of its necessity. In brief, to neglect the education of the people is to fail them both economically and morally. The connection between these two is clear, from Smith's perspective: the fact that neglect of education is bad morality ensures that it is also bad economics. People who have become mutilated in spirit due to the application of the principle of division of labour will work less well even at the small tasks they are given – those tasks, in one sense undemanding, in another make an intolerable demand on the workers.

Additionally Smith notes: 'Men are much more likely to discover easier and readier methods of attaining any object, when the whole attention of their minds is directed towards that single object, than when it is dissipated among a great variety of things.' (*Wealth of Nations*, p.20) On this basis he argues that division of labour should lead to increase in economic efficiency because workers will discover or invent ways in which their own tasks may be better implemented. The thesis that division of labour can be a stimulant to intellectual activity is illustrated by Smith with a tale concerning the contribution that a lazy but bright boy made to a major advance in the design of steam engines. There is reason to doubt Smith's tale but, in any case, as Smith showed himself well aware, if a workforce has become seriously demoralised it will tend to dry up as a source of new ideas. The brightness of the bright workers will have been snuffed out. However, even if the economic argument for the public funding of widespread education is clearly stated in the *Wealth of Nations* it is plain from the *Theory of Moral Sentiments* that Smith places the highest priority on the moral argument; as a result of our natural tendency to sympathise, we would judge demoralising work practices to be morally improper and would sympathise with the workers' resentment at having to engage in such practices. Given the moral philosophical context of Smith's economic theory we must assume that Smith had those moral considerations in mind in the *Wealth of Nations* even while he was stressing the economic argument for the allocation of substantial public funding to education.

Section 6: A general education

In his *Elements of the Philosophy of the Human Mind* Dugald Stewart seeks to identify fundamental requirements of a well-balanced education. His discussion has a modern ring, and indeed can be slotted without effort into a major contemporary debate. I shall attend here to his investigation, and start by noting his acceptance of the Humean doctrine that all the sciences lead back to the concept of human nature, and the consequent doctrine that the study of human nature has a natural priority among all our studies. If this natural priority means anything it surely means that there are special advantages which flow from the study of human nature itself. Stewart believes that there are, and that the chief of them is the light that such study must throw on the subjects of intellectual and moral education. Stewart's preliminary account of the objectives of education is brief: '*First*, to cultivate all the various principles of our nature, both speculative and active, in such a manner as to bring them to the greatest perfection of which they are susceptible; and, *secondly*, by watching over the impressions and associations which the mind receives in early life, to secure it against the influence of prevailing errors; and, as far as possible, to engage its prepossessions on the side of truth.' (*Elements*, p.11)

For Stewart the most important thing is to cultivate the mind to the extent of its capacity, from which it follows that some particular expertise must not be nourished at the expense of other things. Though parallels can be dangerous it is worth noting the parallel with physical development. Someone who regularly exercises, say, the muscles of the left arm and otherwise does little exercise, develops imperfectly because he develops in an unbalanced fashion. And likewise we should not expect to find the highest cultivation of the human mind among those of 'confined pursuits'. A person can of course achieve eminence in his field by concentrating only on that one field. But there is a price to be paid for such emphasis, for the person becomes, in Stewart's dismissive phrase, a 'literary artisan', that is to say, the mental equivalent of the labourer whose physical exertions are of such a nature as to lead to a distorted body in (or with) which the person can therefore never feel comfortable.

However, the kind of concentration that I have been speaking about is not necessarily the most efficient route to excellence in the chosen field, and may well prove to be an obstacle. It is with this in mind that Stewart formulates an important position:

> But it is perfectly consistent with the most intense appli-
> cation to our favourite pursuit, to cultivate that general
> acquaintance with letters and with the world which may
> be sufficient to enlarge the mind, and to preserve it from
> any danger of contracting the pedantry of a particular
> profession. In many cases, (as was already remarked)
> the sciences reflect light on each other; and the general
> acquisitions which we have made in other pursuits, may
> furnish us with useful helps for the farther prosecution of
> our own. (*Elements*, p.12)

Stewart did not need to look beyond his own career to find support for this statement. As a mathematician of considerable accomplishment (sufficient not only to secure him the chair of mathematics at Edinburgh, but also to enable him to return years later to the task of lecturing on mathematics when his successor in the chair was ill) and as a moralist and metaphysician of great distinction, he could see in close-up the advantages that flow from the principle of the broad-based education that he here endorses.

Indeed, had he turned to almost all of the leading lights among the literati he would have found confirmation of his position. Not only were they wide-ranging in their accomplishments; it is easy to demonstrate, in the case of each of them, systematic relations between the various aspects of their work, and it is impossible to believe that their thinking in one field was not influenced by their deep knowledge of cognate (or not so cognate) fields. We are not of course considering solitary geniuses. In the numerous Enlightenment clubs and societies men of disparate and wide-ranging accomplishment set off intellectual sparks in each other, and exemplified the Enlightenment ideal that people should think *for* themselves but not *by* themselves. Nevertheless, by whatever means these creative sparks came to sparkle in their heads, and however much the literati benefited from discussion with their peers, the thinking of each one was hugely influenced by the wide-ranging knowledge and the intellectual skill that he carried about with him. There seems no gainsaying Dugald Stewart's statement quoted above 'In many cases . . . the sciences reflect light on each other; and the general acquisitions which we have made in other pursuits, may furnish us with useful helps for the farther prosecution of our own.'

Stewart is concerned to defend civic virtue. It is after all necessary to have a well-ordered set of priorities, and in that case we should recognise that some things are more important than cultural pre-eminence: 'It ought not to be the leading object of any one, to become an eminent metaphysician, mathematician, or poet, but to render himself happy as an individual, and an agreeable, a respectable, and a useful member of society.' (*Elements*, p.12) Being culturally well-balanced through a broad education has advantages; the person is better adjusted to life in civic society and is therefore happier and is more virtuous in the civic sense of the term. Once persuaded of them, the advantages must seem irresistible.

Stewart offers the following proposition for consideration: 'The most successful and splendid exertions, both in the sciences and the arts . . . have been made by individuals, in whose minds the seeds of genius were allowed to shoot up, wild and free; while, from the most careful and skilful tuition, seldom anything results above mediocrity.' (*Elements* p.14) However, even if the proposition is true, and it is disputable, it would not cut much ice with Dugald Stewart who nailed his colours to the mast in declaring that happiness, respectability and usefulness to society were more important than pre-eminence. Genius is all very well, but happiness and civic virtue are more important, and if Stewart were given a choice between happiness and civic virtue on the one side and genius on the other, he would choose the former. This does not, however, imply that he would rather be uneducated than educated. The contrast is between a rounded education and one which is partial. A rounded education answers much better to the demands of our nature than a partial education does, even if the partiality of our education contributes to our pre-eminence: 'The truth, I apprehend, is that happiness, in so far as it arises from the mind itself, will be always proportioned to the degree of perfection which its powers have attained; but that in cultivating these powers, with a view to this most important of all objects, it is essentially necessary that such a degree of attention be bestowed on all of them, as may preserve them in that state of relative strength, which appears to be agreeable to the intentions of nature.' (*Elements*, p.14)

It is plainly Stewart's view that we are not in practice faced here with an either/or, that is, either genius or civic virtue, with the genius arising from a partial education and the good citizen arising from an education which is more broad-based. He needed only to look at his circle of friends and acquaintances to know that a genius can be the product of a general education, a genius who is also a model citizen. Dugald Stewart, a student of Thomas Reid's at Glasgow, could have conversations daily with Kames, Smith, Black, Hutton, Ferguson, Robertson, Playfair, each a model citizen and a front-rank intellectual. Each of these men, no less than Stewart himself, was widely and deeply knowledgeable, humane, and virtuous in the all-important civic sense of the term, and as such they were living witnesses to the benefits of a general education. In recent decades George Davie, in *The Democratic Intellect* and *The Crisis of the Democratic Intellect*, has emphasised the merits of the generalist approach to education that is strong in the Scottish educational tradition. But we now see that two centuries ago, at the height of the Scottish Enlightenment, Dugald Stewart provided a deep and firm philosophical underpinning to that message.

FIVE

Enlightened Religion

Section 1: Religion and Enlightenment

The concept of Enlightenment with which I have been working has two fundamental elements each of which must prompt, in the mind of anyone who knows the history of Europe, the conjecture, if not the certainty, that Enlightenment and Christianity are not natural allies. Granted that the two fundamental elements of Enlightenment are toleration and the exercise of autonomous reason, respect for the historical realities requires us to recall the record of systematic intolerance practised by the Church in response to people who exercised their autonomous reason in matters of religion.

Institutions, like individual people, tend to act to protect themselves, and the Church is no exception. One of its major enemies is heresy and as a matter of historical record the Church used teaching, censorship and punitive sanctions as means of self-defence against attack from that direction. The Church proclaimed its message, suppressed any message that conflicted with its own and silenced anyone who managed to slip past the protective net and proclaim a message not authorised by the ecclesiastical authorities. The question here is not whether the Church's practices in this direction were justified, though plainly if you see yourself as engaged in the sovereignly important task of saving souls you will think that practically any measure may justifiably be taken to secure success. The question is rather whether the Church, committed to its awesome mission, can sit comfortably with Enlightenment. And the facts just outlined point, on the face of it, to a negative answer. You demonstrate your tolerance by tolerating, not things which you approve of, but things which you do not. By this test, and from the perspective of many leaders of the Enlightenment, the Church was systematically intolerant and was therefore also systematically opposed to Enlightenment. The historic mission of the Church, as making a claim on all souls, was seen as an imperialism without bounds. It was a small part of humanity that believed itself to have the God-given role of appropriating for itself the whole of humanity, and therefore to have the God-given sanction to annihilate whatever stood in its path. There were without doubt many citizens in the Republic of Letters who saw the church in precisely these terms, and therefore saw it as a repressive and in no way a progressive force.

Respect for authority can be mind-numbing in so far as it works against independent thought. From the perspective of the Enlightenment, the Church created and for long periods maintained circumstances, both social and psychological, in which it was psychologically very difficult for those brought up within the faith community not to see the Church as a fount of truth. According to this view many adherents said 'yes', not because they could see that what the Church was saying was true but because they believed the Church to be a repository of the truth that saves and to be a herald of that truth. There may or may not be good arguments for those truths, but if they are salvific then the important thing is not to study the arguments for them, but to believe. Indeed, arguments can be a risky way of introducing people to the truths because if the arguments turn out to be faulty this might shake or even undermine a person's belief in their conclusions, that is, in the saving truths.

Furthermore, the Church accepted that there were mysteries to which it was necessary to give assent even if the propositions encapsulating the mysteries affirmed truths that were beyond demonstration and were even beyond the grasp of the human intellect in this life. Why believe these propositions? Because the Church declares them to be true. But in the Age of Enlightenment that answer was no longer sufficient. Some wanted to know what the evidence was for the truths that save, and they investigated varieties of evidence, because some kinds are stronger than others. If a reasonable person is going to commit himself body and soul to something, dedicate his life to it, then he will first look for evidence of the requisite strength. As a reasonable man he will proportion his belief to the evidence; the stronger the evidence the stronger the belief. The mere fact that somebody else believes the propositions in question is no longer seen to be sufficient evidence, because the reasonable person will want to know what that other person's evidence is. There is, after all, hardly any thought so crazy that you could not find anybody who either believes it or could easily come to do so.

In the Age of Enlightenment, the Age of Toleration, Jews came to be tolerated to a greater degree than had been customary for many centuries; it was the period when the ghetto walls came down, literally and metaphorically, and Jews acquired a much greater degree of civil liberty. For this reason the era is commonly known as the Age of Emancipation. But it was also seen by many as a time of emancipation from the authority of the Church – as if, ironically, the authority of the Church constituted a kind of ghetto walls constraining the intellects of those within. In the eighteenth century, according to this perception, the intellectual faculties of many people managed at last to escape from ecclesiastical control. In the newly tolerant environment there was a flood of philosophical and other sorts of writing on the origins of religion and on the truth (or otherwise) of religious belief.

Hume's judgment about the relation between philosophy and toleration was unequivocal. He speaks of philosophy 'which, as it requires entire liberty above all other privileges, and chiefly flourishes from the free opposition of sentiments and argumentation, received its first birth in an age and country of freedom and toleration, and was never cramped, even in its most extravagant principles, by any creeds, confessions, or penal statutes'. (*Enquiry Concerning Human Understanding*, p.132) He had in mind ancient Greece and particularly the city state of Athens during the fifth and fourth centuries BC, and while writing this passage he must have been painfully aware of the contrast with Scotland during its eighteenth-century struggle towards the sun. He will certainly have known about Hutcheson's problems with the Kirk, for example, the fact that Hutcheson was criticised by the Glasgow Presbytery for 'teaching to his students in contravention to the Westminster Confession the following two false and dangerous doctrines, first that the standard of moral goodness was the promotion of the happiness of others; and second that we could have a knowledge of good and evil, without, and prior to a knowledge of God'. (W.R. Scott, *Frances Hutcheson*, p.84)

It is no wonder that, in a letter shortly after the criticism, Hutcheson wrote of the need to 'put a new face upon Theology in Scotland' (Nov. 1743, W.R. Scott, *Francis Hutcheson*, p.89) The letter was in connection with the candidacy of William Leechman for the divinity chair at Glasgow. Leechman's appointment, which provoked 'the furious indignation of our zealots', to use Hutcheson's description, led, as we saw in Chapter 2, to his being arraigned on a charge of heresy. That he weathered the storm, and indeed in 1761 was appointed Principal of Glasgow University, serves only to underline the intolerance he had had to overcome.

Leechman was by no means the first of Glasgow's eighteenth-century professors of divinity to have come up against the intolerance of the clergy. John Simson (1667–1740), professor of sacred theology at Glasgow during Hutcheson's student days, rejected the dogma of the Incarnation, at least in its usual formulation, and expressed doubts about the doctrine that salvation is possible only for those who have knowledge of Christ. His theology was shaky in other ways also, particularly with regard to his insistence that Christian revelations had to pass a test of rationality if they were to be judged acceptable. These views were intolerable to many ministers. One of Simson's allies, however, was his brother-in-law, Principal John Stirling. But Simson's enemies rose to the occasion, and in 1729 the General Assembly suspended him from all offices of preaching and teaching, and specified that he could not safely be allowed to teach divinity. Principal Stirling protested on his behalf, to no avail.

Simson placed less emphasis on our sinful nature than did the Kirk as a whole, and he perhaps held that standard teachings on our depravity were exaggerated. Whatever his precise views on this matter, it was certainly the belief of Hutcheson that standard teachings on our depravity went much too far; for even the most depraved of us are benevolent. Indeed, in Hutcheson's judgment our benevolence is part of the original constitution of our nature. Some of us may exhibit more of it, some less, but there it is, in some measure or other, in everyone. For Hutcheson therefore it

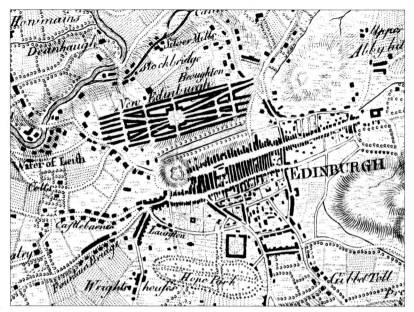

1. Edinburgh New Town in the form of a Union Jack, by James Craig, from John Laurie's Plan of Edinburgh (Reproduced by permission of The Trustees of The National Library of Scotland)

2. 'West Street, called Trongait', by Robert Paul and William Buchanan

3. 'The Origin of Painting', by David Allan

4. 'The Connoisseurs', by David Allan
(National Galleries of Scotland)

5. 'Aberdeen Literati' – an eighteenth-century cartoon

6. Self-portrait of John Kay, greatest of Scotland's Enlightenment cartoonists
(National Galleries of Scotland)

☞ The Public is respectfully informed, that, during the Performance of the New Spectacle of The CATARACT, Places for the Boxes will be let during the Usual Hours at the Box Entrance under the Portico.

This present Evening, MONDAY, February 23. 1824,
Will be performed the Tragedy of

DOUGLAS.

Lord Randolph by Mr DENHAM—Glenalvon by Mr PRITCHARD—Old Norval by Mr FAULKNER,
Young Norval by Master G. F. SMITH,
Whose Performances at the principal American Theatres having gained him the Title of the American Roscius, and having also been received with the most flattering Applause at the Theatre-Royal, Dublin, has visited this City on his Journey to London, to have the honour of appearing in Edinburgh,
Donald by Mr DUFF—Officers by Mr HILLYARD, Mr MILLER, Mr AIKIN, Mr J. STANLEY, Mr M'GREGOR, and Mr POWER,
Anna by Miss EYRE.
Lady Randolph by Miss CAMPBELL,
Being her Third Apperance in this Theatre.

After which will be performed, for the 4th Time in this Theatre, the Melo-Dramatic Spectacle, originally produced at the Theatre-Royal, Drury-Lane, and entitled, The

CATARACT OF THE GANGES,
OR THE RAJAH'S DAUGHTER.

The EQUESTRIAN DEPARTMENT under the Direction of
Mr COOKE,
Whose celebrated Company of Equestrians is Engaged for this Occasion.
The whole produced under the Superintendance of
Mr NORMAN,
From the Theatre-Royal, Covent-Garden, and Director of Spectacle to the Theatre-Royal, Dublin.

Previous to the Spectacle will be performed the celebrated OVERTURE to ZEMBUCA, assisted, with the Permission of their Officers, by
THE BAND OF THE KING'S DRAGOON GUARDS.

Ackbar, *Emperor of Delhi,* by Mr FAULKNER,
Jam Saheb, *Rajah of Guzzerat,* by Mr LYNCH,
Mokarra, *Grand Bramin of the Jahrejah Tribe,* by Mr CALCRAFT,
Iran, *a Young Warrior,* by Mr PRITCHARD,
Mordaunt, *an English Officer,* by Mr DENHAM—Mokayee by Mr MASON,
Jack Robinson, *Servant to Mordaunt,* by Mr STANLEY,
Ambassador by Mr WYNN—The First Brahmin by Mr SMITH—Mahratta Chief by Mr RAE,
Officers by Mr DUFF, Mr HILLYARD, Mr MILLER, Mr POWER, Mr AIKIN, Mr J. STANLEY, and Mr M'GREGOR,
The Princess Dessa, *Daughter to the Emperor,* by Miss EYRE,
Matali, *a Peasant,* by Mrs NICOL—Ulra, *her Daughter,* by Miss NICOL,
Zamine, *the Rajah's Daughter,* by Mrs STANLEY.

EQUESTRIANS BY
Mr COOKE
Mr WOOLFORDE, Mr EVANS, Mr BELL, Mr BUCK, Mr THOMSON, Mr CROSSMAN, Mr USHER, &c. &c

The Scenery, which is partly New, and partly Selected, will be exhibited in the following Succession:
Act I.

1. FIELD of BATTLE after the CONFLICT,
2. EXTERIOR of MOKAYEE's COTTAGE,
3. HALL of AUDIENCE in the RAJAH's PALACE,
4. LAKE and MOUNTAINOUS SCENERY,
5. VIEW in the GARDENS of the RAJAH,
6. GRAND TEMPLE, in which will be introduced

THE GRAND BRIDAL PROCESSION.
Act II.

1. VIEW amidst the MOUNTAINS of GUZZERAT,
2. EXTERIOR of the TEMPLE at JUGGERNAUT,
3. SANCTUARY of the IDOL BRAHMA,
4. ROMANTIC MOUNTAINOUS VIEW,
5. VIEW in the WOOD of HIMMALAYA,
6. The CATARACT, with

THE BATTLE AND TRIUMPH OF THE RAJAH'S FORCES.

☞ On Saturday Evening a numerous and fashionable Audience honoured the Performance of the New Grand Indian Spectacle, entitled,
THE CATARACT OF THE GANGES, OR THE RAJAH'S DAUGHTER,
With unbounded Applause; it will, in consequence, be repeated every Evening this Week after which, it must be withdrawn, to allow the Production of other Hippo-Dramatic Spectacles, Mr COOKE's Engagement at the Theatre-Royal Bath, limiting the one he has formed to a very few Nights.

To-Morrow, by Desire, The BRIDE of LAMMERMOOR, with the CATARACT of the GANGES.
On Wednesday, a favourite Comedy, with the Spectacle of The CATARACT of the GANGES.
On Thursday, by desire, the Comedy of The JEALOUS WIFE,
Mr Oakly by Mr CALCRAFT—Major Oakly by Mr FAULKNER—Russet by Mr MACKAY—Sir Harry by Mr STANLEY,
Lord Trinket by Mr JONES,
Being his First Appearance since his late severe Illness,
Lady Freelove by Mrs EYRE—Mrs Oakly by Mrs H. SIDDONS—Harriet by Miss HALFORD.
After which, the Last Night but Two of The CATARACT of the GANGES, or the Rajah's Daughter,

7. Playbill advertising John Home's *Douglas*
(Reproduced by permission of The Trustees of The National Library of Scotland)

January 9th 1767 Mr Millar gave a Discourse on the Government of Sparta and the Institutions of Lycurgus

January 16th 1767 Dr Trail gave some Considerations on the Changes in the State of human Society introduced by Christianity.

January 23d 1767 This question was considered Can we with safety ascertain the limits of human Knowledge and in what points.

January 30th 1767 What are the most proper Means to be used by a State in order to prevent the necessarys of life from rising to too high a price opened by Dr Reid and conversed upon

February 6th 1767 Dr Wight gave some Observations concerning Persecution on the score of Religion in general and on the Persecutions suffered by the Christians in the early ages in particular

February 13th 1767 Dr Reid gave his Discourse on the Train of Thought in the human Minde

February 20th 1767 The question What is meant by

8. A page of the Minute Book of the Glasgow Literary Society
(reproduced by permission of the Royal Faculty of Procurators in Glasgow)

First Discourse

Page 9

I do not think that Lord Bacon has received from posterity a higher degree of admiration than he deserves.. Nor do I know any instance of hints of discoverys ascribed to him of which he had no Conception.

Did any Man before L Bacon give us the Conception of Philosophy as a Chaste Interpretation of Nature? Did any Man before or after him give so just, so comprehensive, and so Sublime a Conception of it? Was it not he that first taught Mankind to distinguish Theories & Hypotheses the Fictions of human Fancy, from the Oracles of Nature; to revere the last & to put due Contempt upon the first? Did not his Novum Organum give birth to the Art of Induction? Was there ever a Book in the World that delineated an Art so prettily & so minutely before that Art had an Existence? Has not Newton in his Opticks and in his Astronomy followed his precepts, step by step?

His Desiderata in the Book De Augmentis &c His Venalio Paris, His Idols of the human Understanding, His Reflections on the Ancient Philosophy, I admire, & I find very few who admire them so much as I think they deserve, fewer still who have learned so much from them as they might have learned.

In natural Philosophy, the slow Experience of more than a Century and a half hardly lost convinced the Learned that L Bacon taught them at first, that Experiment & just Induction are alone are to be trusted. In the other great Branch of Philosophy, how few are there to this day that seem to think of thee upon of L Bacon.

Had his Principles been known and explained as they ought, could the Cartesian System have filled Europe as it did for half a Century could Leibnetz's System have succeeded it.

It seems to me that Newton & Locke since they came to be known abroad have contributed more to diffuse a true Spirit of Philosophy, than Lord Bacons Writings. His Writings are

3 / II / 3

9. A page from a lengthy manuscript by Thomas Reid
(see Reid, *Correspondence* pp. 211–12)

10. Thomas Reid, by Sir Henry Raeburn
(The Hunterian Art Gallery, University of Glasgow)

11. David Hume, by Louis Carrogis
(National Galleries of Scotland)

12. Elizabeth Gunning, Duchess of Hamilton, by Gavin Hamilton
(In the collection of Lennoxlove House)

13. David Hunter of Blackness, by Sir Henry Raeburn
(National Galleries of Scotland)

14. Margaret Lindsay (Mrs Allan Ramsay), by Allan Ramsay
(National Galleries of Scotland)

15. Mrs Colin Campbell, by Sir Henry Raeburn
(Kelvingrove Art Gallery)

16. James Hutton, detail of a portrait by Sir Henry Raeburn (National Galleries of Scotland)

Siccar Point

17. 'Unconformity at Siccar Point, Cockburnspath', by Sir James Hall

18. Front elevation of William Adam's design for Arniston House, from *Vitruvius Scotus* (Reproduced by permission of The Trustees of The National Library of Scotland)

19. The main entrance to Glasgow College in the 1700s, when Hutcheson, Smith, Reid *et al.* taught there, from James Coutts, *A History of the University of Glasgow* (1909)

is axiomatic that we are so constituted that we can take pleasure in the good fortune of others purely for their sake and not at all for our own. Hence even though their good fortune misses us, and though we derive from it no benefit whatever beyond the pleasure we derive from seeing the happiness of those others who are more fortunate, their happiness is still something that can bring us real joy. Hutcheson's system of moral philosophy is based upon this reading of human nature. We can advance from it to a detailed account of the nature of duty and of the several moral virtues, including justice, and do so without invoking God. Hutcheson was a religious man, a believing and practising Christian, but nevertheless showed how it was possible to construct a moral philosophy that was largely secular. In that sense the Glasgow Presbytery was not far off the mark in ascribing to him the two doctrines, first, that the standard of moral goodness was the promotion of the happiness of others; and second that we could have a knowledge of good and evil, without, and prior to, a knowledge of God.

The two propositions also come quite close to a fair description of the moral philosophy of Hume, whose relations with sections of the Kirk were much worse than Hutcheson's – though Hutcheson, who was a minister of the Kirk and a doctor of divinity, may have found the attack on himself more painful because it came from Scottish presbyterians, who were, in that sense, on his (Hutcheson's) side. Hume's moral philosophy is rigorously secular, a rationally ordered set of propositions forming an overall picture that people who do not believe in a personal God can find persuasive, and that even good Christians might find persuasive because of the sheer strength of the arguments that Hume deploys in support of his doctrines.

Let us say then that Hume sought to demonstrate that a person can live a virtuous life even if he is not a believer – a proposition to which Hutcheson would assent. The question that Hume addressed concerned the extent to which we could construct a sound morality, one appropriate to our human nature, without depending at any point upon the authority of God. This last clause was of course bound to be intolerable to the intolerant, people on the zealous wing of the Kirk, for whom a morality which was not God-centred was an absurdity and a profound wickedness. No doubt there were some among them who would have done to Hume in the 1740s what their predecessors had done to Thomas Aikenhead some fifty years earlier. But the zealots were less in control by the 1740s, while a Moderate party was gaining the initiative, which it finally secured under the leadership of William Robertson, Hugh Blair and others. These latter were the true heirs of Hutcheson, but they also came strongly under the influence of Hume. Increasingly a gentle humanism was to be heard in the pulpits.

The Enlightenment had come to the Kirk in the shape of the Moderate Party, a Party which furnished the Scottish Enlightenment with many distinguished literati, thus helping to give the Scottish Enlightenment a distinctively Scottish voice. It was after all the national church whose voice was being heard in the land – how different from the stridently anti-Christian voice which contributed so much to the tone of the Enlightenment in France where Charles-Louis Montesquieu (1689–1755), Voltaire (1694–1778), Nicolas-Antoine Boulanger (1722–59) and Baron d'Holbach (1723–89), among many others, sought by a variety of logical and rhetorical means to undermine Christianity. The shrill anti-Christian voice heard in France does not indicate that France was a more enlightened country. Far from it. In respect of the central Enlightenment value of toleration, France was a good deal less enlightened than Scotland. It had a much greater distance to travel from a state of religious and political repression, and it is no doubt this that explains the more strident tone of the *philosophes*, the French literati. The comparative lack of toleration in France is easily demonstrated. We need only note that in 1733 Voltaire's *Lettres philosophiques* were burned by the executioner before the Palais de Justice; that in 1746 the *Pensées philosophiques* of Denis Diderot (1713–84) was condemned and it was declared illegal to print, sell or publish the work; and that in 1749 Diderot was imprisoned for publishing his *Lettre sur les aveugles* (*Letter on the blind*). Certain of the *philosophes* engaged the enemy with a good deal less restraint than the cautious Hume was accustomed to show. Nevertheless in his writings on religion in general and on the Church in particular Hume's philosophy has a distinctly French accent, not a Scottish one. He is arguably the least Scottish of the major Scottish thinkers of the Enlightenment, and in that case it may be significant that Hume wrote his *Treatise* while living in France, in the village of La Flèche near the Jesuit College attended a century earlier by Descartes. As contrasted with the French accent of Hume's philosophy, the accent of Hutcheson, Reid, Kames and many others in the common sense school, is unmistakably Scottish.

In the remainder of this chapter I shall focus upon three of the literati. First Hume, who cannot be omitted since his writings on religion are undoubtedly the greatest on the subject produced in Scotland during the Enlightenment. My aim will be to try to identify his position in relation to Christianity in particular and religion in general – is he a deist, an atheist, or what? Secondly, Lord Kames will be considered with a view to determining his position on two central matters, one concerning the illusoriness of human freedom and the other the benevolence of God. And finally I shall offer some thoughts on Hugh Blair, whose sermons from the pulpit drew large congregations and whose collected sermons in printed form were a best seller.

Section 2: *The Natural History of Religion*

In *My Own Life* Hume reports: 'I published at London, my Natural History of Religion along with some other small pieces: Its public entry was rather obscure, except only that Dr. Hurd wrote a pamphlet against it, with all the illiberal petulance, arrogance, and scurrility, which distinguishes the Warburtonian school. This pamphlet gave me some consolation for the otherwise indifferent reception of my performance.' (Hume, *Dialogues and Natural History of Religion*, hereinafter *DNHR*, p.7) Richard Hurd (1720–1808) rose to be Bishop of Lichfield and Coventry and later of Worcester. William Warburton, (1689–1779), dean of Bristol in 1757, the year of publication of Hume's *Natural History of Religion*, was already well known as the author of several works on religion including *The Divine Legation of Moses*. Hume had previously been attacked by him. Writing in February 1754 to John Stewart, professor of

Natural Philosophy at Edinburgh, Hume had remarked: 'When I am abus'd by such a Fellow as Warburton, whom I neither know nor care for, I can laugh at him.' (*Letters*, vol.1, p.186)

Warburton read the *Natural History*, either an advance copy or a proof copy, shortly before its publication and wrote a letter about it to Hume's friend Andrew Millar:

> I supposed you would be glad to know what sort of book it is which you are about to publish with Hume's name and yours to it. The design of the first essay [*The Natural History of Religion*] is the very same with all Lord Bolingbroke's, to establish *naturalism*, a species of atheism, instead of religion ... You have often told me of this man's moral virtues. He may have many, for ought I know; but let me observe to you, there are vices of the *mind* as well as of the *body*; and I think a wickeder mind, and more obstinately bent on public mischief, I never knew. (7 February 1757, Hume, *Letters*, vol.1, p.248, n.2)

Hume commented shortly after to Andrew Millar: 'And any thing so low as Warburton, or his Flatterers, I shoud certainly be ashamed to engage with.' (May 1757, *Letters*, vol.1, p.250) Nevertheless Warburton was saying what many, including many Scottish presbyterians, thought – as Hume knew. He told Smith, who had earlier seen a draft copy, that the *Natural History of Religion* was 'somewhat amended in point of Prudence', adding that 'I do not apprehend, that it will much encrease the Clamour against me'. (Smith, *Correspondence*, p.20) He believed it would not much increase the clamour, because he believed the clamour could not in any case get much louder. To see what in Hume's *Natural History of Religion* was causing the anger will tell us a good deal about a most important area of the Scottish Enlightenment and about its foe.

The work plays a crucial role within Hume's overall philosophical strategy in his confrontation with religion. Two questions may be asked about religious belief: how do we come by it? and what proof is there that it is true? Or, to slant the questions in a Humean way: what is its origin in human nature? and what is its foundation in reason? (*DNHR*, p.134) The questions are very different, and might (and generally do) have very different answers. The fact that something is believed does not imply that it is true, and the fact that it is true does not imply that it is believed. Let us grant then that investigating whether a given proposition is true is a different sort of exercise from investigating why someone believes it. Of Hume's two most sustained investigations of religion, the *Dialogues Concerning Natural Religion* is the first sort of exercise, concerning whether the proposition that God exists is actually true, whereas the *Natural History of Religion* is the second sort of exercise, concerning the social and psychological factors that cause or induce a person to hold the belief.

Briefly stated, the *Natural History of Religion*, the first prong of Hume's two-pronged assault on religion, argues that religion was born of fear, is nourished by fear, breeds intolerance and has precipitated human calamities on an awesome scale. Nowhere does Hume say that God does not exist or that Christianity is false, but all the same the picture is not an attractive one. Indeed it is so horrendous that if it is correct then the only way religion could be defended would be by demonstrating that it, or at least a particular variety of it, *is* true. If we have proof that it is true, then we still might not like it, but we cannot reject what we know to be true. However, the aim of the *Dialogues Concerning Natural Religion* is precisely to expose the inadequacies of available proofs of the existence of God, the fundamental belief of all religions. This is the second prong of Hume's assault. If there is no proof that God exists, then perhaps he doesn't, in which case all those great evils perpetrated in God's name were for naught. Here, then, are the two prongs of Hume's attack on religion. In the remainder of this section I shall focus on aspects of the *Natural History of Religion* and thereafter shall make some comments on the *Dialogues*.

Hume's *Natural History of Religion* begins with a large historical conjecture, namely that polytheism, the belief that there are many deities, preceded monotheism. The evidence that Hume adduces for this conjecture is of two sorts. As regards the first, Hume points out that early accounts of religious belief speak only of polytheistic belief, not monotheistic, and he then deploys the principle that there is a 'natural progress of human thought' as the mind rises from the inferior to the superior and as people rise from barbarity to polite society. If the early peoples who figure in historical records are polytheists then their ancestors would be even more thoroughly sunk in polytheistic belief; they would not have been monotheists who then sank into polytheism in time for historical records to be written. But how does Hume know that one example of the natural progress of human thought is the move from polytheism to monotheism? His answer is that the latter move is from error to truth, and that that move counts as progress. But it is not clear that Hume should be helping himself to this as an example of natural progress, for in the *Natural History of Religion* he does not attempt to prove the truth of the proposition that there is one and only one God.

The second conjecture that Hume deploys in his argument for the historical priority of polytheism is that ancient 'barbarous nations' are much like modern barbarous nations. His argument is from 'our present experience concerning the principles and opinions of barbarous nations'. According to this experience: 'The savage tribes of AMERICA, AFRICA, and ASIA are all idolators. Not a single exception to this rule.' (*DNHR*, p.135) Since historical records of ancient barbarous nations suggest that they were much like the present 'savage tribes' in respect of their idolatry, it is a reasonable conjecture that even more ancient 'savage tribes' were likewise idolatrous.

Religious belief of some sort or other therefore, whether poly-theistic or monotheistic, is very ancient. Why then did it arise? It is useful to distinguish between primary and secondary principles of human nature. We have some principles that well up immediately and by our very nature. Fear wells up at the sight of a threatening thing; likewise a mother's love wells up at the sight of her child. There are many such examples of responses well nigh universal amongst human beings. But religious belief is not like that. Hume reports '. . . it has neither perhaps been so universal as to admit of no exception, nor has it been, in any degree, uniform in the ideas, which it has suggested. Some nations have been discovered, who entertained no sentiments of Religion, if travellers and historians may be credited; and no two nations, and scarce any two men, have ever agreed precisely in the same sentiments.' (*DNHR*, p.134) The first religious beliefs are therefore not primary principles – we do not all look out upon the world and immediately and by a necessity of our nature believe in a deity.

Kames, as against Hume, thought that everyone had a religious belief of one sort or another, and he held that the explanation was that 'the image of the Deity must be stamped upon the mind of every human being' (*Sketches of the History of Man*, vol.2, p.383), an image which is presumably not merely accessible to, but is actually accessed by, all of us. Kames's way of putting the matter suggests that, in a phrase central to the Scottish common sense school of philosophy, belief in a deity is part of the 'original constitution of our nature'. Kames is therefore committed to rejecting Hume's acount of the origin of religious belief in terms of our natural fear of the unknown causes of fearsome happenings.

The question, a crucial one, concerning the universality of religious belief, was also taken up by Ferguson, who did not name Hume explicitly in his discussion, but clearly had him in mind. Ferguson affirms: 'Many operations in nature have been universally looked upon as the exertions of mind or spirit, distinct from man. The most ignorant apprehend such exertions in the little sphere of their own concerns. The more knowing apprehend them in the general order of nature to which their observation extend.' He adds: 'The conceptions of rude minds on this subject are groveling, or require correction; but absolute atheism is an effect of study, and an effort to withstand natural feelings. If successful in any particular instance, it is no more than an exception to the general rule.' (*Institutes of Moral Philosophy*, pp.87–8) Ferguson's position appears to be therefore that nature left to its own devices would produce religious belief, and only a combined exercise of intellect and will can prevent such belief arising. This position conflicts with Kames's, since the latter affirms an unexceptionable universality of belief – the belief is irresistibly attendant upon the grasp that we all have of the image of God stamped on our mind. On the other hand Ferguson's position accords with Hume's, at least in so far as both hold that religion is based on a natural feeling or sentiment. I shall turn now to Hume's account of the way in which this natural sentiment operates.

We observed that Hume held that religious belief or the 'religious sentiment' is not primary – it does not well up immediately in the soul as does, say, a mother's love for her infant or a recipient's gratitude to a benefactor, or a victim's anger at a wanton attack. But if religious sentiment is not primary, it is very close to being so. It is natural to be frightened in the face of destructive natural forces. Our distant ancestors had no idea what the causes of such events were and in response to them the natural human tendency to personify came into play. The idea that we have such a tendency is central to the argument of the *Natural History of Religion*: 'We find human faces in the moon, armies in the clouds; and by a natural propensity, if not corrected by experience and reflection, ascribe malice or good-will to every thing, that hurts or pleases us.' (*DNHR*, p.141) The emphasis is mainly on the negative passions, on fear and dismal apprehension, on vengefulness, severity, cruelty and malice. These, affirms Hume, 'must augment the ghastliness and horror, which oppresses the amazed religionist'. (*DNHR*, p.176) For this reason 'men are much oftener thrown on their knees by the melancholy than by the agreeable passions'. (*DNHR*, p.143) The natural step in the face of these fearsome invisible agents is to appease them, and so religious practice gets under way, with men offering sacrifices to Mars before battle, and to Neptune during a storm at sea.

This helps us to see what Hume means by 'the natural progress of human thought' in relation to religion. With the advance of science we learn that a storm is not deliberately engineered by Neptune, but is instead the natural product of the interplay of wind and waves. We learn that eclipses are not the product of a malicious Zeus but instead have a natural cause. Scientific advance prompts us to abandon belief in the multitude of gods whose existence had been invoked to explain events occurring in various domains, such as the sea, woods, mountains, the air, and so on. This is scientific progress and it will tend to impact on religious belief by prompting in us belief in a single God, creator of heaven and earth and of the laws of nature governing the behaviour of things in the created world. This new religious belief is an advance on the old one because it is a rational response to, or reflection of, advances in scientific understanding of the natural order.

However, Hume does not regard the move from polytheism to monotheism as unqualified progress. This point has to be made since our topic is Enlightenment, and Hume thinks that in a definable way Enlightenment is better served by polytheism for polytheism is comparatively tolerant. A polytheistic religion has numerous deities, each associated with a place, with a type of natural event, or with a human skill, and so on. Different polytheisms tend to have deities for the same sort of thing, and the consequence is that in the ancient world it proved easy to see different religious communities as worshipping the same deities, even though the deities may have had different names in the different communities. Hence in ancient times, when there were many polytheistic religions, there were very few religious wars. Except in certain special cases, toleration was the rule, and religion was, if anything, a unifying force between peoples, a principle of harmony. It had objectionable aspects, as witness the ritual of human sacrifice in which some polytheistic religions engaged. But the suffering caused by such practices was as nothing compared with the monstrous acts committed by modern monotheists in the name of God.

Hume refers to the 'tolerating spirit of idolaters, both in ancient and modern times', and reminds us of Xenophon's tale that when the Delphic oracle was asked what rite or worship was most acceptable to the gods, it replied: 'Those that are legally established in each city.' (*DNHR*, p.161) Hume pays no such compliment to monotheists, for in his view monotheism is naturally associated with intolerance. Each monotheistic sect sees itself as sole guardian of the truth, as the people with whom God is pleased, and sees every other sect as incurring God's displeasure. The outcome of such a self-perception does not accord with the ideals of polite society: 'the several sects fall naturally into animosity, and mutually discharge on each other that sacred zeal and rancour, the most furious and implacable of all human passions'. (*DNHR*, p.161) It is true that some nations with monotheistic religions are tolerant, but to Hume's mind this phenomenon is a reminder that the church (thank heavens) is not the only source of power in the state. The tolerance commonly met with in England and the Low Countries, Hume affirms, is due to 'the steady resolution of the civil magistrate, in opposition to the continued efforts of priests and bigots'. (*DNHR*, p.162)

We have here, therefore, a further argument for the claim, discussed earlier, that religion, if not incompatible with Enlightenment, is at least not its natural ally – though Hume, no doubt to the irritation of his Christian readers, has added the claim that polytheism is, in a crucial respect, more a natural ally of Enlightenment than Christianity could ever be. Given the unremitting hostility he suffered throughout his adult life from the Presbyterian high-fliers, Hume did not need to look much beyond his doorstep in Edinburgh to find empirical evidence for his claims about monotheistic intolerance.

There is a sense in which the *Natural History of Religion* puts religion on the defensive. For if Hume is right about the origin of religious belief then he has undermined the claim that the near-universality of belief in the existence of a deity is hard evidence for the truth of the belief. We need to take seriously the term 'natural' in the title of the dissertation. Hume seeks to demonstrate that the belief is natural. We have a natural fear of hidden causes and have also a natural tendency to personify them. Even if what he terms the 'sentiment of religion' is not as immediate as certain other sentiments, such as a mother's love for her child, the sentiment of religion rises from the deep well springs of human nature; it does so in almost everybody and does so quite unbidden. That's us. The near-universality of belief in a deity points to near-universal features of human nature, while at the same time carrying no implication whatever for the truth, or otherwise, of what is believed.

Section 3: Why dialogue?

Granted that even if there were no deity there would none the less be a natural tendency to believe that there is one, let us take the next step, that of asking not how we come by the belief in a deity, but instead whether the belief is true. This latter question calls for a different kind of approach; we must seek a proof, a demonstration of the belief. That investigation is made in Hume's *Dialogues Concerning Natural Religion*, which eventually appeared in 1779, three years after his death.

That publication date is misleading. Hume had almost certainly drafted about eleven-twelfths of the *Dialogues* sometime between 1749 and 1751. It is almost certain that he wrote the *Natural History of Religion* around 1750. Hume was, therefore, working intensively on the question of the reasonableness of belief in a deity while at the same time investigating the question whether occurrence of the belief could be given a purely naturalistic explanation, that is, an explanation saying nothing about reasonableness and focusing entirely on natural causation. His reply in the *Dialogues* is that there is nothing reasonable about the belief in a deity and, as we have seen, his reply in the *Natural History of Religion* is that there is a purely naturalistic explanation for such a belief. Writing to his publisher William Strahan about the *Dialogues*, Hume reported: 'Some of my Friends flatter me, that it is the best thing I ever wrote.' (*Letters*, vol.2, p.323) Hume probably agreed with his friends. Why, then, was he willing to publish the *Natural History of Religion*, a work that he must have known would make uncomfortable reading for his fellow citizens, and yet was not willing to publish the *Dialogues*? One possible answer is that he was not satisfied with the early draft of the *Dialogues*. That is suggested by the fact that he was revising it even on his deathbed. On the other hand it may be that he was revising it because he had good reason not to publish it; it was therefore lying around available for revision. I think that the latter suggestion is correct, and that Hume judged that even though the time was ripe, though barely ripe, for the *Natural History*, it was not yet ripe for the *Dialogues*. For the *Dialogues* was patently a more destructive work. Whereas the *Natural History* left open the question of whether there is evidence that God actually exists, the *Dialogues* confronts the question head on and, in a series of brilliant, destructive arguments, demonstrates the utter failure of any available argument that might be thought to have a chance.

The book is one of the glories of the Scottish, and indeed the European, Enlightenment, a profound meditation on the existence of God. If, as many have claimed, Hume was an atheist, this fact about him (if it is a fact) does not prove that the book must be fatally flawed; it simply proves that an atheist can make a profound contribution to the philosophy of religion. In fact I do not believe that Hume was an atheist. But I shall come to that point later. First the *Dialogues*.

The fact that the *Dialogues* is in the form of a dialogue is biographically and philosophically significant. As regards the biographical significance, a philosopher writing a monograph writes in his own name. If he presents a thesis, argues in favour of it and defends it against objections, then, unless told otherwise, we are entitled to assume that he accepts the thesis. He might not do so, of course, but we are entitled to suppose that he does – unless there are counter-indications. In a dialogue, on the other hand, the matter is more complex. If, as in the *Dialogues Concerning Natural Religion*, there are three principal interlocutors, each disagreeing with the other two on a wide range of issues, it might be that just one of the interlocutors represents the author's own views, but it might be that the author has distributed his own views between two or all three characters. It follows that if one of the characters rejects a widely accepted thesis, the author can seek to blunt any criticism of himself by supporters of that thesis by pointing out that it was after all just one of the characters in the dialogue that rejected it; it was not the author.

Of the three principal interlocutors one, Cleanthes, has an 'accurate philosophical turn', the second, Philo, is a 'careless sceptic', and the third, Demea, is 'inflexibly orthodox', (*DNHR*, p.30) and the three disagree about most things relating to arguments for the existence of God. Almost certainly one reason Hume had for writing his masterwork on religion in dialogue form was that he could put his arguments into the public domain while leaving himself at least some small chance of diverting, in the way just described, some small amount of criticism. For though it is true that one of the interlocutors, Philo, makes many points that indicate he is a sceptic in matters of religion, why identify Hume with Philo rather than with the 'accurate' Cleanthes or even with the 'inflexibly orthodox' Demea? In fact Hume well knew how slight was his chance of mollifying a religious mob that was in any case baying for his blood. Towards the end of the *Natural History of Religion* Hume had written: 'Examine the religious principles, which have, in fact, prevailed in the world. You will scarcely be persuaded, that they are any thing but sick men's dreams.' (*DNHR*, p.184) The high-fliers of the Kirk could hardly avoid taking such judgments personally. Philo, though more measured in his tone than is Hume speaking in his own name in the *Natural History*, sounded altogether too much like Hume. And so Hume opted for posthumous publication. Nevertheless the contents of the *Dialogues* were known to a number of Hume's friends in his own lifetime, since he showed them copies. Indeed as early as 1751 Hume was writing about the book at length to Gilbert Elliot of Minto.

In the *Dialogues* Hume is even more circumspect than so far indicated. For we do not find him reporting the dialogue. His tactic is to remove himself yet further from the conversation by giving to a fourth person, Pamphilus, who had been present at the dialogue between Philo, Cleanthes and Demea, the role of sending to his friend Hermippus a report of what had been said. Hume could hardly have detached himself more than he did from the arguments and doctrines discussed. All, of course, to no avail. It was after all Hume who had written the book, including Philo's dangerous and disturbing arguments, presented at length and in great detail, that neither Cleanthes nor Demea, speaking for the opposition, quite managed to match. And we should remind ourselves that, on the evidence, it was Adam Smith's desire for a peaceful life that prevented Smith from publishing the *Dialogues*. Hume seems to have anticipated the difficulty. In his will he had charged Smith with the publication of the work, but three months before his death he had written to Smith about the *Dialogues*: 'I am content, to leave it entirely to your Discretion at what time you will publish that

Piece, or whether you will publish it at all.' (Hume, *Letters*, vol.2, p.318)
In the end it was Hume's nephew David Hume who stepped in and
arranged the publication. Hume's circumspection in using the dialogue
form was not enough for Hume nor in the end even enough for Smith.

I referred above to the philosophical significance of the dialogic
form of the *Dialogues*. In the introduction to the conversation the
narrator Pamphilus affirms: 'Any question of philosophy . . . which
is so obscure and uncertain, that human reason can reach no fixed
determination with regard to it; if it should be treated at all; seems
to lead us naturally into the style of dialogue and conversation. Reasonable men may be allowed to differ, when no one can reasonably
be positive.' (*DNHR*, p.30) Pamphilus thereupon stresses the fact
that as regards the question of the nature of God, his attributes,
decrees and providential plan: 'human reason has not reached any
certain determination: But these are topics so interesting, that we
cannot restrain our restless enquiry with regard to them; though
nothing but doubt, uncertainty and contradiction, have, as yet, been
the result of our most accurate researches.' Hume recognised that
there were powerful and mutually opposed arguments in the field
of natural religion, and in all probability was sceptical whether a
definitive answer would ever be forthcoming. In these circumstances
why not lay out the opposing positions, giving each the strongest
arguments available, and leaving it to the reader – not to adjudicate
but to recognise the size of the problem?

As to the size, Philo speaks of 'those who think nothing too
difficult for human reason; and presumptiously breaking through
all fences, profane the inmost sanctuaries of the temple'. It is at
least arguable that Hume thought that the fundamental problems of
religion were indeed too difficult for human reason, and that we are
therefore not entitled to place our confidence in 'this frail faculty of
reason' in respect of these sublime and abstruse matters which are
'so remote from common life and experience'. (*DNHR*, p.33)

Section 4: *Dialogues Concerning Natural Religion*

Hume was brought up in the Calvinist tradition, and when he
reacted against it he knew from the inside what it was he was

reacting against. Yet a lingering doubt remains concerning Hume's philosophical relation to Calvinism. I do not wish to argue that Hume was a crypto-Calvinist – that would be several steps too far – but I shall suggest later that there are features of Hume's attack on religious belief with which Calvinists could feel at home if they paused to consider his position with due care. However, this measure of agreement should not be exaggerated. Even if it is there, and even if, as I suspect, Hume was well aware of it, there is between the two sides a disagreement of cosmic proportions. First a comment on the battleground.

Natural religion, nowadays commonly called natural theology, is the investigation, by reason unaided by revelation, of God's existence and nature. The term 'natural' is doubly appropriate in this context for, first, it is used in contrast to 'revealed by God' as this phrase is used particularly of the revelations reported in holy scriptures. The question for the natural theologian, therefore, is not what we can learn about God by reading holy scriptures, but what we can learn about him by a rational enquiry which is not supported by such aid. Secondly, most natural theology has consisted of an investigation of the natural order with a view to gleaning from it evidence that God exists and also evidence that he has a particular nature; and in at least two ways, which I should now like to spell out, revelation is not far from such an enquiry.

For first, theologians believe that God *reveals* himself in nature to the extent that the natural order displays signs of its createdness – as if God left his handprint on his work, a handprint consisting of, for example, the marks of a cosmic intelligence. Indeed many theologians of the Enlightenment era welcomed the work of Isaac Newton as proof positive of a cosmic creator. Throughout the *Dialogues* Hume's three interlocutors address the question of what, if anything, is to be learned about God by a study of the natural order. If by such a study we do learn things about God and his nature, such as that he exists and is wise, good and powerful, then God may be said to have indirectly revealed to us these facts about himself, 'indirectly' because he has done so by the mediation of nature.

The second of the ways in which revelation is not far from natural religion is simply this, that to a large extent it is revelation that sets the agenda of natural theologians. People read in the Bible about the existence of God and about his nature. They could then assent to those religious propositions as an act of faith. Such an act is partly, and perhaps primarily, an act of will. But the question naturally arises as to how many, if any, of those propositions could be demonstrated. For if a demonstration were forthcoming then even without the aid of the will one could give one's assent. Intellect would do the assenting by itself. The Bible does not furnish us with demonstrations; rather it furnishes us with many propositions about God, and people then undertook the task of finding rational support for them.

Looking for arguments to support propositions in which you in any case believe is a perfectly respectable intellectual exercise – one need only think of Bertrand Russell's three hundred and sixty-four pages devoted to a proof that $2 + 2 = 4$. No less respectable is the search by theologians for proofs of such propositions as that God exists, that he is powerful, wise, just, merciful, and so on. Hume affirms: 'A wise man, therefore, proportions his belief to the evidence.' (*Enquiry Concerning Human Understanding*, p.110) If the evidence for the existence of God, and for his wisdom and so on, is strong, then it is reasonable to proportion your belief to that evidence and believe accordingly. The question addressed in the *Dialogues* is simply: what is the quality of that evidence?

The character of the three interlocutors emerges early. Cleanthes argues that the adaptation of means to ends is evident throughout nature, and in this respect nature resembles human contrivances perfectly. In human contrivances we find clear evidence of a designer. In nature likewise. As Cleanthes puts the point: 'Since therefore the effects resemble each other, we are led to infer, by all the rules of analogy, that the causes also resemble; and that the Author of nature is somewhat similar to the mind of man; though possessed of much larger faculties, proportioned to the grandeur of the work, which he has executed.' (*DNHR*, p.45)

Demea is appalled at this line of argument. He believes that, in so far as the conclusion establishes a likeness of God to humans (or perhaps, rather, of humans to God), it implies that God is as it were a human being on a grand scale. But God is no such thing. Such a deity as figures in the conclusion of Cleanthes' argument is simply not God. To believe in such a deity is therefore not to believe in God, for which reason Demea complains to Cleanthes: 'you give advantage to atheists, which they never could obtain, by the mere dint of argument and reasoning'. (*DNHR*, pp.45–6) Demea is not against the use of reason in the sphere of religion, but he is against the design argument. He believes that God's existence can be demonstrated, and later in the *Dialogues* he presents a proof. But he thinks that Cleanthes' proof, a version of the design argument, seeks to do the impossible, namely, give us humans an insight into the divine nature. For Demea, God is ineffable; we can know *that* he is, but not *what* he is. There is thus a strong hint of mysticism in Demea's position, which he manages to combine with a measure of rationalism.

In a sense, Philo, Hume's *persona* in the *Dialogues*, is more on the side of Demea than of Cleanthes, at least to this extent, that Philo, like Demea, thinks the design argument a hopeless instrument for learning anything about God. His reason is that the argument relies on a supposed analogy between the natural order and human artifacts, and yet the analogy is so slight as to be vanishingly small. We have seen many houses being built, and so, when we come across a house we have not previously seen, we assume that someone has built it even though we have not actually seen it during the construction stage. This newly seen house is so like the many houses we have seen people building that we can reasonably claim an exact analogy between this house and the others. Likewise by analogy we can reasonably argue from the fact of the circulation of blood in many people to the fact of the circulation of the blood in *this* person, for *this* person is sufficiently similar to the people in whom the blood is known to circulate. But can we argue from the circulation of the blood in frogs to the circulation of blood in people? Surely the analogy is rather weak. Furthermore, can we argue from the circulation of the blood in people to the circulation of sap in trees? Surely the analogy is far too weak to permit such a conclusion.

Well, thinks Philo, this last case is much like Cleanthes' claim that one can argue from human contrivances to the order of nature. As Philo states to Cleanthes: 'But surely you will not affirm, that the universe bears such a resemblance to a house, that we can with the same certainty infer a similar cause, or that the analogy is here entire and perfect. The dissimilitude is so striking, that the utmost you can here pretend to is a guess, a conjecture, a presumption concerning a similar cause.' (*DNHR*, p.46)

Philo's chief criticism of Cleanthes is in effect that the latter has altogether too narrow a perspective. We have so far discovered a large number of principles of origination and of change in the universe, principles relating to chemical compounds, to plants, to animals, and to us humans also, for we humans are principles of change – we have new ideas, plan things, and so on. We have no reason to believe that we know more than a tiny fraction of the principles that are actually in operation in the universe. By what right do we pick certain features of our own life and ascribe those features, albeit greatly magnified, to a being responsible for the origin of the entire universe? Who knows what there might be elsewhere that could serve as a no less plausible model? The possibilities are endless. Philo writes: 'When nature has so extremely diversified her manner of operation in this small globe; can we imagine, that she incessantly copies herself throughout so immense a universe? . . . A very small part of this great system, during a very short time, is very imperfectly discovered to us: And do we thence pronounce decisively concerning the origin of the whole?' (*DNHR*, pp.50–1) Of course if we had witnessed worlds being made we would have a useful basis for making inferences about the origin of our world. But in the absence of such experience it is not enough to say that though we haven't seen worlds being made we have at least seen people building houses and working to the plans of architects, and we believe that that is a sufficiently close analogy for making inferences about the universe. The analogy, as said earlier, is vanishingly small. It is the basis of bad theology.

Of the three interlocutors in the *Dialogues* Philo has the most to say (60 per cent of the words of the first draft were said by

Philo), 85 per cent of the revisions Hume made were to Philo's contributions, and when Hume revised the work on his deathbed it was Philo's part that he worked on. The evidence points irresistibly to the conclusion that Philo is Hume's *persona*.

But the situation is more complex. In March 1751 Hume gave a 'Sample' of the *Dialogues* to Gilbert Elliot of Minto and his accompanying comment to Elliot is worth quoting at length for the light it sheds on Hume's attitude to the rationality (or otherwise) of belief in God.

> You wou'd perceive by the Sample I have given you, that
> I make Cleanthes the hero of the Dialogue. Whatever you
> can think of, to strengthen that Side of the Argument, will
> be most acceptable to me. Any Propensity you imagine I
> have to the other Side, crept in against my Will . . . I cou'd
> wish that Cleanthes' Argument could be so analys'd as to
> be render'd quite formal & regular. The Propensity of the
> Mind towards it, unless that Propensity were as strong &
> universal as that to believe in our Senses & Experience,
> will still, I am afraid, be esteem'd a suspicious Foundation.
> Tis here I wish for your Assistance. We must endeavour
> to prove that this Propensity is somewhat different from
> our Inclination to find our own Figures in the Clouds, our
> Face in the Moon, our Passions and Sentiments even in
> inanimate Matter. Such an Inclination may, & ought to be
> controul'd, & can never be a legitimate Ground of Assent.
> (Hume, *Letters*, vol.1, p.153)

This interesting passage is open to several interpretations, but one that is plausible is that Hume is saying that there is a natural propensity of the mind to see the world as bearing the marks of having been designed. The propensity is neither as strong nor as universal as our propensity to believe that there is an external world, but there is at any rate more to the propensity than there is to our inclination to see clouds as forming human shapes, or to see the moon as having the shape of a face. In light of this fact about our propensities, Hume is asking Gilbert Minto for help in understanding how it is that our belief in design is better founded than our belief in human shapes in the clouds or faces in the moon.

Cleanthes of course would say that the belief in design is well founded. It is therefore important to note that at the end of the *Dialogues* Pamphilus, who is reporting the conversation, declares that 'upon a serious review of the whole, I cannot but think, that PHILO's principles are more probable than DEMEA's; but that those of CLEANTHES approach still nearer to the truth.' (*DNHR*, p.130) Nevertheless this is the view of Cleanthes' pupil Pamphilus; the question I am addressing concerns the view not of Pamphilus or Cleanthes, but of Hume.

I think that Hume's position on matters of religion is the same as his position on matters of metaphysics and morals. He was a sceptic. In particular he was sceptical about the power of reason to provide demonstrations of many things that we find ourselves believing. He speaks about the frailty of reason, and about our tendency to give it tasks for which it is simply not fitted. The problem with discussions within natural religion is the tendency of reason to take flight into regions where it utterly lacks the support of experience. The point is that in the absence of that support we are in no position to adjudicate on the truth of the conclusions. The wings of reason flap vigorously in the experiential void and actually take us nowhere while seeming to bear us aloft to distant and magical realms.

On the last page of the *Dialogues* Philo speaks movingly of the predicament of the natural theologian who seeks insight into the divine nature, and it is too easy to say that this could not be the voice of Hume:

> Some astonishment indeed will naturally arise from the greatness of the object: Some melancholy from its obscurity: Some contempt of human reason, that it can give no solution more satisfactory with regard to so extraordinary and magnificent a question. But believe me, Cleanthes, the most natural sentiment, which a well-disposed mind will feel on this occasion, is a longing desire and expectation, that Heaven would be pleased to dissipate, at least alleviate, this profound

> ignorance, by affording some more particular revelation to
> mankind, and making discoveries, attributes, and operations
> of the divine object of our Faith. (*DNHR*, pp.129–30)

If a duly slanted scientific study of nature does not yield up
evidence of the existence of God and of his attributes, is there
another route that holds out promise? Historically, one important
line of thought is that within a given faith community miracles are
taken to confer validity on a divine revelation. Hume tackled this
idea by enquiring into the strength of the evidence for miracles and
concluded that belief in miracles is unreasonable. The outcome was
an argument against the reasonableness of belief in miracles. Hume
held that a miracle is an event contrary to natural law, and that it
is always more probable that the witnesses to an alleged miracle are
speaking falsely than that the event occurred. The point for Hume
was that the evidence to support the claim that nature proceeds
in a law-like way is so strong as to overwhelm any evidence to
the contrary. In December 1737 Hume sent a draft of his essay
on miracles (of which the final version is *An Enquiry Concerning
Human Understanding*, sect.10) to Lord Kames, explaining that he
was holding back from publishing it because it was an essay 'which
I am afraid will give too much offence, even as the world is disposed
at present'. (*Letters*, vol.I, p.24) He was right.

It should be noted, as not all of Hume's critics noted, that in the
essay Hume does not deny the existence of miracles any more than in
the *Dialogues* he denies the existence of God. His point in each case
concerns not what actually exists but what we have reason to believe
exists. Calvinism comes in many forms, but among them there is
one which is sceptical about the power of reason to deliver answers
to the basic questions of religion. Such scepticism does not in itself
commit the sceptic to an anti-religious stance; it simply leaves him
rejecting the claim that there is a rational basis to religious belief.
Which prompts a question concerning what other sort of basis there
might be. The short answer of course is faith. Nevertheless it should
be stated plainly that although Hume seems to have been impressed
by the drawing power of the appearance of design in the universe

there is no evidence that Hume had any religious faith whatever. That does not, however, justify the attribution of atheism to him. Though convinced that theists could not draw successfully on reason in support of their position, Hume was also sure that atheists were no better placed. Both theists and atheists would be flapping their wings in the experiential void. For many Calvinists Hume's arguments for the frailty of reason in its attempts to investigate God would be welcomed as support for their position that a fallen human being, sunk in depravity, cannot reach upward to the divine except by a free act of will, an act of faith, by which, in love and contrition, he recognises that he is wholly in the hands of God and cannot be saved except by a merciful and gracious God whose love goes out to meet the love of his fallen creature.

This additional and typically Calvinist step was of course not taken by Hume; but he certainly helped to clear the ground for it by his critique of the powers of reason. From this point of view Hume's critique is less damaging to theists, those who believe in a personal God and rely for their belief at least in part on faith, than it is to deists, those who believe in God only in so far as his existence can be proved. For a theist can retain faith in the revelation which, directly or otherwise, he has been vouchsafed, whereas the deist, whose belief has only the support of reason, will be left with his deism cut from under him if he reads Hume's arguments and finds he has to accept them.

This, however, would hardly endear Hume to the high-fliers of the Kirk. Much as Hume publicly rejected atheism and acknowledged his scepticism to be not about God's existence but only about the powers of reason deployed in the cause of religion, the high-fliers would see no difference that mattered between, on the one hand, a combination of Humean scepticism and a lack of faith and, on the other hand, atheism. The two stances have the same effect – namely a person who refuses to subscribe to the reality of a personal God. Nothing good in such a person could come near to counterbalancing the terrible error he lives through his refusal to believe. For this reason many people took almost as a personal affront Adam Smith's report that Hume had died in tranquility. Hume was not entitled to an easy death, and surely Smith was spreading lies. Yet a few months before his death Hume wrote that if he had a choice it would be the most recent period of his life that he would choose to live again; he possessed during it, he said, ardour in study, gaiety in company, and no abatement in his high spirits. And he added: 'I consider, besides, that a man of sixty-five, by dying, cuts off only a few years of infirmities: And though I see many symptoms of my literary reputation's breaking out at last with additional lustre, I know, that I had but few years to enjoy it. It is difficult to be more detached from life than I am at present.' (*My Own Life* in *DNHR*, p.9) Further evidence of Hume's equanimity as the end approached is furnished by Adam Ferguson in a letter to Smith on 18 April 1776: 'You have heard from Black of our worthy friend D. Hume. If anything in such a case could be agreeable, the easy and pleasant state of his mind and spirits would really be so.' (Ferguson, *Correspondence*, vol.1, p.143)

James Boswell, who had known Hume since 1758, wrote a remarkable report, 'An account of my last interview with David Hume Esq'. Boswell quizzed the dying philosopher regarding his beliefs about the possibility of an after-life. Did Hume not believe in salvation? 'He answered it was possible that a piece of coal put upon the fire would not burn; and he added that it was a most unreasonable fancy that we should exist forever. That immortality, if it were at all, must be general; but a great proportion of the human race has hardly any intellectual qualities; that a great proportion dies in infancy before being possessed of reason; yet all these must be immortal; that a porter who gets drunk by ten o'clock with gin must be immortal; that the trash of every age must be preserved, and that new universes must be created to contain such infinite numbers. This appeared to me an unphilosophical objection, and I said "Mr Hume, you know spirit does not take up space".' The document tells us a good deal about Boswell, but it also sheds light on Hume's state of mind. Hume's words are not those of a man in fear of his own forthcoming demise; in handling Boswell's blunt approach Hume displayed both philosophical alertness and also good humour. All the evidence, then, from Smith, Black, Boswell and others, points to Hume's state of mind at the end as wonderfully in accord with the philosophy he had been developing over the previous four decades.

Though the *Dialogues* were published without a dedication there is a hint in Hume's correspondence that he had considered dedicating the work to Hugh Blair. The dedication would have been a poisoned chalice to any dedicatee, and especially to the minister of the High Kirk, but there is reason to believe that Hume's words on the matter are not to be taken seriously. On 29 September 1763 Blair had written to his friend, then en route to France. He congratulated Hume on 'going to a Country where you will want nothing of being worshipped, except bowing the Knee to you . . .' In religion alone, continues Blair, the *philosophes* may consider you 'as being somewhat bigotted . . . But had you gone but one Step farther – I am well informed, in several Poker Clubs in Paris your Statue would have been erected. If you will show them the MSS of certain Dialogues perhaps that honour may still be done you. But for Gods sake let that be a posthumous work, if ever it shall see the light: Tho' I really think it had better not.' (Hume, *New Letters of David Hume*, quoted pp.72–3, fn.4) Hume replied a week later: 'I have no present thoughts of publishing the work you mention; but when I do, I hope you have no objection of my dedicating it to you.' (*New Letters*, p.72) Hume may have been serious, but it is more likely that he was simply enjoying teasing his old friend.

Section 5: Kames in trouble

We saw in Chapter 2 that David Hume was not the only member of his family who had to face the wrath of a section of the Church, for his kinsman the Reverend John Home ran into serious trouble on account of his play *Douglas*. In addition there is also the case of Henry Home, Lord Kames, who was attacked because of his opinions about God and human nature expressed in his *Essays on the Principles of Morality and Natural Religion*, published in 1751. Kames took the precaution of publishing the *Essays* anonymously, but their authorship was an ill-kept secret. It is appropriate here to comment on Kames in light of what has now been said about Hume's *Dialogues*. In the year of the publication of the *Essays* Hume wrote to Michael Ramsay: 'Have you seen our Friend Harrys Essays? They are well wrote; and are an unusual instance of an obliging method of answering a Book. Philosophers must judge of the question; but the Clergy have already decided it, & say he is as bad as me. Nay some affirm him to be worse, as much as a treacherous friend is worse than an open Enemy.' (*Letters*, vol.1, p.162)

One ire-inducing feature of Kames's doctrine derives from his acceptance of the principle that every event has a cause. From this principle it follows that whatever happens does so by causal necessity. Yet we have to set against the claim of universal causality the no less compelling claim that we are free. But if we are free we surely are not causally necessitated, and hence the universal claim made on behalf of causality must be false. Kames's solution to this apparent contradiction is that our feeling that we are free conceals from us the necessity of our acts, and he adds: 'A feeling of liberty, which I now scruple not to call deceitful, is so interwoven with our nature, that it has an equal effect in action, as if we were really endued with such a power.' (*Essays*, p.204) In short, we are really necessitated, but by the deceitfulness of our nature we cannot help acting as if we are free.

But if we have been so made that our nature systematically deceives us, then it must have been the intention of our maker that we be systematically deceived, in which case our maker is a deceiver. It is, however, possible to argue in the opposite direction, by starting with the premiss that the Christian God is not a deceiver. And from that premiss it surely follows that Kames does not believe our maker to be the Christian God. Kames is therefore no Christian. He is perhaps even an atheist – like his kinsman David Hume. In light of such considerations, pamphlets strongly hostile to Kames were composed by hardliners in the Kirk. Sad to say, philosophers also pitched in. James Beattie, in a letter to Mrs Elizabeth Montague about Kames's *Sketches of the History of Man*, wrote: 'Nor will it appear surprising, to some of us at least, that he should exert himself in subverting Christianity, at the same time that in words he professes to honour it. I cannot conceive of anything more flagitious, or more unmannerly than this conduct, which among our infidels is now so common. It puts me in mind of that miscreant who "betrayed the son of man with a kiss".' (quoted in Ross, *Lord Kames*, pp.344–5) And years later John MacFarlane, Minister of Canongate Church in Edinburgh, wrote to Kames: 'When I read the first Edition of your Lordships Essays I was a very young man educated with very narrow and illiberal Notions both of men & things. You will not be surprised that I was taught to regard you as an Arch Heretic & all your writings as coming from a suspected hand.' (quoted in Ross, *Lord Kames*, pp.153–4) Kames, who was a deeply religious man, and who had indeed been a Commissioner to the General Assembly, survived calls for his excommunication, though no doubt he was wounded by the ferocious attacks made upon him by sections of the Kirk.

Beattie's extraordinary comparison of Kames with Judas is all the more impressive testimony to the narrow perspective of many leading Scottish churchmen in view of the considerable space that Kames devoted to establishing the existence and the benevolence of God. Here I shall make some comments on Kames's teaching on divine benevolence. My chief purpose is to give further indication of the nature of Kames's theology and also to show how very far he departs from Hume despite taking a thoroughly Humean principle as his starting point. In any case both what Kames said, and also the fact that he said it, matter, for the Enlightenment was a public battleground of ideas, and the hardest fought battles were over religion. Kames's writings on natural (that is, rational) religion are the kind of thing that we need to know if we are to grasp the character of the Scottish Enlightenment.

In the *Dialogues Concerning Natural Religion* and in other writings also Hume had deployed the principle that if a cause is known only by its effect then we ought to assign to the cause nothing beyond what is necessary to explain the effect. For example, we see many good things in the world and this might prompt us to ascribe goodness to the cause of the world. But in that case, applying Hume's principle, we are not logically compelled to assign infinite goodness to the cause of the world; we should instead ascribe to the cause just as much goodness as is necessary to explain the goodness in the effect, that is, in the world. Since the world contains not only much that is good but also much that is bad, the evidence does not indicate an infinitely good cause. Put otherwise, you do not need to be perfect to produce something imperfect, and the world is undoubtedly imperfect.

This approach is that of the empirical scientist, who looks around the world in search of rational support for a thesis. And indeed in a sense theology is here being treated as an empirical science. This is undoubtedly Hume's approach and in effect Kames agrees with Hume and so, like Hume, asks what we actually find when we look around us. But Kames deploys his sensory experience to very different effect. He reports that there is in the world so much that is good as contrasted with what is evil that that preponderance provides assurance of the existence of a benevolent cause of the world, a benevolence which we can acknowledge 'without giving way', as Kames puts the point, 'to the perplexity of a few cross appearances, which, in matters so far beyond our comprehension, ought rationally to be ascribed to our own ignorance, not to any malevolence in the Deity'. (*Essays*, p.353) The 'few cross instances' therefore are so few that it is more reasonable to suppose them not to be so cross after all, and to suppose them instead to be fully compatible with the hypothesis of an omnibenevolent God.

Whether they are as few as Kames declares is open to dispute, as he knew even as he was penning those words. So he set out to defend himself. Not everything is perfect, but what sort of world would it be if everything were perfect? We humans are not perfectly wise, or perfectly good, or perfectly happy. But then, that is us according to nature. Beings perfectly wise, good and happy would not be human beings. Are we to say that the world would be a better place if it contained no human beings? And indeed other animals also lack the perfections just mentioned. Would the world be better if there were no animals in it? And perhaps no plants either? Kames on the contrary lauds the rich variety of creation. Admittedly that richness is bought at a price but, as Kames maintains, it is a price worth paying. For that reason we must conclude that some of the 'cross instances', properly understood, are evidence for, not against, the benevolence of the creator.

Pain, for example, in Kames's view is not purely a bad thing. It functions as a monitor of what is hurtful or dangerous. Without pangs of hunger we would starve, and more generally our preservation depends routinely on our feeling a pain and acting against its cause. In that sense some evils are, in Kames' phrase, 'necessary defects in a good system'. (*Essays*, p.365) But these are natural evils. What about so-called 'moral evils'? God has given us a free will, and freely we will evil as well as good. God as the creator of our will is therefore responsible for the evil that we will, and is therefore not a perfectly good God. Surely a good God would have so created us that we would not act in evil ways and therefore he would have created us without a free will. Some might reply, however, that moral evil is the consequence of our free will, and that our free will is such a precious thing that if the price the world has to pay for it is moral evil then that is a price worth paying. But Kames does not like this reply for, as he says, 'it is a very possible supposition, that man might have been endued with a moral sense, so lively and strong as to be absolutely authoritative over his actions'. (*Essays*, p.366) With such a moral sense we would will freely but always and by our nature will on the side of virtue and the good. In that case why did not God make us like that?

In reply to this important question (a question often asked even today in writings on the relations between morality and religion) Kames in effect invokes his idea that the rich variety of the created world is itself one of the most glorious features of the world. In particular a world that does not contain beings like us is the poorer for that, and is therefore to that extent defective. Hence our presence in the world is an argument in support of the claim that God is benevolent, not an argument against. Kames writes:

> to complain of a defect in the moral sense, is to complain that we are not perfect creatures. And if this complaint be well founded, we may with equal justice complain, that our understanding is but moderate, and that in general our powers and faculties are limited. Why should imperfection in the moral sense be urged as an objection, when all our

senses, internal and external, are imperfect? In short, if this
complaint be in any measure just, it must go to the length,
as above observed, to prove, that it is not consistent with
the benevolence of the Deity to create such a being as man.
(*Essays*, pp.366–7)

Kames's main idea in this line of argument is that even though
we are imperfect a world without us would have a gap in it, would
be deprived or defective. It needs us to help it be complete, and our
world is therefore a better place on account of our presence. Hence
a perfect world, or at any rate a world that is as perfect as a world
can be, must contain some imperfect creatures. It should be said,
however, that, interesting as this idea is, it would not have impressed
Hume who was starting to write his *Dialogues Concerning Natural
Religion* just at the time when Kames was preparing his *Essays
on the Principles of Morality and Natural Religion* for publication.
Hume would certainly have questioned Kames's description of the
evils of this world as 'a few cross instances'; for Hume the evils run
too wide and too deep to be no more than a few cross instances, and
he could hold this even without accepting the Calvinist doctrine of
the radical depravity of humankind.

Hume's response to Kames therefore is that there is no way to
account for the cross instances if the creator is an infinitely good
God whose power likewise is without limit. To say, as Kames
does, that we see only part of the picture and that if we saw the
whole picture, as God assuredly does, we would see that the cross
instances were not so cross after all – to say this is, from Hume's
perspective, to miss the philosophical point that we cannot argue
from the existence of just a few cross instances to the existence of
an infinitely benevolent and powerful God. Even one cross instance
creates a problem, but the instances are in fact numerous and in many
cases very cross indeed. In his *Dialogues*, Hume's mouthpiece Philo
speaks to Cleanthes in these terms: 'But allowing you, what will
never be believed; at least, what you never possibly can prove, that
animal, or at least, human happiness, in this life, exceeds its misery;
you have yet done nothing: For this is not, by any means, what we

expect from infinite power, infinite wisdom, and infinite goodness.
Why is there any misery at all in the world? Not by chance surely.
From some cause then. Is it from the intention of the Deity? But
he is perfectly benevolent. Is it contrary to his intention? But he
is almighty.' (*DHNR*, p.103) At least in his *Essays on the Principles
of Morality and Natural Religion* Kames appears to have no answer
to Hume's argument.

Section 6: The view from the pulpit of St Giles

The intellectual concerns about God that motivated Hume, Kames
and others among the philosophically minded literati are to be
contrasted with the pastoral concerns of those literati (many of
them philosophers), such as Hugh Blair, who occupied the pulpit. No
doubt most people did not care much about the validity or otherwise
of proofs of God's existence, or proofs of his omnibenevolence, but
they did want to live reasonably godly lives, and it was the minister's
job to help them manage it. A chief vehicle for such help was the
sermon. A good deal can be learned about the character of the Scottish Enlightenment by a consideration of the sermons of the period.
Many are interesting as revealing what the Enlightenment was up
against in Scotland, and many others are interesting as revealing
the particular character possessed by Enlightenment values when
informed by the distinctive spirituality of the moderate wing of
the Kirk. Hugh Blair was eminent among the preachers of the
Scottish Enlightenment and I should like to provide indication of
the kind of message he sought to convey to his congregation at
St Giles.

Blair's sermons, though not totally lacking in theological content,
do not contain any very heavy metaphysics about God. The
overwhelming concern in the sermons is the godly life, and
the godly life is spelled out in terms of the stoic virtues of
self-discipline and of patience in adversity. This is a Christian
stoicism since our patience is to be supported by our faith in
a future state in which the good Lord will reward those who
have walked in his ways. It should be noted that Blair writes
within the context of a rather long tradition of Christian stoicism

amongst Scottish thinkers. One thinker of particular interest in this context is Florence Wilson from Moray who studied in Paris from 1526 and formed a friendship there with the great humanist George Buchanan. Wilson knew well the writings of Erasmus and seems also to have been influenced by Martin Luther's reformist colleague Philip Melanchthon (1497–1560). Wilson's principal work is *Dialogus de animi tranquillitate* – *Dialogue on Tranquility of Mind* (Lyon 1543). A tranquil mind is one at peace with itself, one in which the passions are under the control of reason, under control not in the sense that the agent manages to refrain from acting on his more violent passions but in the sense that the passions are themselves of a calm and gentle nature. The passions have been 'sedated', to use Wilson's term.

These ideas are developed in great detail in Blair's sermons, and it is therefore of interest that an edition of Wilson's *Dialogue on Tranquility of Mind* was published in the 1740s at the behest of the Principal of Edinburgh University, William Wishart, and that a poem by Blair appears in the edition. It is also of interest that Blair delivered a sermon entitled *On Tranquility of Mind* (*Sermons*, vol.2, pp.224–33) Here, however, I shall focus on his sermon *On our Imperfect Knowledge of a Future State* (*Sermons*, vol.1, pp.40–53) where he gives a distinct shape to certain of Wilson's themes. His text is: 'For now we see through a glass, darkly' (1 Corinthians xiii, 12), and the text is puzzling. Scripture directs our attention to the fact of a future state, that is, the state of our life after death, and our very nature directs our attention to the fact of our future life. Yet we are vouchsafed very little knowledge of it. Blair declares: 'We are strangers in the universe of God' (*Sermons*, vol. 1, p.40) meaning by this that we are ignorant of what surrounds us. We know little enough of the perceptible world, and even less of the spiritual world we inhabit. What is life like in our future state? We see it, if at all, through a glass, darkly. But why not clearly? Would that not be better for us, because if we were vouchsafed a clear vision of the glories that await us, we would not be afflicted by distress and fear. Blair is sure, however, that we would not be better for knowing, because the knowledge would have disastrous practical consequences. Bewitched by the vision of the glorious future state, we would stagnate in this life. We would neglect the activities that support the order, and promote the happiness, of society. There would no longer be any spirit of enterprise. Impatient of our confinement within this tabernacle of dust, declares Blair, and languishing for the happy days of our translation to those glorious regions which were displayed to our sight, we would sojourn on earth as melancholy exiles. In a word, we would no longer be fit to inhabit this world.

The present dispensation, by which we have some knowledge, though very imperfect, of the future state, ensures that we retain a lively interest in this world and are also motivated to prepare ourselves for our life after death. Difficulties and temptations face us and by progressive discipline we develop the virtues of fortitude, temperance and self-denial. We learn to be moderate in our prosperity and patient in adversity, and if we saw through a glass, clearly, these virtue would never be developed. Blair affirms that: 'this life is no other than the childhood of existence' (*Sermons*, vol. 1, p.47), and just as we educate a child at a pace suitable to its stage of development, so also we are educated in this life in a way appropriate to our abilities and capacities. Our childhood education that fits us for adulthood is an analogy of the lifelong education that fits us for eternity.

Blair began the sermon by wondering why we are not given a clear view of the future state. His reply reveals that he occupies a position very close to that of Kames which we considered in the previous section. To complain that we are not from the start possessed of knowledge of the future state is like complaining that we are not born with an eagle's wings nor born with eyes with microscopic power. It is in effect to complain that God created human beings. (*Sermons*, vol. 1, p.47) Given the kinds of beings that we are, we have been vouchsafed by God as much as we can cope with, or are fitted to receive; more would destroy us. Or, as Blair declared to his congregation: '. . . the hand of Infinite wisdom hath in mercy drawn a veil over scenes which would overpower the sight of mortals'. (p.50) The message of the sermon is that, instead of peering into the future in search of knowledge that we are in fact not fitted to receive, we should concentrate on that which is according to our abilities and capacities, living a virtuous life, attending to 'all the studies and pursuits, the arts and labours which now employ the activity of man, which support the order, or promote the happiness of society'. (p.44) The message of the sermon is ultimately directed to the practical side of life. We are being told how to behave: 'Inhabitants of the earth, we are at the same time candidates for heaven. Looking upon these as only different views of one consistent character, let us carry on our preparation for heaven, not by abstracting ourselves from the concerns of this world, but by fulfilling the duties and offices of every station in life.' (p.52)

Blair's formidable talent as an orator is on display in his sermons, and they remind us that his other principal post was that of regius professor of rhetoric and belles lettres at Edinburgh University. His lectures at Edinburgh demonstrate that he had a deep knowledge of the classical texts on rhetoric, and his students would have known that he could practise what he preached. All the sermons make a strong appeal to the intellect – they are, in accordance with Aristotle's prescription in his *Ars Rhetorica*, first and foremost exercises in sound argumentation. But the listener's attention is held not simply by the luminous clarity of the arguments but also by the brilliant use of language, for example the deployment of metaphors that stop you in your tracks. Blair's message for his congregation at St Giles was especially that the true Christian is strong in faith and in civic virtue, a person who loves God and loves his neighbour, and whose steady promotion of the happiness of society is a step towards the reward bestowed upon the faithful remnant at the end of days.

David Hume would of course have been sceptical about the theological framework of Blair's sermons; but their practical message, the only part of the sermons that the congregation could act on, would have met with Hume's full approval. We should not however forget that, in presenting his ideas on society and morality within a theological context, Blair is more representative of the ethos of the Scottish Enlightenment than is the sceptic Hume. Yet for all the differences between them they were close friends. One might even see their friendship as a celebration of the Enlightenment virtue of tolerance, for the credulity that Hume found in Blair and the incredulity that Blair found in Hume could not shake the bond of affection.

SIX

Enlightenment in the Arts

Section 1: Whaur's yer Wullie Shakespeare noo?

During the Scottish Enlightenment the arts were in full swing. Painters, poets, novelists, architects, town planners, landscape gardeners, composers and instrumentalists – they all contributed to the cultural ferment. Playwrights too played their part, as is evidenced by the contemporary report of the effect on Edinburgh of John Home's *Douglas*: 'The town was in an uproar of exultation, that a Scotchman should write a tragedy of the first rate.' (Hook, *History of Scottish Literature*, p.312) No doubt, however, the cry from the stalls at the first performance of the *Douglas*, 'Whaur's yer Wullie Shakespeare noo?', went a few paces beyond the evidence. Yet Hume, with reference to *Douglas*, wrote to its author: 'But the unfeigned tears which flowed from every eye, in the numerous representations which were made of it on this theatre; the unparalleled command, which you appeared to have over every affection of the human breast: These are incontestable proofs, that you possess the true theatric genius of Shakespear and Otway, refined from the unhappy barbarism of the one, and licentiousness of the other.' (Hume, *New Letters*, p.41, n.) Elsewhere, however, as we shall see, Hume offered a strong, philosophically significant criticism of the play. Meantime it should be noted that that outburst from the stalls, as theatrical in its own way as was the performance that prompted it, was motivated by a pride in Scotland's artistic achievements. And, however embarrassingly unworthy of such pride *Douglas* may have been, there were many other works produced by Scots in Scotland that were as fine of their kind as anything produced anywhere in Europe and were fully worthy of that pride.

It is beyond dispute that the geniuses working in philosophy and the sciences were matched by men (as indicated in Chapter 2, all the Scottish Enlightenment geniuses were men) in such fields as literature, painting and architecture. Despite the best efforts of the

Reverend John Home of Athelstaneford, there do not seem to have been many geniuses associated with the Scottish theatre, perhaps because of the ferocious hostility towards the theatre (as opposed to literature, painting and architecture) shown by significant sections of the Kirk and by those they influenced. Here one is reminded of the theatre in Carrubber's Close in the Canongate, Edinburgh, founded by the poet Allan Ramsay in 1736 which one year later the magistrates closed down. The closure was due to pressure from an alliance of ministers, magistrates and professors (shame on the professors), who invoked the 1737 Licensing Act which required theatres wishing to stage plays (as opposed to other sorts of performances, such as concerts) to hold a Royal Patent, something that could not be accomplished except by an Act of Parliament.

Long before the Carrubber's Close affair Allan Ramsay had already been in serious trouble with the magistrates. In 1725 they had raided his lending library, the first in Scotland, because, as Robert Wodrow reported: 'all the villainous profane and obscene books and playes printed at London by Curle and others, are gote doune from London by Allan Ramsay, and lent out for an easy price, to young boys, servant weemen of the better sort, and gentlemen, and vice and obscenity dreadfully propagated'. (Wodrow, *Analecta*, vol.3, p.515) Ramsay, it should be added, had been tipped off about the raid and had removed from the library all the works that he thought the magistrates would judge off-message. We are dealing therefore with a man who knew as well as anyone the risks of association with the theatre. Nevertheless he persevered and his *The Gentle Shepherd* (1725), written in Scots, and the greatest play in Scots written in the century or so after Lindsay's *Ane Satire of the Thrie Estatis* (1602), played to packed houses and also ran to numerous editions.

It took a long time to wear down the Kirk's opposition, but it was eventually charmed into submission. In 1781 Mrs Siddons came to Edinburgh to star in several theatrical productions including Home's *Douglas*. Her performances were hugely popular – for one of them, in a theatre seating 600, there were 2000 applications for tickets. Evidently the ministers were not immune. Alexander Carlyle, a mine of gossipy information about the Scottish Enlightenment, claimed:

'. . . when the great Mrs Siddons first appeared in Edinburgh during the sitting of the General Assembly, the court was obliged to fix all its important business for the alternate days when she did not act, as all the younger members, clergy as well as laity, took their stations in the theatre on those days by three in the afternoon.' (Carlyle, *Autobiography*, pp.338–9) It would of course be a quite natural thing for young ministers, concerned with the quality of their pulpit oratory, to take a close interest in Mrs Siddons's techniques of voice projection. But whatever the motivations involved, and bewitchment cannot be excluded in all cases, with the arrival of Mrs Siddons the war waged by the pulpit on the theatre in Scotland was effectively lost, and by 1800 Scotland boasted nine permanent theatres. (see Cameron in Hook, *History of Scottish Literature*)

Section 2: Scots in Rome

In contrast with the long-drawn defensive campaign that the theatre had to sustain, practitioners in the other arts had the opportunity to hone their skills in comparative peace. Not surprisingly the dearth of good playwriters was more than balanced by the large number of top quality people elsewhere. There were no finer portraitists in Europe than Allan Ramsay (son of the poet) and Sir Henry Raeburn, nor finer an architect than Robert Adam.

Ramsay, Raeburn and Robert Adam studied in Italy, Ramsay indeed returning three times, a reminder that during the Enlightenment there was in Continental Europe a large diaspora of Scottish artists. The chief destination of the Scots was Rome, always a high point of the 'Grand Tour' but particularly important for Scotland's artists; there was indeed in Rome during that period a veritable colony of Scottish painters. Its most prominent member was Gavin Hamilton (1723–98), a native of Lanark and graduate of Glasgow University, who paid his first visit to Rome in 1745 to study under the portrait painter Agostino Masucci, before returning briefly to Britain in the early 1750s to practise as a portraitist. His *Elizabeth Gunning, Duchess of Hamilton* (Lennoxlove House, Haddington)(plate 6), painted during this brief period in Britain, is a fine, delicate portrait which exploits also his brilliant skill at representing sumptuous drapery. The work suggests that Hamilton would have made a highly successful career as a portraitist had he stuck to the task. Instead he returned to Rome where historical painting preoccupied him. In at least one major historical painting, his *Wood and Dawkins discovering Palmyra* (1758, Glasgow University), he included portraits of the two explorers, but this was a rare display of his skill as a portraitist after his return to Rome. Hamilton was on friendly terms with many distinguished Italian artists, such as Piranesi and Canova; to the latter he gave advice, which was welcomed and acted on, regarding matters of artistic style. He was also host to many Scots on the Grand Tour.

John Aikman of the Ross, writing in 1767 to John Forbes, father of the painter Anne Forbes, said of her future teacher: 'Mr Gavin Hamilton ... is what the Italians call the Premiero, and we call the Principal, in the Academy of Painting at Rome, and all the young students apply to him for Direction and Instruction in their Studies ... He is a sweet blooded gentleman, and being the most renowned of all the History Painters of this age is highly respected at Rome.' (Macmillan, *Painting in Scotland*, p.33) The Accademia di San Luca, to which John Aikman was referring, was a major attraction for Scottish painters seeking to widen their artistic horizons.

Though Hamilton spent most of his working life in Rome he was very much a part of the Scottish Enlightenment, this for several reasons, the most obvious being that he was a Scot, educated in Scotland, and expressing his roots and upbringing. Secondly, he was a central figure of the Scottish community in Rome, many members of that community being young artists who studied under him and took their skills back with them to Scotland. Among the many Scots in Rome during the period in question were Robert Adam, David Allan, Alexander Runciman and his brother John, James Clerk, Alexander Nasmyth, Anne Forbes, James Nevay, Colin Morison, John Baxter, the sculptor William Jeans, John Brown, Richard Cooper; and Archibald Skirving who painted a memorable portrait of Gavin Hamilton (*c.*1795, National Gallery of Scotland). As Duncan Macmillan notes (*Painting in Scotland*, p.43), they were quite a crowd; and there is ample evidence that Hamilton, an open and generous spirited man, was happy to give them help and support. Any assessment of Hamilton's contribution to the artistic life of Scotland has to take into account the contribution made by the generation of Scots who came under his aegis.

Thirdly, there are features of his art which are closely related to philosophical ideas that flourished in Scotland during the Scottish Enlightenment; and here we must recall that at Glasgow University Hamilton was a pupil of Francis Hutcheson. As we saw in Chapter 5, Section 1, Hutcheson's philosophy was naturalistic at least to the extent that he sought to found the concepts of human virtue and moral obligation upon a non-religious basis. Hutcheson did indeed believe in God, a personal God, but he believed also that it was possible to construct a comprehensive account of our virtues and our obligations, including an account of the bindingness of our obligations, without resort to revelation. We do not, for example, need to resort to Exodus xx to explain why we ought not to kill, commit adultery or steal. A careful study of human nature would enable us to see, without raising our eyes to heaven, why such acts are impermissible. There is, therefore, in Hutcheson's system a careful eschewing of the supernatural. Granted that there would not be beings with a human nature unless God had so willed it, the question arises whether we need to invoke God in order to account for the moral dimension of our social relations. Hutcheson's unequivocal answer is 'no', and it is for that reason that it is appropriate to describe his ethical theory as naturalistic.

The paintings of his pupil Hamilton are likewise naturalistic in the sense of deliberately eschewing the supernatural. I say 'deliberately' because, on an obvious reading of the narratives that Hamilton illustrates, the supernatural elements have a prominent role. Given the pervasive influence of the gods in the *Iliad* it could only have been by choice that in Hamilton's enormous canvases illustrative of the Homeric narrative the divinities of Homer have absolutely no place. Hamilton treats his characters as real live human beings and portrays them in their reactions to each other in a range of dramatic, tragic and heartrending contexts, as they bid farewell, grieve, supplicate, rage, and generally do things that people do when living on the outer edge of their emotions, all but dominated by passion while yet seeking to impose rational structure on their acts. In these narrative paintings – Achilles raging over the loss of Briseis, Hector saying farewell to Andromache, Achilles mourning Patroclus, Achilles avenging himself on the body of Hector, Priam pleading with Achilles for Hector's body, Andromache grief stricken as she lies prostrate over Hector's body – Hamilton was, in his own way, doing what the philosophers of the Scottish Enlightenment were doing; he was investigating human nature. He observed the ways in which people react to each other in a wide variety of contexts, and portrayed those reactions. The outcome is a convincing representation of a range of passions. James Boswell, while visiting Hamilton's studio in Rome in 1765, saw the canvas of Achilles venting his fury on Hector's body, and wrote in his diary the brief comment 'superb'.

In this naturalistic approach Hamilton was fully in tune with Hutcheson's ethical teaching. The two men stayed within a secular humanistic framework (which was in effect the same framework to which Hume and Smith, both devotees of Hutcheson, also remained faithful). Of course the *dramatis personae* of the *Iliad* are in an obvious way larger than life. These products of poetic genius are not small-minded people, they are king-sized, with king-sized passions and king-sized behaviour to match – even Achilles sulking in his tent has a king-sized sulk. And this added dimension, licensed by the muse, is duly represented by Gavin Hamilton. But the human actions and passions he portrays are none the less human despite the magnification. As represented by Hamilton, the passion of Priam, supplicating before Achilles, is profoundly human, and all the more so for its heroic scale. The gods are nowhere in sight, and their presence could not enhance the emotional intensity of the work. This is human drama at its most dramatic, a master painter's contribution to the great philosophic project of the Scottish Enlightenment, the study of human nature.

Section 3: Painting and education

George Turnbull, regent at Marischal College, Aberdeen, is a significant figure in the history of Scottish philosophy both because of his direct contribution to the literature of the school of common sense philosophy and also because of his influence on various of his pupils, most importantly Thomas Reid. Turnbull had a good deal to say on moral philosophy and natural philosophy, on the relation between the two, and the relation of art, particularly painting, to both of them. In developing his ideas on the unity of these three fields, Turnbull was arguably as seminal a figure for the Scottish Enlightenment as was his contemporary Hutcheson, though the latter is commonly thought to have been, in the simplistic phrase, the 'father' of the Scottish Enlightenment. (Wood, 'Science and the pursuit of virtue')

Turnbull's writings on art were informed by his deeply philosophical perspective. His chief work in the field, *A Treatise on Ancient Painting* (1740), was written expressly as advice to those about to set out on the Grand Tour, and Turnbull had at least two main objectives in mind in penning the book for the tourists.

First, the best answer to the question 'Why go on such a Tour?' is 'education'; a tourist should not go to enjoy himself, except in so far as the pleasure he aims at is an element in or a consequence of his proper appreciation of objects of high cultural value. In that case he should have an educational grounding sufficient to enable him to derive the most from the high culture of the cities he visits. Hence the *Treatise* conveys detailed information both of the lives of the painters of ancient Greece and Rome and also of their works. We learn not only what they painted but also what other ancient writers thought of those same works. The tourist, armed with Turnbull's book, would have an excellent idea of what to look at, and also of what to look out for in order to get a due sense of the quality of the works. One feature of the book is the large set of plates of ancient paintings, plates Turnbull acquired with the help of Allan Ramsay the younger, and which he uses as a guide to his commentaries on the originals.

Secondly, the book was written with the aim of promoting moral, and particularly civic, virtue, especially among the élite of Scottish culture, but also more widely among the citizenry. The idea of promoting civic virtue by writing on ancient painting might seem bizarre to us; but we need to attend to Turnbull's arguments, and in that case we should begin by noting that for Turnbull there are two sorts of object of human enquiry. First there are truths, 'that is, real Connexions in Nature or Facts', and secondly there are the various ways in which we can be brought to understand the truths or feel them. These ways are all linguistic, in a broad sense of the term. I say it is a broad sense because among the languages Turnbull lists as a means of bringing us to grasp the truth are oratory, poetry, all the arts of design, painting and sculpture. This established, Turnbull articulates an important principle: 'And therefore if right Education ought to teach and instruct in Truths, and in the various good Methods or Arts of conveying Truths into the Mind; no sooner is one led to the Discovery of any truth, than he ought to be employed in comparing and examining several different ways by which it may be unfolded, proved, embellished, and enforced by Oratory, Poetry, or Painting.' (*Treatise*, p.ix) Among the truths that Turnbull has especially in mind are those concerning morality: 'But one Point aimed at in this Treatise is to shew how mean, insipid and trifling the fine Arts are when they are quite alienated from their better and nobler, genuine Purposes, which, as well as those of their Sister Poetry, are truly philosophical and moral: that is, to convey in an agreeable manner into the Mind the Knowledge of Men and Things; or to instruct us in Morality, Virtue, and human Nature.' (*Treatise*, p.xv)

Turnbull believed ancient paintings to be a priceless resource for eighteenth-century Scottish society on account of their portrayal of the moral virtues. The ancient painters found their own way of representing the virtues so forcefully, in such attractive colours, that the paintings were, in Turnbull's view, a powerful argument to adopt the corresponding lifestyle. This is not of course to say that we cannot appreciate beauties in a painting while yet giving no thought to the moral significance of what is portrayed. But not to give such thought is to miss the rhetorical significance of the painting. Rhetoric is the art of persuasion by speech, and since Turnbull believes that painting is a kind of language or speech, and believes also that a painting can persuade us of a moral truth, he is therefore committed to the view that a painting can be a piece of rhetoric, a persuasive argument on behalf of virtue. It was Turnbull's hope that by a duly focused education in the arts, but especially in painting, young Scots on the Grand Tour could come under the influence of the rhetoric of ancient painting and be persuaded of the merits of such classical virtues as dignity and humanity, of courage and magnanimity, of temperance and justice. To be persuaded about such things is not merely intellectual assent to an argument; it is an assent of feeling, and those persuaded will therefore be motivated to embody those virtues in their lives. Such grand tourists, most of whom in the nature of the case were drawn from the upper rungs of society, would return eager to exercise power in the name of civic virtue and they would therefore help to ensure that Scottish society proceeded along the path of sound morality. From this point of view Turnbull's *Treatise on Ancient Painting* must be classed as a contribution to the general programme of improvement that characterised the Scottish Enlightenment from its earliest days.

In light of comments in Section 2 of this chapter it might be added that Hamilton's Homeric paintings, which are portrayals of high drama, charged with emotion and with a moral significance made all the deeper by the rawness of the emotion, are powerful exercises in moral rhetoric, an eighteenth-century version of the kind of thing that, according to Turnbull, was accomplished with particular brilliance in classical antiquity.

Earlier I stressed the naturalism of Hamilton's painterly vision, a vision naturalistic partly in virtue of its refusal to give space to the host of Homeric divinities. We find just such a naturalism in Turnbull's aesthetic writings also. What is at issue here is an aesthetic naturalism, a portrayal of nature but through the eye of the artist, an eye turned outward to what is aesthetically pleasing in nature and turned inward to an idea of a composition which, even if not precisely found in all its detail in nature, is not any the less natural and is aesthetically pleasing. I should like to explore this 'aesthetic naturalism' since the doctrine, common in the Scottish Enlightenment, reinforces the claim that philosophy, which is assuredly central to the Scottish Enlightenment, is assuredly central also to the aesthetic thinking of the period.

Turnbull writes:

> what superior Pleasures one must have, who hath an Eye formed by comparing Landscapes [i.e. landscape paintings] with Nature, in the contemplation of Nature itself in his Morning or Evening Walks, to one who is not at all conversant in Painting ... he will feel a vast Pleasure in observing and chusing picturesque Skies, Scenes, and other Appearances, that would be really beautiful in Pictures. He will delight in observing what is really worthy of being painted; what Circumstances a good Genius would take hold of; what Parts he would leave out, and what he would add, and for what Reasons (*Treatise*, p.146)

There are two kinds of object here: one the actual scene spread out before the spectator, and the other a mental composition, a concept of what is physically before the spectator except for changes he has mentally made to it, whether by addition, by subtraction, or otherwise. The latter exercise is of particular interest to Turnbull, for the ability to conceive things which do not actually exist in nature but which are fully congruent with nature is a crucial ability of the creative artistic imagination. The painter can paint the landscape that is before him, yet alter the relative sizes of the fields, or make the hills seem closer, or bathe the whole in a different light. But, in Turnbull's view, the changes must be kept within bounds. Even if what he paints is not precisely faithful to what he sees, it must at least be credible. That is, such a scene as he paints must be possible in nature. If he bathes the scene in a Wordsworthian 'light that never was on sea or land', this will detract from the aesthetic value of the painting.

This rather broad concept of nature, encompassing not only what does occur naturally but also what can occur even though it does not in fact do so, allows Turnbull to develop the idea of painting and poetry as more philosophical than history is. History, on this reading, is constrained to a faithful representation of the facts, that is, of what actually happened, and as such has to eschew the amplitude of vision characteristic of painters and poets, who can deal directly with universal features of our experience. A painter explores human nature, imagining people in unusual or unlikely, but still possible, situations, and thinking about the ways in which they might express their humanity in those situations. Thus, the painter, remaining within the bounds of the naturally possible, can explore the gamut of emotions between the extremes of love and hate, of pride and humility, of rage and calm, of hope and despair. As Turnbull puts the point: 'the imitative Arts become Magnifiers in the moral way, by means of chusing those Circumstances which are properest to exhibit the Workings and Consequences of Affections, in the strongest Light that may be, or to render them most striking and conspicuous. All is Nature that is represented, if it be agreeable to Nature.' (*Treatise*, p.147) It is of course precisely because he sees painting as having the ability to function as a magnifying glass to the moral dimension of our lives that Turnbull regards the study of painting as having such educative power; and since he finds in ancient painting so many examples of appropriate portrayals of virtue and vice, that is, virtue portrayed in a good light and vice in a bad, he sees the study of ancient painting as a potent educative force on behalf of the good.

Before leaving the topic of Turnbull on the portrayal of nature I should like to note, briefly, that one person who picked up this ball and ran with it was Turnbull's student George Campbell. Campbell's *Philosophy of Rhetoric* (1776) contains a discussion of different sorts of use of speech, and the different ways in which we evaluate the truth or otherwise of what is said. We do not look for truth in poetry or in fictional writings as we do in history. History aims to report events that actually occurred; plainly novels do not, and in general neither do poems. Nevertheless, in one way or another, novels, works of fiction, do articulate truths, and indeed must do so if they are to be acceptable even as works of fiction. This idea is explored illuminatingly by Campbell. I quote a lengthy passage since its theme in fact opens up a principle of unity for all the arts, and bears directly on points already made about Hamilton and Turnbull, and even John Home:

> Nay, even in those performances where truth, in regard to the individual facts related, is neither sought nor expected, as in some sorts of poetry, and in romance, truth still is an object to the mind, the general truths regarding character, manners, and incidents. When these are preserved, the piece may justly be denominated true, considered as a picture of life; though false, considered as a narrative of particular events. And even these untrue events may be counterfeits of truth, and bear its image; for in cases wherein the proposed end can be rendered consistent with unbelief, it cannot be rendered compatible with incredibility. Thus, in order to satisfy the mind, in most cases, truth, and in every case, what bears the semblance of truth, must be presented to it.
> (*Philosophy of Rhetoric*, bk.I, ch.4)

It is with considerations such as these in mind that Hume offered John Home criticisms of the play *Douglas*. Hume focused on Glenalvon, the villain of the play, and on Lord Barnet (later renamed 'Lord Randolph' so that London playgoers should not associate his name with the village outside London): '*Glenalvon's* character is too abandoned. Such a man is scarce in nature . . . *Lord Barnet's* character is not enough decided; he hovers betwixt vice and virtue, which, though it be not unnatural, is not sufficiently theatrical nor tragic.' (Hume, *Letters*, vol.1, p.215) And to the Comtesse de Boufflers Hume wrote: 'The value of a theatrical piece can less be determined by an analysis of its conduct, than by the ascendant which it gains over the heart, and by the strokes of nature which are interspersed through it.' (Hume, *Letters* vol.1, p.452) Hume therefore makes the same demands of fiction as does Turnbull.

Let us say, then, that there is a difference between being believed and being credible, and correspondingly between being disbelieved and being incredible. An episode in a novel will not satisfy us if we do not believe that the episode could have happened. Since the work is one of fiction we do not come to it looking for nothing but the truth, but the story must not exceed the bounds of possibility. Likewise a character in a novel must be believable – the character sketch will not satisfy us unless we think that, even if no such person, one precisely answering to the description in the novel, actually ever lived, there at least could have been such a person. The reason why the portrayal of such possibilities is sufficient to satisfy us is that we humans are naturally truth-seeking creatures, and fiction at a certain level of abstraction contains truths, perhaps not individual or singular truths, whether about *this* event or *this* person, but certainly universal truths. When Campbell speaks about statements that have a semblance of truth, he has in mind truth of the universal sort, which is after all truth of sorts, and indeed is particularly important for us in countless contexts where it is precisely a message of universal validity that we are seeking to convey. Alexander Pope, writing about Achilles' response to the supplication of Priam, comments: 'His anger abates very slowly; it is stubborn, yet still it remits: had the poet drawn him as never to be pacified he had outraged nature, and not represented his hero as a man but as a monster.' Here again the point is that the poet has had to portray the naturally possible, for to do otherwise, to have 'outraged nature', would have diminished his work. Duncan Macmillan has pointed out that Gavin Hamilton's portrayal of Achilles' response to Priam accords closely with Pope's interpretation. (Macmillan, *Painting in Scotland*, p.39) Achilles relents, not because of divine intervention but because of something natural and indeed fully human – his anger is beginning to abate. Great fictional characters, Ulysses, Hamlet, Don Quixote, are great partly because of their archetypal quality. There is something of them in all of us; they embody in a supreme way a quality for which we all by nature strive, and in that sense they are not fictional, but alive, even larger than life. And it is for this reason that we truth-seeking creatures find great works of fiction so satisfying. To call such works 'fiction' is already to miss the main point about them. A poet or novelist must aim for truth at this universal level even if not at truth at a level at which the historian aims.

There is a whole theory of literature in the remarks of Campbell that I have just quoted. But, as we have now seen, the remarks are equally applicable to painting, and in a sense are foreshadowed in Turnbull's *Treatise*. Painting is potentially an immensely powerful resource on behalf of moral education because a painting can speak at a universal level about fundamental moral truths, can speak of the immeasurable value of justice, temperance, mercy and humility. It can also convey the despicable nature of the forms of moral vice, the cruel, lecherous or cowardly dispositions that shape the corrupt soul. In the hands of a great artist a painting can convey such a message, not merely in the sense of representing a virtuous or a vicious act, but of representing one in such a way that the painting persuades us of the truth of the moral universal we see in the painting. In one and the same sense of 'orator' a great painter is no less an orator than were Demosthenes and Cicero. Paint can talk as loudly as words and as persuasively. There are fashions in art appreciation as in most other things, and Gavin Hamilton is not much in fashion these days. But he spoke powerfully and persuasively to his contemporaries about universal features of the human spirit, passion on a grand scale, and virtue and vice on the same scale. Hamilton, as we observed, did not seek to invoke the gods on Olympus. His paintings, about the heights to which we can soar and the depths to which we can sink, deliver a powerful message from within the humanistic framework that he set himself. These are themes at the heart of the Scottish Enlightenment.

Section 4: Portraiture

We have many ways of studying human nature, and many ways of presenting our findings. Biologists, physiologists, neurologists, psychologists, social anthropologists, ethnologists, sociologists, economists, and others, make a scientific contribution – I use the term 'scientific' in a suitably broad sense. Philosophers also make their contribution, and perhaps philosophy (or at least some philosophy) should be brought under the heading 'science' in this broad sense. Hume's *Treatise of Human Nature* is undoubtedly philosophy, although Hume saw himself as doing a science of sorts in the book, as is made clear by the subtitle: *Being an Attempt to Introduce the Experimental Method of Reasoning into Moral Subjects*.

But there are others, creators of non-scientific works, who also have interesting things to tell us about human nature. Among them are poets, playwrights and novelists. Nor can we rule out the possibility that, to some people at least, some truths about human nature can be conveyed better by poetry, plays and novels than by overtly scientific expositions. However, it is not only in literary genres that human nature can be explored. As a medium for the portrayal of the whole gamut of human passions, music is arguably no less appropriate than the genres already mentioned. And of course there is also painting. I have said enough for the present about Hamilton's king-sized representations of king-sized narratives about king-sized passions, and in this section shall focus on rather smaller paintings, mostly portraits of individuals, though some group paintings will be mentioned. It might be added that it was not only painters who produced portraits of outstanding artistic value during the Scottish Enlightenment. I have in mind particularly James Tassie (1735–99), who worked in the medium of glass-paste medallions, using a paste he had patented. He has given us strong and abiding images, a white paste profile in relief, of many of the leading figures of the Enlightenment, such as Hume, Smith, Reid, Hutton and also, happily, the greatest Scottish portrait painter of his day, Henry Raeburn. However, for the remainder of this section, in speaking about portraitists it is painters that I shall primarily have in mind.

The task of a portrait painter is in a sense as far removed as is possible from the task of philosophers analysing human nature. Whereas the philosopher considers human nature in its universality, the portrait painter considers human nature in its individuality. The portraitist seeks to convey something about the subject, enabling us to recognise him, not just in respect of a physiognomic peculiarity, but in respect of the person's distinct personality, for the subject is not just *a* person, but *this* person. Once the artist has got the 'likeness' then, so to say, the work starts, for the subject's inner qualities, or some of them, have to be represented: the person's gentleness or sharpness, confidence or diffidence, and so on. So the painter has us taking in the shifty glance of a shady character or the open gaze of an upright citizen. The list of personal qualities is inexhaustible.

From it the portraitist extracts sufficient to say something about humanity, yes, but humanity as instantiated in *this* individual.

Let us consider the portrait of Margaret Lindsay, Allan Ramsay's second wife (National Gallery of Scotland, Edinburgh), looking at the painter. (plate 8) In March 1752 Ramsay eloped with Margaret, daughter of Sir Alexander and Lady Lindsay of Evelick. Later that year she gave birth to twins, Alexander and Amelia, who did not survive long. In February 1754 she gave birth to a son, Alexander, who died aged one. In September 1758 she gave birth to a girl, Charlotte, who survived to adulthood. It has been suggested by Alastair Smart that it was in a spirit both of thankfulness for the fact that his wife remained in good health after the birth, and also of thankfulness for the infant's survival, that in around 1759 Ramsay painted Margaret's portrait (Smart, *Allan Ramsay*, p.155) Hers is a clear, confident, friendly gaze, responsive to the painter, who is assuredly gazing at her in as friendly a way. The portrait is in a sense a portrait of a relationship, and especially of the mutual affection that infuses it, and yet only one of the two subjects is 'in the painting'. The painter does not need to be there on the canvas. He is already there, a presence that we can read in her eyes, in the expression of her face, and in the relaxed way she is turning towards her husband. Margaret Lindsay is there before the painter, and therefore also before us, in her uniqueness. (Macmillan, *Painting in Scotland*, p.27)

In many portraits, perhaps in most, the subject is looking at the artist. In general, however, the subject's attitude to the artist is irrelevant – it is not part of what is being represented. This is obviously true of the numerous formal portraits of high dignitaries portrayed by Ramsay, where indeed he would be stepping seriously out of line by suggesting in the portrait that the subject has condescended to have any attitude to him whatsoever – he was after all only a painter (no doubt the reason, or one of the reasons, why his second wife's well-born parents objected to his marrying their daughter). But that is part of the point of his portrait of her. Allan and Margaret had been through a good deal together, and they were if anything strengthened as a close and affectionate couple by their misfortunes. In this famous portrait the subject's attitude to the painter is all important.

I should now like to draw attention to one more portrait, in crucial ways very different from that of Margaret Lindsay. In 1796 Henry Raeburn painted Thomas Reid (the painting is in Fyvie Castle, with Raeburn's copy of the Fyvie painting in Glasgow University Hunterian Gallery). (plate 5) The portrait, a quiet, restrained and moving account of the subject, captures something essential in him. Unlike Margaret Lindsay, gazing in an open and welcoming way at the artist, Reid's eyes are directed elsewhere, or nowhere. He was a thinker, perhaps the greatest philosopher of the Scottish Enlightenment. He had also been actively interested in mathematics all his life, had worked at the cutting edge of mathematics, and at the very end of his life was still worrying away at advanced problems in mathematics. This portrait was painted a few months before his death at the age of eighty-six, and in the painting he is a man living inside his head. The look is not a mindless vacancy. In his own way Reid could see a good deal further than most people, and he knew far more about what we like to think of as reality than most of us do; and it is that Thomas Reid who is portrayed. Raeburn portrayed many professors and scientists, almost always with papers, books or scientific instruments as studio props, as witness the portraits of James Hutton, William Robertson, Hugh Blair, Adam Ferguson, John Robison and John Playfair. But, for Reid, Raeburn provided no props. He gives us instead the thinker with his thoughts. I believe that the thoughts of Reid are important for an understanding of Raeburn's technique, and in the next section I shall take steps towards justifying that assessment.

Section 5: The craft of painting

The first of Thomas Reid's masterpieces, *An Inquiry into the Human Mind on the Principles of Common Sense* (1764), is devoted to an analysis of sensory perception, of our sensory faculties and of what we can learn of the world by means of them. Unlike almost all previous studies of sensory perception, which were dedicated simply to the sense of sight, Reid investigates all five senses. Each of the senses gives us access to a different aspect or feature of the world. What we learn of an apple by tasting it, we cannot learn by the senses of sight, hearing, touch or smell. A full account of the physical world therefore requires attention to the deliverances of all the senses. No doubt there is something special about sight in that by sight we can in a flash gain more information about the world than we can as quickly by means of any other of the senses. But that of course does not imply that philosophers are justified in studying sight to the exclusion of all the other senses.

I want to focus on the fact that we can in many cases, just by using our eyes, know immediately what something feels like, or tastes or sounds like. We do not of course *see* tastes and sounds, but we quickly enough learn to associate the deliverances of the various sensory modalities with the deliverances of our eyes. There is, therefore, a difference between what we know and what we see. This is a distinction of the utmost importance for painters, and Thomas Reid explores the distinction in detail, paying special attention throughout to the significance of the distinction for the craft of painting.

In a nutshell, Reid believes that a painter should paint what he sees rather than what he knows. Once he has done this the viewer of the painting should then 'read' the painting and interpret it, just as we ordinary spectators of the visible world 'read' this world of sights and bring to bear our knowledge of the world, gained by the use of all our sensory receptors, in order to form a sound interpretation of it. What is it that we learn by the use of our other senses that we cannot learn by the use of sight itself that is of importance to painters? Reid's answer is that most importantly our awareness of the three-dimensionality of space comes from the sense of touch not of sight. As a result of our handling of objects and simultaneously looking at them, we learn that it is one and the same object that is both seen and touched, and the knowledge that we acquire of an object by touching it we can come to apply to the object merely by looking at it. Distance of an object from the viewer is, therefore, first judged by whether it is at arm's length or less, and we learn to *see* the object as being, say, at arm's length from us, even though, had we only a sense of sight, we could never even have formed a concept of something as being at a distance from us.

Much of what we perceive is treated by us as a sign of something else, and in such a way that we do not even notice that we are treating the sensory data as signs. For example, if an object occupies steadily less of our visual field, we do not necessarily judge that the object is really diminishing in size; we might instead treat its apparent diminution as a sign that the distance between us and the object is increasing. Reid has a good deal to say about this relation between the sign and the knowledge we have as a result of our interpretation of the sign. Mastery of the craft of painting involves mastery of the art of distinguishing between the sign and what it signifies, and reproducing the sign, not the significate, on canvas. I shall now unpack these ideas, and in doing so shall follow closely Reid's line of argumentation. (Reid, *Inquiry* ch.6; excerpted in Broadie, *The Scottish Enlightenment: An Anthology*, pp.273–82)

Suppose we walk about a room looking all the time at a book lying in the middle of it. We are a foot away from the book and then move four yards from it. Sometimes our shadow falls on it, on all or on part of it. Throughout this time we judge that it is one and the same book, and that its qualities have not changed – it is the same size, the same shape, the same colour. Yet the visible appearance of the book, the appearance that it makes to us, must be changing all the time that we are moving in relation to it. And this in several ways.

First, the appearance of the colour changes as our distance from the book alters. Let us imagine the cover has a tartan design. As we move away, the various distinct colours appear less distinctly, and gradually become so blurred that we cannot distinguish the multitude of colours that is really there; instead the cover appears to be only a homogeneous bluish colour. By the same token the geometric complexity of the tartan becomes blurred. The squares and rectangles disappear from sight, and the contents of the book cover appear geometrically undifferentiated. What we *see*, the appearance that the book cover makes to us, changes, but what we *know*, that the book cover is tartan, does not change.

Secondly, the shape of the book appears different as we walk round it. But of course we do not judge its shape to have changed. It is 'really' the same, only 'apparently' different. From one perspective it appears rectangular, from another hexagonal. Again, what we see changes, and yet we know that nothing has really changed.

Thirdly, as regards the magnitude of the book, as we double our distance from the book its visible appearance halves. And yet we know that it is still seven inches by five by one. What we know of its magnitude, namely that it is the same size however far away we are from it, is not what we see, namely something that looks smaller the greater our distance from it.

Fourthly, if we relied purely on sight we would not learn that the book has three dimensions. To the eye the book has length and breadth only. As mentioned earlier, Reid seeks to demonstrate that it is only by bringing to bear what we learn by touch that we can interpret what we *see* as having depth. Reid was greatly interested in work that had been carried out in previous decades on people born blind who acquired sight. According to reports of scientific authorities, after they have gained their sight such people are at first not able to judge distances from the eye, that is, to judge whether A is further from the eye than B is. This has to be learned and cannot just be *seen*.

Reid's point is clear, and is developed partly by the imaginative experiment of thinking through what could be learned about the world by a person newly granted his sight. Reid's conclusion is that, though we think that there is something special about sight in terms of how much more we can learn about our world using sight rather than any other of the senses, we do not sufficiently take into account the extent to which the knowledge we gain by using our eyes is *acquired* knowledge, gained by customary association of our sight with the use of our other senses. Reid sums up this point:

To a man newly made to see, the visible appearance of objects would be the same as to us; but he would see nothing at all of their real dimensions, as we do. He could form no conjecture, by means of his sight only, how many inches or feet they were in length, breadth, or thickness. He could perceive little or nothing of their real figure; nor could he discern, that this was a cube, that a sphere; that this was a cone, and that a cylinder. His eye could not inform him, that this object was near, and that more remote. The habit of a man or of a woman, which appeared to us of one uniform colour, variously folded and shaded, would present to his eye neither fold nor shade, but variety of colour. In a word, his eyes, though ever so perfect, would at first give him almost no information of things without him. They would indeed present the same appearances to him as they do to us, and speak the same language; but to him it is an unknown language. (Reid, *Inquiry*, pp.84–5)

A painter, in Reid's view, has to identify the signs by which we judge things to be distant, and he must seek to represent those signs. This task of identification is difficult, since we are so accustomed to moving straight from the sign to what is signified by it that we hardly attend to the sign at all. Yet these visible signs are all-important for the painter. To attend to one example already cited, the more distant an object is, the more degradation there is in the appearance of its internal parts; increased distance is there correlated with increased uniformity of the object's visible appearance. Hence one way for a painter to represent an object as distant is for him to paint it with an appropriate degree of indistinctness. If he wishes to represent two men, one further into the background than the other, it is not sufficient that the painting of the more distant man be four inches high and that of the closer be eight inches. If the two are portrayed with equal distinctness the one will seem only to be a dwarf or Lilliputian, and not more distant. The appearance of the more distant figure must also be more blurred.

It follows from this, as Reid notes, that it is easier for a painter to indicate that an object is at a distance if it is an object of a kind known to have a complex colour structure than if it is known to be of a uniform colour. For if it has a complex colour structure then the painter need only present it with a blurred or fairly uniform colour to indicate distance, whereas it is not so easy to represent by blurring of colour an object which in any case is of a unifom colour. In the latter case the quality of that uniform colour should be taken into account. For example, the quality of the air can make a difference. Reid comments: 'The colours of objects, according as they are more distant, become more faint and languid, and are tinged more with the azure of the intervening atmosphere.' (Reid, *Inquiry*, p.182)

The quality of the intervening atmosphere interests Reid as commentator on the craft of the painter. He notes that in Italy and Sicily, where the air is particularly pure, distant things seem less distant than they would in other climes. This is, on Reid's account, because with the greater clarity of the air comes a more precise perception of the details of the distant things, and it is the clarity of the details that gives a clue as to how far away things are. They surely cannot be so far away if they are seen with such clarity. So Reid adds: 'The purity of the Italian air hath been assigned as the reason why the Italian painters commonly give a more lively colour to the sky, than the Flemish. Ought they not, for the same reason, to give less degradation of the colours, and less indistinctness of the minute parts, in the representation of very distant objects?' (Reid, *Inquiry*, p.183)

To take up a last point about the contrast between seeing and knowing, I should like to consider further Reid's distinction between the sign and the thing signified. Though a piece of cloth is really a uniform colour, its colour does not necessarily appear to us as uniform. It may be partly in sun and partly in shade. Yet, seeing the way the cloth lies, with the sun shining on only part of it, we immediately judge it to be of unifom colour. The difference in visible appearance of the two parts is exactly what we, experienced observers of the world, would expect of a piece of cloth that is really of uniform colour if the cloth were laid out in that particular way. To take the opposite case, if part of the cloth were in sun and part in shadow, and yet the visible appearance of the whole cloth were uniform, we would instantly judge the two parts to be of different shades. For how else could we explain the fact that the part in shade appeared to be as bright as the part in direct sunlight? Reid thinks that most of the time, in fact almost all the time, we ordinary people do not notice the discrepancy between appearance and reality. Faced with the appearance we treat it as a sign of something else and immediately focus on what the sign signifies, namely, on what we fondly think of as reality. So we hardly notice that one part of the cloth appears to be darker than the other. All we notice, that is, all we *attend to*, is the fact that the cloth must really be of a uniform colour. But, as Reid notes, there is a profession in which the difference between visible appearance and visible reality needs to be noted, and that is the profession of painting. How else is the painter going to represent the fact that the piece of cloth, partly in sun and partly out of it, is in fact of a uniform colour except by copying the visible appearance of the cloth, and painting the bit in shade as darker than the bit in the sun?

I emphasise this last point because some of Raeburn's most spectacular effects are got by a systematic application of the principle here at issue. There is, for example, a good deal to be written about the hats Raeburn painted, or rather about the shadows cast by their brim. In the portrait of David Hunter of Blackness (National Galleries of Scotland, Edinburgh) (plate 7) the entire forehead and the subject's right eye are very dark indeed, in sharp contrast to the rest of the face. To a lesser extent we see the same effect in Raeburn's most famous portrait, that of the skater, the Reverend Robert Walker (National Galleries of Scotland). Perhaps the most remarkable example is in the portrait of Anne Campbell, Mrs Colin Campbell of Park (Kelvingrove, Glasgow) (plate 9) in which her jet black hat, a sign of her widowhood, casts a shadow which envelops her forehead, her eyes and the bridge of her nose. In the upper part of her face the only relief from this shadow is an extraordinary painterly effect, a hallmark of Raeburn's; the flesh above the eyes and below the eyebrows is in light reflected from the bright white collar of the sitter. The effects here described are examples, executed by a genius, of the distinction between what we see and what we know. We might well say that the relation between Reid and Raeburn is that between theory and practice, for nothing could better exemplify Reid's philosophy of perception than Raeburn's paintings. Whether Raeburn actually read Reid's philosophy of perception is not recorded, but Raeburn was a close friend of Dugald Stewart who was himself both a pupil of Reid and an authoritative commentator on Reid's philosophy. It is almost certain that Raeburn was well acquainted with Reid's teaching in this area, especially in view of the fact that Reid repeatedly invokes the practice of painters in the course of his expositions of his theory of perception.

Dugald Stewart wrote an *Account of the Life and Writings of Thomas Reid*, in the course of which he mentions Reid's visit to Edinburgh in 1796 from his home in Glasgow: 'His countenance was strongly expressive of deep and collected thought; but, when brightened up by the face of a friend, what chiefly caught the attention was a look of good-will and kindness. A picture of him, for which he consented, at the particular request of Dr Gregory, to sit to Mr Raeburn, during his last visit to Edinburgh, is generally and justly ranked among the happiest performances of that excellent artist.' (p.31)

The encounter between Reid and Raeburn in 1796 in Edinburgh was a magical moment, one to give pause to any philosopher or painter. Two geniuses of the Scottish Enlightenment faced each other in Raeburn's studio, one of them dedicated to the study of human nature in its universality and the other to the representation of human nature as individuated in each of us, that is, human nature as it is ordinarily encountered. The conversation between the two men is not recorded. But Reid must have known that Raeburn did not need to be encouraged to paint what he saw rather than what he knew. Raeburn had been acting according to that injunction for years, and did so again when the ancient but intellectually still formidable Reid sat for him. Whatever the conversation that passed between the two men, the artistic product of the meeting was a masterpiece, a formidable synthesis of philosophy and the painter's art. (see Plate 5)

Section 6: Hutcheson's aesthetics

Philosophers of the Scottish Enlightenment did not invent aesthetics – the philosophical study of beauty, the sublime, and related categories – but they did make a highly significant contribution. Hutcheson's was important, partly in respect of his solutions to problems, and partly in respect of his map of the field. Hume learned a great deal from Hutcheson's work in this area but came to very different conclusions. Their writings are of much more than merely historical interest, and here I shall make comments on some salient points that arose in the debates.

My starting point is Hutcheson. He completed his studies at Glasgow University in 1717 and returned to Ireland where in due course he opened a Dissenting Academy in Dublin. In 1725 he published *An Inquiry into the Original of our Ideas of Beauty and Virtue*, and in 1725–6 published *Reflections upon Laughter*. These are his major works on aesthetics, though his other writings, principally on moral philosophy, make frequent reference to aesthetic matters, in view of his conviction that aesthetic categories have a moral dimension. Indeed 'moral beauty' is a central concept of Hutcheson's. Hence by the time Hutcheson was elected to a philosophy chair at Glasgow University in 1729 he had already worked out his most significant ideas on aesthetics, though once in the chair he gave priority to the revision of some of those ideas and the reinforcement of others.

Hutcheson believed that we have an aesthetic sense, also called an 'internal sense'. The claim might seem odd, but less so if Hutcheson's conception of a 'sense' is brought to bear: a sense is 'every determination of our minds to receive ideas independently on our will, and to have perceptions of pleasure and pain'. (Hutcheson, *Philosophical Writings*, p.115) I open my eyes and see a book; the visual sensing or experience is an immediate and natural effect of my looking at the book. I cannot look at it and by an act of will refrain from seeing it. Likewise I cannot unplug my ears and by an act of will not hear the din from the nearby radio. I can by an act of will keep my eyes shut, or keep the plugs in my ears. But so long as I do not have the plugs in I will immediately hear the racket that fills my sound space, and so long as I open my eyes I will immediately see the book that is right in front of me. There are two elements here. One is the immediacy of the reaction and the other is the fact that the will is not engaged; the perceptual effect is by purely natural means. It is Hutcheson's contention that we likewise *sense* the beauty, sublimity or grandeur of a sight or of a sound. The sense of the thing's beauty, so to say, wells up unbidden. I see a sunset, and a sense of its beauty immediately wells up in me. Associated with that sense, and perhaps even part of it – Hutcheson does not give us a clear account of the matter – is the pleasure that we take in the thing. We *enjoy* beautiful things and that enjoyment is not merely incidental to our sensing their beauty.

A question arises here regarding the features, or elements, of a thing that cause us to see it as beautiful and to take pleasure in it. Hutcheson suggests that a beautiful thing displays unity (or uniformity) amidst variety. If a work has too much uniformity it is simply boring. If it has too much variety it is a jumble. An object, whether visible or audible, requires therefore to occupy the intermediate position if it is to give rise to a sense of the object's beauty. I shall explore this proposal by considering appropriate ways to deal with what appears to be a serious problem with it. The problem is this: there is surely not much room for dispute over whether or not an object displays uniformity amidst variety, and in that case why is there so much disagreement between us in our judgments about whether given objects are beautiful?

In reply we should start from the fact that for Hutcheson the sense of beauty is universal; that is, it is part of what he calls the 'frame of our nature', an original human endowment. We all, or almost all, have this sense just as we are all, or almost all, born with a sense of sight. Hutcheson dwells on this last point, which he believes can be too easily overlooked as a result of the common emphasis on the extent of disagreement on aesthetic matters. Of course such disagreement exists but, as he points out, it would not exist if we did not at least agree in applying aesthetic categories to the things we perceive. That is agreement at a most fundamental level.

But why do we not agree more than we do? We are all, according to Hutcheson, responding to the same thing – unity amidst variety. This is the standard of taste, which we can use to check the correctness or otherwise of a person's judgment about the beauty or the ugliness of an object. Nevertheless, whether we find something beautiful depends not only on whether we perceive unity amidst variety in the thing, but also on the associations that the thing arouses in our mind. If an object that we had found beautiful comes to be associated in our mind with something disagreeable this will affect our aesthetic response; we might even find the thing ugly. Hutcheson gives an example of wines to which men acquire an aversion after they have taken them in an emetic preparation: '. . . we are conscious that the idea is altered from what it was when that wine was agreeable, by the conjunction of the idea of loathing and sickness of the stomach.' (Hutcheson, *Philosophical Writings*, pp.8–9) And our aesthetic response can also be affected in the opposite direction. It is this mechanism of association that Hutcheson invokes to explain the fact of disagreements over aesthetic matters.

On this matter his position may seem extreme, for he goes so far as to say the following: 'But there appears no ground to believe such a diversity in human minds, as that the same simple idea or perception should give pleasure to one and pain to another, or to the same person at different times, or to say that it seems a contradiction that the same simple idea should do so.' (p.9) Part of what he is saying or implying here is that if two people have the same visual experience and if the thing experienced carries the same identical associations for the two people, then they will have the same aesthetic response to the visible object. This position is very difficult to disprove, since if two people do in fact disagree about the aesthetic merit of an object, it is always open to Hutcheson to say that the object produces different associations in the two spectators. This may, however, be another way of saying that Hutcheson's position on this matter is vacuous – that he has so described what occurs that nothing can count as evidence against his claim.

Section 7: Hume on the standard of taste

In the preceding section we considered the idea that uniformity amidst variety is the standard of taste, the standard by which we measure the beauty or sublimity of a thing. I should like now to focus more closely on the idea of a 'standard of taste', first asking whether there is such a standard, and then probing more deeply the question of what it is (if it exists).

In reply to the question whether there is a standard of taste, it seems possible to argue both that there must be one and also that there cannot be. The principal justification for the claim that there must be one is that no-one thinks that everyone's opinion is just as good as everyone else's; we each think that we are right on many matters of taste and that those who disagree with us are therefore wrong. But we surely cannot think this unless we have in mind a standard of taste and think that our judgment measures up to the standard whereas any judgment contradicting ours fails to measure up to the standard. In short, we can and do dispute about taste, and can only do so on the assumption that there is a standard to which an appeal can be made.

On the other hand, the principal justification for the claim that there cannot be a standard of taste is precisely that there is so much dispute on matters of taste. If indeed there is a standard and we all appeal to it, then why is there so much disagreement? The situation therefore is paradoxical in that the opposite sides of the question of whether there is a standard of taste appeal to precisely the same fact, namely the measure of disagreement on matters of taste. Hume's essay 'Of the standard of taste' (*Essays*, pp.226–49) begins by emphasising the fact of disagreement. Within our own small circle of acquaintances we find many disagreements on matters of taste: 'But those, who can enlarge their view to contemplate distant nations and remote ages, are still more surprized at the great inconsistence and contrariety.' (*Essays*, p.227) Hume here brings his empirical method to bear, and does so in a way characteristic of the amplitude of vision of the Scottish Enlightenment. The evidence regarding the existence or non-existence of an accessible standard of taste is immeasurably strengthened if the evidence encompasses not only the local facts but also the situation in distant places at distant times. What this ample vision indicates is that the local disagreement in taste is representative of a wider problem, that either many human beings have trouble gaining access to the standard of taste or, more radically, no such standard is accessible to us.

Indeed in Hume's view the measure of disagreement is greater than it might at first appear to be. He writes: 'Every voice is united in applauding elegance, propriety, simplicity, spirit in writing; and in blaming fustian, affectation, coldness, and a false brilliancy.' But this unity is only language-deep. The very word 'elegance' implies approval, and the very word 'affectation' implies disapproval. But as soon as we describe a work of art as 'elegant' we will find someone rejecting our judgment. We and our opponents all approve of elegance, but are instantly divided on the question of whether *this* is elegant.

It should be said at once that Hume believes that there is a standard of taste, and bases this belief on the consideration on which I have already focused, the fact that we each of us think that we are right in our judgments of taste and that therefore people who disagree with us are wrong. This is an empirical fact about us, and of course the empiricist Hume, seeking 'to apply the experimental method of reasoning to moral subjects', respects this fact. In a key sentence he affirms: 'It is natural for us to seek a *Standard of Taste*; a rule, by which the various sentiments of men may be reconciled; at least, a decision, afforded, confirming one sentiment, and condemning another.' (*Essays*, p.229) For Hume, a judgment of taste articulates a sentiment or feeling. A work of art delights or enthrals us, or moves us in some other way. But whichever sentiment or feeling is engaged when we encounter the work, we cannot judge it beautiful if it leaves us cold. Some might say that one person's sentiments on aesthetic matters are as good as another person's, but Hume rejects this approach, holding instead that in relation to any work of art some aesthetic responses are demonstrably more appropriate or fitting than others – 'demonstrably' given the role of argument in discussions on the aesthetic merits of works of arts. In the arguments we produce we seek to demonstrate the propriety, indeed the reasonableness, of our judgments.

It is noteworthy that our arguments are not, or at least not generally, about high-level aesthetic principles but instead are much more focused on the details of the works that we are judging. This feature of our supporting arguments is recognised by George Turnbull, whose *Treatise on Ancient Painting* must have been well known to Hume. Turnbull believes that we can ask of a painting, any painting, such questions as:

> Have all the Parts a just relation to the principal Design? Doth it clearly strike, or is the Sight splitted, divided, and confounded, by Parts; either not essential, or not duly subordinated to the Whole? Is the Colouring proper to the Subject and Design; and is it of a proportional Character throughout the Whole, to that of the principal Figure? Doth the same Genius and Spirit reign throughout the Work? Is there a sufficient and well-chosen variety of Contrasts? Is there too little or too much? ... By these and such like Questions ought Pictures, as well as Poems to be tried and canvassed. (*Treatise*, p.93)

All these are questions that are directed to the particular work of art. The point here is that if you judge a painting beautiful and another person judges to the contrary, you can defend your position by pointing out things about the painting that your protagonist might have missed, such as the fact that the colouring is proper to the subject, that there are well-chosen contrasts, and that one part of the painting is a nicely judged counterpoint to another part. By making these points, and therefore by rational means, we can induce the other to change his mind about the merit of the painting. If in light of these observations about the paintings he decides he was wrong and we were right, this surely implies that he has decided that his judgment did not in fact measure up to a standard of taste on which we and he agree. What is this standard? For Hutcheson it was unity amidst variety. Hume offers a different line.

Hume's famous dictum, 'Reason is, and ought only to be the slave of the passions, and can never pretend to any other office than to serve and obey them' (*Treatise*, p.415), was deployed by him in the course of his discussion of moral judgments. Such judgments 'are more properly felt than judged of', he tells us, and it is therefore appropriate to think of Hume as a sentimentalist about matters of morality. But it should be noted that he does not say that reason has no role to play in morality. It has one – it is the slave of the passions. But that is not a negligible or despicable role. If passion is the master then reason is the slave, and in this, as in most other cases of the master–slave relation, the master cannot cope without the slave. The master is dependent on the slave, at least as much as the slave is dependent on the master. Within Hume's philosophy the doctrine 'reason is the slave of the passions' is applicable to almost all aspects of our experience of the world, and is certainly no less applicable to our aesthetic than to our moral judgments. When we make a judgment of taste it is our feelings, sentiments or passions, we can call them what we will, that are in the driving seat, but they cannot cope without reason, which moves in on the immediate sentimental response to a work of art and proceeds to adjust that sentiment, by bringing to bear the sorts of considerations that George Turnbull enumerates. The clear proof that reason has a role is the fact that we think it appropriate to mount a rational defence of our aesthetic judgments.

In light of Hume's examples it is plain that he would be prepared to mount such a defence on behalf of the claims that John Bunyan is inferior to Joseph Addison, and that John Ogilby (a seventeenth-century verse translator of Homer and Virgil) is inferior to Milton. Hume affirms: 'Though there may be found persons, who give the preference to the former authors; no one pays attention to such taste; and we pronounce without scruple the sentiment of these pretended critics to be absurd and ridiculous.' (*Essays*, p.231) That Hume thinks it absurd and ridiculous to say that Bunyan is better than Addison sheds an interesting light on Hume's own literary values, but for the present I wish to attend instead to his reference to 'these pretended critics'. That they subscribe to the absurd and ridiculous literary claims at issue is proof of the hollowness of their claim to be critics. A good critic would be able to demonstrate the superiority of Addison over Bunyan. A question arises therefore as to the qualities of a good critic; for once we have identified some good critics, we can evaluate our own aesthetic judgments by seeing whether our judgments measure up to theirs. How, then, are we to recognise a good critic? This question turns out to be essential to Hume's entire aesthetic theory. In a nutshell, his doctrine is that the judgment of the good critic is the standard of taste. Hume therefore enumerates the qualities of the good critic, and he finds five. The list is not, so to say, worked out from first principles, but by empirical means.

There are rules regarding what sorts of things will give aesthetic pleasure, but they can be formulated only on the basis of experience. They are 'general observations, concerning what has been universally found to please in all countries and in all ages'. (*Essays*, p.231) Hume does not enumerate the rules he has in mind, but it is reasonable to suppose that they relate to the sorts of features of works of art that Turnbull invokes when he invites us to ask of a painting such questions as: 'Have all the Parts a just relation to the principal Design? . . . Is the Colouring proper to the Subject and Design?' This is not to say, however, that works which accord with the rules will in fact always please us. It is the finer, not the grosser, emotions that are engaged in our adequate response to the beauties of a work of art, to paintings, poems, sonatas, and so on, and a person who is not in a suitable frame of mind will not judge well. Deep depression, wild hilarity, barely controlled rage, savage jealousy and seething hatred incapacitate our faculty of aesthetic judgment, by diminishing our receptivity to the subtleties, the delicately balanced relationships, the finely judged distinctions, of the work of art. In a word, while these big emotional states are in control of the spirit there is simply no room in the spirit for the necessary delicacy of sentiment.

The situation is somewhat as with physical taste, for a person with a delicate, refined sense of taste can recognise the various ingredients in the food. Others are simply unable to pick out those ingredients. Hume adds: 'Where the organs are so fine, as to allow nothing to escape them; and at the same time so exact as to perceive every ingredient in the composition: This we call delicacy of taste, whether we employ these terms in the literal or metaphorical sense.' (*Essays*, p.235) This emotional fine tuning of the spectator, his 'delicacy of taste', is the first quality of the good critic that Hume lists.

The second quality of the good critic is that he is well practised in the exercise of his critical powers. He has frequently surveyed and contemplated works of the relevant kind, and only by such experience has he learned what to look out for. The good critic also frequently surveys an individual work and each time sees more in it, assuming of course that there is more to be seen. His judgment of the work is plainly sounder as a result. The third quality of the good critic is this, that he is experienced in making comparisons with other, related kinds of works of art. Without such experience the critic might well give undue weight to superficial or frivolous features of the work being judged. Fourthly, the good critic is unprejudiced in his judgment. If the artist is a dear friend of the critic, then the latter must somehow distance himself from this relationship if he is to give a fair judgment of the painting. Likewise, if he hates the painter, he must distance himself from this fact. In short, the good critic is what Adam Smith terms an 'impartial spectator', but he is in this case an impartial spectator in relation to the art work being judged. If the critic fails in this task, 'his taste evidently departs from the true standard; and of consequence loses all credit and authority'. (*Essays*, p.240) Fifthly, and finally, in this list of qualities of the good critic, he must have 'good sense'. This quality is required if a critic is to judge the fittingness of works of art in relation to their end. For example, in assessing a rhetorical performance the critic's good sense should tell him that he should take into account the nature of the audience for whom the performance was originally intended. Thus Hume sums up the character of the good critic in these terms: 'Strong sense, united to delicate sentiment, improved by practice, perfected by comparison, and cleared of all prejudice, can alone entitle critics to this valuable character; and the joint verdict of such, wherever they are to be found, is the true standard of taste and beauty.' (*Essays*, p.241)

It is not clear whether Hume's account of the standard of taste is sound, and in particular it has seemed to some that he is open to the charge of begging the question, that is, of antecedently accepting the very thing he is proposing to prove. He lists the virtues of a good critic, but why should we say that these are the virtues of a good critic if not because we believe that someone with these virtues is more likely to be right in his aesthetic judgments? If this is correct then we need to know which aesthetic judgments are correct before going in search of the qualities that a good critic possesses. On the face of it then we require to have criteria of sound aesthetic judgment antecedently to having criteria of a good critic, yet Hume evidently seeks to base the criteria of sound aesthetic judgment on the concept of a good critic, and not vice versa. In short, Hume silently assumes he knows the criteria of sound aesthetic judgment, on the basis of which criteria he sets up a concept of a good critic, on the basis of which he then develops the criteria of a sound aesthetic judgment. If this is Hume's line of thought he is surely begging the question. This criticism of Hume may be unfair, and there are some who think it is. It is not however my purpose to plunge into the depths that beckon here. It is enough for present purposes to have given some indication of Hume's hugely influential account of the standard of taste.

I should like to end by deploying an insight of Turnbull's in relation to a distinction between Hutcheson and Hume that has not been much noted. Hutcheson makes a number of references to the beauties of nature, and his aesthetic theory is designed to take into account the fact that we apply aesthetic categories no less to nature than to human artifacts. On the other hand, all Hume's examples in his essay 'Of the standard of taste' are human artifacts. In fact they are all literary; they are by poets, playwrights, essayists and so on. George Turnbull, like Hutcheson, discusses the beauties of nature, but does so in such a way that it is clear he is thinking of them almost as if the objects of our gaze are artifacts. I have already noted his exclamation: 'what superior Pleasures one must have, who hath an Eye formed by comparing Landscapes [i.e. landscape paintings] with Nature, in the contemplation of Nature itself in his Morning or Evening Walks, to one who is not at all conversant in Painting ... He will delight in observing what is really worthy of being painted; what Circumstances a good Genius would take hold of; what Parts he would leave out, and what he would add, and for what Reasons'. (*Treatise on Ancient Painting*, p.146) The observer is looking at nature through a painter's eyes. It is almost as though he is seeing nature within a picture frame. Nature, as thus experienced, is viewed as a painting, a human artifact. Turnbull, writing of the person well instructed in painting, adds: 'Nature would send such a one to Pictures, and Pictures would send him to Nature.' (*Treatise*, p.146) We find here, clearly delineated near the start of the Scottish Enlightenment, an account of a concept that would in due course loom large in aesthetic theory, the concept of the 'picturesque', something in nature, but seen in terms of its potential for forming the subject of a painting, nature therefore as simultaneously natural and artificial. Few of the later writers on aesthetics had more interesting things to say on this subject than did Turnbull.

SEVEN

Science and Enlightenment

Section 1: Science and its unity

Numerous major scientific advances were made during the Scottish Enlightenment and in this chapter I shall try to present a picture of the effervescent scientific scene. This will not be a whirlwind tour of the sciences and the scientists, but rather an attempt to say something about the intellectual context within which some few of the big ideas were generated. These will be a few ideas among many, for we could focus on Colin Maclaurin's mathematical advances and his highly original work on the movement of tides, William Cullen's chemical discoveries, Joseph Black's discoveries of latent heat and specific heat, James Watt's invention of the improved version of the Newcomen steam engine, or John Robison's remarkable discovery of the inverse square law of electric force. I shall restrict myself in the remaining four sections to comments on a handful of matters, first Adam Smith's account of the nature of scientific discovery, then the theological dimension of Maclaurin's account of Newtonian mechanics, next Thomas Reid's exposition of non-Euclidean geometry, following which I shall consider James Hutton's epochal work on the forces which govern geological change. What I shall be attending to in those four sections is merely illustrative of the many discussions that marked out Scotland as in the forefront in Europe in the field of the physical and mathematical sciences in the eighteenth century. I shall begin, however, with some comments on human nature and the Scottish Enlightenment concept of the unity of the sciences.

The people responsible for the big scientific advances were interesting and unusual. Nevertheless, as I have said earlier, the Scottish Enlightenment would be of little or no consequence now were it not for the sheer intellectual quality of the thinkers, and it is therefore on this that I shall be concentrating in this chapter on the science of the age, while at the same time making clear that there are also important social and personal contexts within which this memorable thinking was done. I shall also attend, though briefly, to aspects of the relation between science and religion in eighteenth-century Scotland. Any belief we might have that science and religion are somehow in mutual conflict has to confront a well-developed and utterly contrary belief that was firmly entrenched in the heart of the Enlightenment in Scotland.

One important belief held by many literati was that the sciences form a unity. They were seen as having a unity at least in the sense that knowledge gleaned from one can be deployed to secure results in another. Dugald Stewart provides an example: 'The modern discoveries in astronomy and in pure mathematics, have contributed to bring the art of navigation to a degree of perfection formerly unknown. The rapid progress which has been lately made in astronomy, anatomy, and botany, has been chiefly owing to the aid which these sciences have received from the art of the optician.' (*Elements*, p.9)

But the doctrine of the unity of the sciences incorporated deeper, more metaphysical considerations than those indicated by Dugald Stewart, and at the heart of these 'deeper considerations' was the concept of 'human nature'. The concept was extensively studied, both because of its intrinsic importance and also because it was seen as forming a principle of unity of all the other sciences and therefore as providing a fruitful starting point for exploration within the other sciences. Famously at the start of his *Treatise of Human Nature*, Hume argued for the claim that human nature is such a principle of unity: ''Tis evident, that all the sciences have a relation, greater or less, to human nature; and that however wide any of them may seem to run from it, they still return back by one passage or another.' (*Treatise*, p.xv) Some indication of Hume's justification for his claim is immediately provided: 'Even *Mathematics, Natural Philosophy, and Natural Religion*, are in some measure dependent on the science of MAN; since they lie under the cognizance of men, and are judged of by their powers and faculties.'

We look out upon a world whose contents are accessible to us by our senses or our intellect; and we see what we see, and in the way we see it, because of the peculiar character of our human faculties and powers by which these things are accessible. How the world looks to beings with different faculties we do not know and can hardly even guess. All we can talk about is our world. That is the world that is the object of our scientific investigations, and of course the content of our science is in substantial measure shaped by the fact that the scientific investigators are human.

In fact Hume devotes a pivotal section of the *Treatise*, 'Of scepticism with regard to the senses' (*Treatise*, bk.1, part 4, sect.4), to arguing that the world in which we humans live, and which we know by means of our human faculties, is largely a creation of one of those faculties, that of imagination. We receive the data provided by the senses and the data is the raw material out of which we construct our world. It is an imaginative act that we perform without realising that we are performing it, but if we did not perform it we would live in a chaos of sensory data that lacks the coherence necessary to constitute a world. Since our natural scientific investigations are of the world that is largely a product of our own mental activity it follows immediately that natural science has, as Hume puts it, 'a relation, greater or less, to human nature'. It is therefore not surprising that Hume concludes: 'There is no question of importance, whose decision is not compriz'd in the science of man; and there is none, which can be decided with any certainty, before we become acquainted with that science.' (*Treatise*, p.xvi) Thereafter the *Treatise* is a detailed investigation of human nature, and the investigation is carried out according to scientific procedures appropriate to the natural sciences, for Hume is expounding a *science* of human nature, and reaches his conclusions by employing methods of the sort that scientists use to conduct investigations in any other areas of the natural world. In particular Hume proceeds by experiment and observation. For this reason it can be argued that there is a further layer of unity in the sciences, for the sciences constitute a unity not only in so far as they all lead back to human nature, but also in so far as progress is made in them only by means of a strict adherence to the rules of experiment and observation. Now we see that even the science of human nature, to which all the other sciences lead back, has to be pursued by the same methods as those employed in, say, physics.

During the Scottish Enlightenment, human nature was investigated in a variety of ways, as we have observed throughout this book. One of the greatest achievements of the Scottish Enlightenment was the philosophy of Thomas Reid, which is chiefly dedicated to an exposition of the concept of human nature, particularly of our faculties of sense perception, memory, concept formation, judgment, reasoning and will. He attends throughout to the belief system that everybody has and the lack of which would make someone significantly less than human in a most crucial respect. This belief system is composed of a set of principles of common sense, principles which are original features of our constitution, and which cannot be proved, because they are basic or foundational. It is only because we already have them that we are able to prove anything whatsoever.

Reid used a variety of methods, particularly introspective and linguistic, to achieve his results. To take one of the host of available linguistic examples that Reid deploys to telling effect, he notes that we speak of the mind primarily with the aid of active forms of verbs. Thus, we think, imagine, remember, conceive, judge, reason, and so on. The active form of verb comes more naturally than the passive, and this is indicative of the fact that the mind is an active principle, not passive as is dead matter. In constructing a model of the human mind therefore it is appropriate to think of the mind not as a substance which has various qualities or attributes, but as an agent which has the power to engage in various kinds of act. Thoughts are not things in the mind, as if the mind is some kind of mental space within which aggregates of mental particles, thoughts, are located; but instead thoughts are acts in which the mind engages. According to Reid, all this, and a good deal besides, can be learned about the human mind by close attention to language, and especially to grammatical features of language, such as active and passive forms of the verb, the tenses of the verb, singular and plural forms of nouns, relations between nouns and adjectives, and so on.

Linguistic science is therefore according to Reid an invaluable research tool in the project of providing a scientific account of human nature.

The linguistic studies of many other literati also bear witness to an interest in the exploration of the concept of human nature by linguistic means. Perhaps the most prolific in this field was James Burnett, Lord Monboddo, author of a multi-volume study, *Of the Origin and Progress of Language*. Hugh Blair's extensive writings on literary style explore, among other topics, the way different figures of speech, metaphor, simile and so on, can be deployed systematically to reflect or express different emotions. Adam Smith's important treatise on the origin of language contains, as we observed earlier, an analysis of the thought processes of primitive people who look out upon a strange world and try to classify things, and George Campbell's brilliant study of language in his *Philosophy of Rhetoric* shows ways in which linguistic science is immediately applicable to the study of human nature.

The study of history also was recognised as a means of investigating human nature. In an earlier chapter we saw aspects of this point at work. In particular it proved necessary to attend to the famous statement by Hume:

> Mankind are so much the same, in all times and places, that history informs us of nothing new or strange in this particular. Its chief use is only to discover the constant and universal principles of human nature, by showing men in all varieties of circumstances and situations, and furnishing us with materials from which we may form our observations and become acquainted with the regular springs of human action and behaviour. These records of wars, intrigues, factions, and revolutions, are so many collections of experiments, by which the politician or moral philosopher fixes the principles of his science . . .'
> (*Enquiry Concerning Human Understanding*, pp.83–4)

Although later in this chapter I shall be considering writings on astronomy, mathematics and geology by three great figures of the

Scottish Enlightenment, all three saw their scientific writings as contributing in a variety of ways to an understanding of human nature.

Section 2: The psychology of scientific discovery

To make a scientific discovery is to engage in a particular sort of act, and during the Scottish Enlightenment, a movement which engaged in a good deal of self-reflective and self-critical thinking, the nature of such creative acts was itself held up for scrutiny. These self-reflective investigations produced numerous interesting insights. On 16 April 1773 Adam Smith wrote to Hume:

> As I have left the care of all my literary papers to you, I must tell you that except those which I carry along with me there are none worth the publishing, but a fragment of a great work which contains a history of the Astronomical Systems that were successively in fashion down to the time of Des Cartes. Whether that might not be published as a fragment of an intended juvenile work, I leave entirely to your judgment; tho I begin to suspect myself that there is more refinement than solidity in some parts of it ... Unless I die very suddenly I shall take care that the Papers I carry with me shall be carefully sent to you. (Smith, *Correspondence*, p.168)

Smith had been ill, or at least had thought he was ill – he had a marked tendency throughout his life to hypochondria – at the time he wrote the letter, and the illness might have been the reason why at about that time he appointed Hume as his literary executor. Hume would no doubt have followed Smith's instructions to the letter, but Hume (the older man by a dozen years) died first. The two men who eventually inherited Hume's mantle as Smith's literary executors, namely Joseph Black and James Hutton, were scrupulous in the performance of their duties, to the extent that shortly after Smith's death in 1790 they destroyed by fire sixteen volumes of his manuscripts. We have little idea as to the contents of those volumes and, so far as we know, Black and Hutton destroyed them wholly unread.

Among the papers they were not asked to destroy was the manuscript on the history of astronomy which was exercising Smith's mind when he wrote to Hume in 1773. Black and Hutton duly published this work in 1795, under the title *The Principles which lead and direct Philosophical Enquiries; illustrated by the History of Astronomy*. There is strong evidence that most of the work was written in the period between 1740 and 1746 when Smith was a student at Balliol College, Oxford, and in that case the *History of Astronomy* was finally published some half a century after most of it had been composed. We have to suppose therefore that for the discussion of science and scientific methodology that we find in the *History of Astronomy* Smith did not draw on his close personal knowledge of the great Scottish scientists, such as his two literary executors, who were his contemporaries. Even less did he benefit from the scientific experts who taught him at Balliol, for there were none there; indeed Smith was appalled at the low quality of the dons at the college, a low quality that must have seemed to him all the more striking in light of his happy experiences at Glasgow where he had been taught by men of very high calibre indeed, including Francis Hutcheson, Robert Simpson, professor of mathematics, and Robert Dick, professor of natural philosophy.

The last two may have contributed to the confident tone of Smith's writing on astronomy. Dugald Stewart reports: 'Dr Maclaine of the Hague, who was a fellow-student of Mr Smith's at Glasgow, told me some years ago, that his favourite pursuits while at that university were mathematics and natural philosophy; and I remember to have heard my father remind him of a geometrical problem of considerable difficulty, about which he was occupied at the time when their acquaintance commenced, and which had been proposed to him as an exercise by the celebrated Dr Simpson.' (Stewart, *Account of the Life and Writings of Adam Smith*, pp.270–1) There is no doubt that Adam Smith, like many of the great men of the Scottish Enlightenment, was a quality performer in several fields, and that, though now remembered as an economist and a moral philosopher, he had received a very solid grounding in mathematics and physics. Smith's *History of Astronomy* is a major statement, despite his remark to Hume, quoted above, that 'I begin to suspect myself that there is more refinement than solidity in some parts of it'. The *History* is particulary remarkable both for its account of the psychology of scientific discovery and also for its account of the manner in which science stands in relation to the truth. I shall consider here what Smith has to say on both of these topics – topics of lively concern in the present day no less than they were during the Enlightenment. Indeed some of his insights in this field have a thoroughly modern ring.

Smith seeks to identify the motive that prompts us to think scientifically, the motive that leads us to ask scientific questions and that then sustains our search for the answers. We might have imagined that Smith would give an answer in terms of the exercise of the faculty of reason, for if science is not from start to finish a rational exercise then it is surely nothing. But we should recall that Smith's great work on ethics is *The Theory of Moral Sentiments*. He emphasises the role of the sentiments in our practical lives, and might fairly be said to have down-played the role of reason in that same field. Put otherwise, he caught hold of Hume's famous dictum: 'Reason is, and ought only to be the slave of the passions, and can never pretend to any other office than to serve and obey them' (*Treatise*, p.415) and ran with it. Well, he certainly ran with it as far as his ethical theory is concerned. What I wish to stress is that on an obvious interpretation he also applied that dictum to his account of the psychology of scientific discovery. To deploy large, if rather crude, categories in his psychological story, Smith is a sentimentalist not a rationalist. As regards our moral life it is always sentiment that motivates us, that actually gets us moving; and likewise in our scientific work. But for Smith there is no big contrast here between the practical life on the one side and science on the other. He is thinking of science as on the side of practice, because it is something we *do*, and since sentiment motivates all our practices, it also motivates our scientific thinking. To be more precise, his answer to the question of what motivates us to engage in scientific thinking is that it is a set of related but mutually distinct sentiments which come into play successively as the scientific exercise begins, and is maintained. In the practice of science, sentiment is in the driving seat from start to finish.

Smith is not making what would be a bizarre claim, that science is through and through an exercise of sentiment. He had read a good deal of science and was well aware that a scientific paper contains premises, proceeds by the systematic application of rules of inference, and draws its conclusions accordingly. The whole piece of work has a rational structure, and will be judged by scientists on the basis both of the correctness of the data, and also of the quality of the application of the rules of inference to those data. Sentiment is not present in any form as part of the content of the paper. But Smith is not here writing about the outcome of the process, or activity, of scientific discovery, that is, about the content of the scientific paper; he is instead writing about the process or activity that leads up to the finished article. His claim is that this process relies heavily on sentiment. Someone might have the *intellectual* potential to be a scientific genius, but if he is not sufficiently motivated, that is, if he does not respond in the appropriate sentimental way to the natural world, his scientific potential will not be realised.

Smith believed that the first step in the process of scientific discovery is surprise. According to his analysis of the concept, surprise, though a sentiment, is not one sentiment among all the others; it can come in the form of any of the sentiments. On perceiving something unexpected we respond with a sentiment which comes upon us suddenly and unbidden. The sentiment might be of the agreeable or of the disagreeable variety; it might be very faint or very violent. The crucial point about it is its abruptness. To be surprised is to undergo an abrupt change in sentiment, no matter of what kind the sentiment may be, in response to the perception of something unexpected. Hence, if we come across an unexpected happening and have absolutely no emotional reaction to it then we are not surprised by the happening. How great the surprise is depends in part on the state of mind antecedent to the perception of the unexpected. If the emotion that comes upon us abruptly and unbidden is the opposite to the one already in place, as when a grief-stricken person receives good news and is suddenly smitten with joy, the surprise is the greater on account of the contrast with the previous state. Surprise therefore is to be measured not in terms of the intensity or violence of the emotion, but in terms of the size of the abrupt change that takes place in the person's spirit.

Not all surprise, however, prompts us to scientific thinking. We need to consider also the different sorts of thing that might occasion surprise, and Smith focuses upon two sorts. First, we are by nature classificatory animals. We see things as *of a kind*. This is a plant, that a table, and so on. But occasionally we are presented with something new and singular, and we cannot classify it. As Smith says: 'The imagination and memory exert themselves to no purpose, and in vain look around all their classes of ideas in order to find one under which it may be arranged.' (*History*, in *Essays*, p.39) This fluctuation from thought to thought in search of the class of which the thing is a member, plus the accompanying emotion as we pursue the objective, are conjointly termed by Smith 'wonder'. He adds: 'What sort of thing can that be? What is that like? are the questions which, upon such an occasion, we are naturally disposed to ask.' The term 'wonder' is a technical term in this context. Smith is not referring to an open-mouthed mindless wonderment. A central element in his concept of 'wonder' is an intellectual act. The person who wonders is asking a question; he is not just gaping at a thing, but is wondering *what* the thing is. He is in an inquisitive mode. The scientist is surprised at what he sees, but does not stop there – he starts asking questions.

As regards causes of surprise there is a second sort of cause also to which Smith directs our attention, namely a sequence of events. There are countless customary sequences. A glass tumbler falls and it breaks; a piece of paper placed on a fire goes up in flames. We have seen such sequences a million times and for us there is nothing in them to hold our attention. When we see the first item in the sequence the imagination immediately, and in a customary way, produces an idea of the second item. There is what Smith calls 'a natural career of the imagination'. Consequently when the second item in the customary sequence happens we are not surprised. We see the tumbler fall on concrete and of course we are not surprised that it breaks. How can it not? Glass always breaks when it lands on concrete. It is 'natural' that it do so. But then one day a tumbler lands without breaking, and of course we are surprised, and immediately wonder why two events that were always joined are suddenly disjoined. This obstacle to 'the career of the imagination' prompts the question 'why?' and if we start investigating nature in search of an answer we are launched upon a scientific project.

There are, however, differences between people. I said that *we* are not surprised that a glass tumbler breaks when it lands. But I should have said 'most of us are not surprised'. There are those who might be given pause by the breakage, and see that there is something to wonder about, namely why it is that when a glass tumbler lands on concrete it is the glass that breaks and not the concrete. People who ask such questions are the real scientists, the ones who are looking for answers when the rest of us have not even thought to ask the questions. In their case there is not the same smooth and easy transition of the imagination that is to be found in most of us. They do not allow customary thinking, or at least customary movements of the imagination, to drag them around, but instead realise that the customary sequence itself conceals a problem. It calls for explanation no less than does the failure of the sequence. If a full explanation is provided the wonder stops, since to wonder is in part to ask a question, and once we have the explanation we have the answer to the question. Smith writes: 'Thus the eclipses of the sun and the moon, which once, more than all the other appearances in the heavens, excited the terror and amazement of mankind, seem now no longer to be wonderful, since the connecting chain has been found out which joins them to the ordinary course of things.' (*History*, in *Essays*, pp.42–3) Smith's example here is of course apposite in a *History of Astronomy* which leads up to a paean of praise for Newton's *Principia* (the *Mathematical Principles of Natural Philosophy*): 'His system, however, now prevails over all opposition, and has advanced to the acquisition of the most universal empire that was ever established in philosophy.' Newton's system is 'the greatest discovery that ever was made by man'. (*History*, in *Essays*, pp.104–5)

This successful outcome of surprise and wonder leads directly to a third sentiment, that of admiration, in particular, admiration of the natural order. Having discovered a new principle of unity amidst the diversity of natural phenomena, nature presents itself to us as an even more magnificent spectacle than we had previously found it to be. Where we had seen disparity we now see coherence. This consideration leads Smith to make a statement remarkable for the eighteenth century, though not so uncommon today:

> Let us examine, therefore, all the different systems of nature, which, in these western parts of the world, the only parts of whose history we know any thing, have successively been adopted by the learned and ingenious; and, without regarding their absurdity or probability, their agreement or inconsistency with truth and reality, let us consider them only in that particular point of view which belongs to our subject; and content ourselves with inquiring how far each of them was fitted to sooth the imagination, and to render the theatre of nature a more coherent, and therefore a more magnificent spectacle, than otherwise it would have appeared to be. (*History*, in *Essays*, p.46)

Smith comes impressively close to detaching the scientific project of western culture from questions of truth, as if it is not truth that the scientist is after. Instead what he looks for is a set of principles that enables him to see the disparate, and apparently chaotic mass of phenomena as a coherent whole. It is plain that for Smith any scientific advance, even Newton's, is defeasible in the sense that we cannot be sure that at our next glance at the natural world we will not be confronted with a phenomenon that agitates the imagination by preventing a smooth passage from one event to the next, expected, event in a customary sequence. On this account the aim of science is the practical one of soothing the imagination, rather than the theoretical one of getting at the truth; as if one of our goals in life is peace and quiet, and science is one of the instruments by which this is to be achieved. Smith is therefore not simply saying that truth is not the ultimate goal of science. On the reading of Smith that I am proposing, he is saying that truth is not even an intermediate goal. On the contrary the ultimate goal is the soothing of the imagination and the intermediate goal is the achievement of coherence. It is therefore significant that although Smith judged Newton's inverse square law of gravitational attraction to be 'the greatest discovery that ever was made by man', Smith nowhere says that the law is true, for he was aware of the fact that however effective the law is at enabling us to see the phenomena as a coherent system, phenomena might yet be discovered that are incompatible with the Newtonian picture of the universe.

Earlier I sought to provide a context for Smith's thoughts on scientific discovery by directing attention towards a famous dictum of Hume's: 'Reason is, and ought only to be the slave of the passions, and can never pretend to any other office than to serve and obey them.' (*Treatise*, p.415) We now see that crucial to Smith's entire account of the psychology of scientific discovery is his perception that the desire for calm or peace of mind, is a fundamental human motive, and that that desire, as well as driving much else, also drives science. Science, in short, is deployed to serve and obey the desire by soothing the agitated imagination. It is easy to resort to slogans in speaking of the Enlightenment. We can describe it as an Age of Reason in contrast with the preceding Age of Faith, and we can speak about the Enlightenment's reliance on rational insight in contrast with the reliance that medieval writers placed on earlier authorities. This section provides evidence that this crude picture needs to be greatly finessed. For here at the heart of the Scottish, and therefore of the European, Enlightenment we find a powerful argument for the need to qualify the ascription of rationality to scientific thinking, the kind of thinking that is surely the most rational of all. No doubt scientific progress is a march of reason but during the Scottish Enlightenment it was thought to be a march of reason to the drum beat of sentiment.

Section 3: Theology and Newtonian science

In the preceding section, reference was made to the relation between the Glasgow mathematician Robert Simpson and his pupil Adam

Smith. Another pupil of Simpson's, one of his earliest at Glasgow, was Colin Maclaurin, who would in due course be recognised as among the most powerful mathematicians in Britain. In 1714, at the age of fifteen, Maclaurin graduated Master of Arts at Glasgow after publicly defending his thesis, 'Power of gravity', and in the process displaying a formidable and precocious grasp of Newtonian physics, as witness Newton's own approval of Maclaurin's thesis. In 1717 he was appointed to the chair of mathematics at Marischal College, Aberdeen. It was a time of massive changes in the two colleges of Aberdeen. The Jacobite uprising of 1715 was still very close, and a number, perhaps most, of the teachers at the colleges had been Jacobite sympathisers. In the post-1715 climate it was decided that a clearout of the sympathisers was sound policy, and in Marischal in particular there remained in post only the classicist Thomas Blackwell, whose conspicuous loyalty to King George led to his elevation to the principalship of the college. Maclaurin, once in post, dedicated himself to mathematical research, publishing during his period at Marischal the masterly *Geometria Organica* (1720), and two substantial research papers. They were works of sufficient substance and originality to help secure for him a fellowship of the Royal Society when he was only twenty-one. But in contrast with his work in the more purely cerebral areas of mathematics we know that he was constrained in his experimental scientific work by the lack of funds in Marischal and by a consequent shortage of scientific instrumentation (Wood, *The Aberdeen Enlightenment*, ch.1), a shortage which no doubt played a part in his eventual departure for the wealthier Edinburgh. By the time of his translation to the Edinburgh chair he had already become a firm friend of Sir Isaac Newton, who greatly admired Maclaurin as a person and as a mathematician.

In Edinburgh the professor of mathematics, James Gregory, was sick, and Maclaurin thought to join Gregory in his work with a view to occupying the chair in his own right in due course. Newton wrote to him on this matter. The letter says a great deal in a short space: 'I am very glad to hear that you have a prospect of being joined to Mr James Gregory in the professorship of mathematics at Edinburgh, not only because you are my friend, but principally because of your abilities, you being acquainted as well with the new improvements of mathematics as with the former state of those sciences; I heartily wish you good success, and shall be very glad of hearing of your being elected; I am, with all sincerity, your faithful friend, and most humble servant.' (Chambers, *Biographical Dictionary*, vol.3, p.533) With Newton's permission, Maclaurin used the letter as testimony, and the letter proved irresistible to the appointing committee. So in November 1725 Maclaurin moved to Edinburgh, and stayed there till 1745.

Just as the Jacobite rebellion of 1715 created, in a sense, the opening for Maclaurin's academic career, so also the Jacobite rebellion of 1745 was responsible for bringing his career and indeed his life to a premature close. With the Jacobite army approaching Edinburgh, Maclaurin, who had given lectures on, and researched, the sciences of fortification and of gunnery, was given the task of designing and superintending the construction of the city's defensive response, its walls, trenches, barricades and batteries. His role gave him a high profile as an anti-Jacobite and was therefore potentially dangerous. Consequently, with the fall of Edinburgh he fled to England, to York where he was the welcome guest of the Archbishop. His physical exertions had been immense during that period and they weakened a constitution that was in any case not strong. In York he completed the dictation of his *An Account of Sir Isaac Newton's Philosophical Discoveries* and died, in June 1746, aged forty-eight.

I shall here draw upon material in *An Account of Sir Isaac Newton's Philosophical Discoveries* to expound Maclaurin's own perspective on natural philosophy, one which he shared with Newton. The perspective in question is essentially theological. Maclaurin's colleague in Aberdeen, George Turnbull, had written of 'the moral perfections of [Nature's] Creator and Governour, which are clearly manifested by the Frame, Constitution and Laws of Nature', and adds: 'And then it is that the Study of Nature must afford the highest Joy, when we feel the same Temper and Disposition prevailing in our own Minds which Nature displays.' (*Treatise of Ancient Painting*, pp.135–6) Here Turnbull both indicates his support for a version of the argument from design for the existence of God, and also hints at a religious motivation for doing natural science. Turnbull states briefly a position that Maclaurin develops at some length in his *An Account of Sir Isaac Newton's Philosophical Discoveries*, and he feels free to develop it because it is his own position and also Newton's.

Maclaurin acknowledges that every useful art has a connection with natural philosophy, and that 'the unexhausted beauty and variety of things makes it ever agreeable, new, and surprizing'. (*Account*, p.3) This is a motive for studying nature, though not the most important: 'But natural philosophy is subservient to purposes of a higher kind, and is chiefly to be valued as it lays a sure foundation for natural religion and moral philosophy; by leading us, in a satisfactory manner, to the knowledge of the Author and Governor of the universe. To study nature is to search into his workmanship: every new discovery opens to us a new part of his scheme.' (*Account*, p.3) Through a study of the universe considered as an effect, we learn about the existence and nature of its cause. Put otherwise, scientific study yields up to us a higher conception of God. In particular, according to Maclaurin, we learn of the power, wisdom and goodness of God. As regards the first of these attributes, divine power, Maclaurin focuses on the difference between it and all kinds of created power and in particular gravity, the greatest power of all, as that by which every particle of matter in the universe is attracted to every other. But of course the power of gravity diminishes with distance – every particle attracts every other *inversely* as the square of the distance between them. And in contrast there is the power of God, 'that mighty power which prevails throughout, acting with a force and efficacy that appears to suffer no diminution from the greatest distances of space or intervals of time'.

Much in accord with Adam Smith's discussion of the psychology of scientific discovery, Maclaurin refers in the opening paragraph of his *Account* to the motive of surprise, but he also discusses the role of admiration where this is in response to the unity we discover amidst

apparently infinite diversity and in response also to the vastness of
the created order: 'Even all the systems of the stars that sparkle in the
clearest sky must possess a small corner only of that space over which
such systems are dispersed . . . After we have risen so high, and left
all definite measures so far behind us, we find ourselves no nearer to
a term or limit; for all this is nothing to what may be displayed in
the infinite expanse, beyond the remotest stars that ever have been
discovered.' (*Account*, pp.15–16) The microscopic also, no less than
the macroscopic, has to be considered in assessing the powers of the
experimental scientist: '. . . it appears, that the subdivisions of the
particles of bodies descend by a number of steps or degrees that
surpasses all imagination, and that nature is unexhaustible by us on
every side . . . When we perceive such wonders, as naturalists have
discovered, in the minutest objects, shall we pretend to describe
so easily the productions of infinite power in space, that is at the
same time infinitely extended and infinitely divisible?' (*Account*,
pp.16–18)

Yet the fact that experimental scientists will never deliver all
the answers, and may perhaps by way of an answer put together
no more than a few fragments of a story whose totality is beyond
our reach, is no motive for abandoning the task. For there is, in
Maclaurin's view, a religious motive which trumps all others:

> As we arise in philosophy towards the first cause, we
> obtain more extensive views of the constitution of things,
> and see his influences more plainly. We perceive that we
> are approaching to him, from the simplicity and generality
> of the powers or laws we discover; from the difficulty we
> find to account for them mechanically; from the more and
> more complete beauty and contrivance, that appears to us
> in the scheme of his works as we advance; and from the
> hints we obtain of greater things yet out of our reach.
> (*Account*, p.22)

By his works, therefore, shall we know him. It was, however, within
about a year of the publication of Maclaurin's *Account of Sir Isaac
Newton's Philosophical Discoveries* that David Hume started work

on his *Dialogues Concerning Natural Religion*, a book which placed in the dock exactly the kind of theological reasoning that Maclaurin had deployed and which submitted such reasoning to an onslaught of philosophical questioning from which it has hardly yet recovered. However, as regards his religious stance, Maclaurin was a much more typical figure among the scientific literati than was Hume.

Section 4: The blind geometer

From the start of the Scottish Enlightenment, Aberdeen made an immense contribution, and in the earlier stages of the movement Aberdeen's contribution was arguably at least as great as that of either Glasgow or Edinburgh. We have already considered the contribution by Maclaurin and should recall that George Turnbull was an ally of Maclaurin's on faculty. In 1727 the mathematics chair left vacant by Maclaurin was given to John Stewart. All these were major figures. At least two and probably all three of them taught the young student Thomas Reid. Turnbull taught him Newtonian mechanics and much else besides, and Stewart and probably also Maclaurin taught him mathematics. Common sense philosophy, the dominant philosophy of the Scottish Enlightenment, was first developed in Aberdeen and was then broadcast round Scotland, becoming in due course the dominant philosophy in the other universities. It is that philosophy for which Enlightenment Aberdeen is perhaps best known, but we should not lose sight of the fact that Aberdeen was host to some of the best mathematicians in the country, and in this section I shall consider an extraordinary moment in the Aberdeen Enlightenment, when a brilliant piece of Aberdonian mathematical research was deployed, to devastating effect, in the service of common sense philosophy.

Reid received a thorough grounding in the mathematical sciences, and his lectures at King's College, where he became a regent in 1751, ranged across Euclidean geometry, algebra, fluxions, applied mathematics, mechanics, astronomy, electricity, magnetism, hydrostatics, pneumatics, physical optics, catoptics and the theory of vision. (Wood, *Reid Studies*, vol.2, p.28) And if, as mentioned earlier, he took an active interest in mathematics throughout his life, he seems to have been particularly concerned with Euclidean geometry and especially with Euclid's account of the straight line and of parallel lines. He was no doubt interested in Euclidean geometry for its own sake, but he also had a philosophical agenda which stood to be served by that interest, and that agenda, much to the fore in his *Inquiry into the Human Mind*, was directed to the rebuttal of Humean scepticism. Hume believed that our knowledge of the sensible properties of the world can be gained only by the exercise of the appropriate senses, so that for example an understanding of the tangible properties of the world cannot be gained by a person who lacks a sense of touch, and that an understanding of the visible properties cannot be gained by one born blind. This belief is basic to Hume's empirical philosophy. Reid, however, claims that Hume's belief is false, and he uses his skills as a geometer to demonstrate the claim.

His demonstration is based on the fact that someone born blind can glean a good deal of knowledge of the visible world, and the argument culminates in the development of a geometry of the visible, as opposed to the tangible world. This geometry serves therefore a philosophical agenda (though not only a philosophical agenda). For on the one hand if Hume is right it is impossible for a blind person to form a conception of the visible world, and on the other hand Reid demonstrates that a blind person can form just such a conception. The Humean form of empiricism, which gives rise inevitably to a thoroughgoing scepticism, is thereby undermined, thus creating space within which common sense philosophers can develop their own positive solution to philosophical problems.

Reid's claim is not that a blind person, left to the direction of his own senses alone, can learn a great deal about the visible world, but instead that a blind person can form a conception of many features of the visible world once these features are explained to him. As Reid puts the point: 'there is very little of the knowledge acquired by sight, that may not be *communicated* to a man born blind.' (*Inquiry*, p.78, my italics) One piece of evidence that Reid had for this claim was the fact that Nicholas Saunderson, the blind professor of mathematics at Cambridge, whom Reid and John Stewart had met in Cambridge in 1736, was able to form a formidably wide range of conceptions of features of the visible world. For example, he could conceive that a body moving directly from the eye or directly towards it may appear to be at rest, that the same motion may appear quicker or slower according as it is nearer to the eye or further off, that a plane surface, in a certain position, may appear as a straight line, and that a circle seen obliquely will appear an ellipse. Reid also shows that, even if a blind person would never, by himself, form a conception of light, he could, under instruction from others, learn almost everything we sighted people know about it, such as the minuteness and velocity of its rays, its ability to pass through glass and other dense materials, its reflexibility and so on, in fact all that we know about the physics of light. Even if under instruction he would not come to conceive how colours appear to us (though analogies with the other senses might be of some small help in that direction), there are other visible qualities of physical objects that he could conceive, and I shall now turn to these in order to explain a major intellectual triumph of the Scottish Enlightenment.

In Chapter 6 Section 5 I discussed Reid's account of the craft of the painter, and particularly his insight that a painter should paint what he sees, not what he knows. Then I emphasised the difference between on the one hand the colour that something really has and on the other hand the apparent colour of the thing, a colour which varies as the conditions in which it is observed varies. Now I wish to attend to the fact that we could make the same moves in respect of a thing's shape or figure, and in particular we can distinguish between the real figure that a thing has and its apparent or visible figure, the figure as it appears to us or as we actually see it. Thus a flat disk whose flat surface faces the eye, and which is so positioned that its centre is directly before the eye, will appear circular; but if the disk is tilted so that it is at an oblique angle to the eye it will appear elliptical, and if it is edge-on to the eye it will appear as a straight line. Its real figure has remained the same – that is, there has not been any real change in the shape of the object – but its visible figure changed as the disk rotated. It was Reid's contention that this difference between the real figure and the visible figure can be understood by a blind person, and that a blind mathematician would be able to calculate the visible figure of an object, the appearance that the figure of the object makes to the eye, if he knows both the real figure of the object and also the object's precise position in relation to the eye. He would for example be able not only to conceive but also to demonstrate that a flat disk positioned at an oblique angle to the eye would appear elliptical. Furthermore he would be able to understand why it is that the visible figure diminishes as the object recedes from the eye, and why the diminution is proportional to the distance, so that for example a visible line diminishes to a tenth its previous size when it recedes to ten times the distance.

It might be said in reply to all this that the blind geometer is not forming any concepts that are specific to the sense of sight, for he could learn all these facts purely on the basis of his sense of touch. It is at this point that Reid pulls his rabbit out of the hat. He argues that the geometry we construct on the basis of the world we learn about from the sense of touch is very different indeed from the geometry of the world we learn about by sight. And to demonstrate this he constructs his remarkable geometry of visibles, in which he shows that the geometry of Euclid is the geometry of tangible figures, and propositions true in Euclid's geometry are false of visible figures. We have to stir up our imaginations to follow Reid's line of reasoning. Let us imagine we are nothing more than an eye, a point-sized eye, in the middle of a hollow sphere, and that a line starts at the north pole of the hollow sphere and heads straight south down the inner surface of the sphere in a visibly straight line. That is, the appearance that the line makes to the eye is dead straight. The line reaches the south pole and continues up still visibly straight, that is, still appearing straight to the eye, and finally reaches the north pole at which point of course the line has arrived at the point from which it started. Something utterly non-Euclidean has happened. According to Euclid, however far a straight line is projected it will never return to its starting point. But a visible straight line will return to itself. So visible straight lines are not like tangible straight lines, that is, they are not like the straight lines of Euclidean geometry.

Furthermore, suppose that, having inscribed that visible straight line through the poles, another line is projected round the equator. The eye at the centre watches it on its trajectory and to the eye the line looks straight. It does, after all, deviate neither to right nor left, that is, neither to north nor south. Eventually the equatorial line returns to itself, though it has not at any stretch appeared not to be straight. This latter line must have cut the polar line at two places. But that is impossible from the perspective of Euclidean geometry, for according to Euclid two straight lines cannot cut each other at more than one point, and here we find two straight lines, that is, visibly straight lines, cutting each other twice. Hence, again, the geometry of visible figures is non-Euclidean. Reid goes on to demonstrate a number of theorems in this new geometry, for example, that if two lines are parallel, that is, everywhere equidistant from each other, then they cannot both be straight; that a circle may be parallel to a straight line; and that the internal angles of a triangle, whose three sides are straight, must add up to more than 180 degrees.

It is not necessary here to go deeply into this strange new geometry. It is enough to recognise that this geometry of the visible world is different from the Euclidean geometry of the tangible world. The blind geometer has sensory knowledge of the world by touch, not sight. Yet he can understand all these propositions about visible figures, propositions about the visible shapes that things have. Therefore he can form concepts that he simply could not form if Hume is correct.

In light of the strange, but perfectly intelligible, propositions concerning straight lines and parallel lines that Reid asserts in his geometry of visibles, it is of particular interest to note that Reid worried away at Euclid's account of straight lines and parallel lines throughout his adult life. (Wood, *Reid Studies* vol.2) The fact that there are things to worry about in that area was common knowledge among mathematicians. Nobody else, however, seems to have conducted precisely the psychological exercise of imagining an eye at the centre of a hollow sphere, and on that basis devising the geometry of the objects that such an eye would see, nor by any other means does anyone else seem to have arrived at the startling system of non-Euclidean geometry that Reid develops in the *Inquiry into the Human Mind*.

It would be easy to fall into anachronism here. Non-Euclidean geometry was a major theme of nineteenth-century mathematics, and some of the greatest contributions to it were made by men who saw their geometries as on a par with Euclid's, in the sense that they believed both that Euclidean space is just one among many possible spaces, each with its own geometry, and also that it is the needs and purposes of the scientists that determine which geometry they should apply. Thus, for example, Einstein used the geometry not of Euclid but of Riemann, because Einstein believed space to be curved and Riemannian geometry, in contrast with Euclid's, describes a curved space. Reid's position contrasts with the one I have just ascribed to the great nineteenth-century geometers, for Reid did not doubt that Euclid's geometry was the geometry of the 'real' world, the world that is known by touch, the world of 'common sense'. I do not believe that Gauss, Riemann, Lobachevsky, and others of the nineteenth century who constructed non-Euclidean geometries, would have said that Euclid's geometry was privileged among geometries in being the one which is of the real world. In that philosophical sense, it is therefore inappropriate, because anachronistic, to include Reid with the subsequent non-Euclideans.

If, however, we set aside consideration of philosophical agendas and focus solely on the mathematics, then Reid was undoubtedly a non-Euclidean pioneer. Nevertheless, in trying to determine what kind of task Reid was engaged in when he constructed his geometry of visibles, his philosophical agenda must hold centre stage, because in constructing that geometry he had a very precisely defined philosophical target, namely the central tenet of Hume's empiricism, that (in Humean language) 'impressions precede ideas', so that it is, for example, impossible to have an idea of a visible object unless one has previously had perceptual experience of similar visible objects. With the Reidian geometry of visibles, mathematics is at work in the service of several things, for example, the science of perspective. But it is at the service of philosophy more than of anything else. Why Reid thought that the 'real' world is primarily the world we know by touch rather than the world we know by sight, is an interesting and, in the context of his philosophy, an important question. But I shall not pursue it here. I have said sufficient for my present purpose, which was chiefly to describe Reid's remarkable invention and to give some indication of his motivation. It was also part of my purpose to say something, even if very little, about the contrast between Reid and some great mathematicians of the nineteenth century. That also is a topic that would bear extended scrutiny.

Section 5: The age of the earth

In Section 3 I referred to Colin Maclaurin's description of deep space: 'Even all the systems of the stars that sparkle in the clearest sky must possess a small corner only of that space over which such systems are dispersed . . . After we have risen so high, and left all definite measures so far behind us, we find ourselves no nearer to a term or limit; for all this is nothing to what may be displayed in the infinite expanse, beyond the remotest stars that ever have been discovered.' (*Account*, pp.15–16) In this section I shall be speaking about the discovery, made during the Scottish Enlightenment, of the temporal analogue of deep space, which has since been named 'deep time', a discovery made by one of Maclaurin's students. In 1725, as we noted, Maclaurin transferred from Marischal College to Edinburgh, with a view to being elected professor of mathematics. There he taught James Hutton, who has a better claim than anyone else to being named the father of modern geology. Hutton had attended the High School at Edinburgh before matriculating at the university in 1740 aged fourteen. He enrolled as a humanity student but his principal interests were strongly on the side of science. He used to speak in later years of his great admiration for Maclaurin's lectures. He also expressed gratitude to the professor of logic, John Stevenson, not because of the quality of his logic but, sad to say, because of his knowledge of chemistry, which may indeed have been slender. However, in the course of a logic lecture, Stevenson illustrated a point in logic by referring to some chemical facts, namely 'that gold is dissolved in aqua regia, and that two acids which can each singly dissolve any of the baser metals, must unite their strength before they can attack the most precious'. After a brief sojourn in a law firm, Hutton became a medical student in Edinburgh (1744–7), following which he transferred to medical studies in Paris for two years and finally, in 1749, he spent a few months in the University of Leiden, where he submitted a thesis on the circulation of the blood, and was duly awarded a doctorate of medicine.

In Edinburgh he had carried out experiments with a fellow student James Davie on the production of sal ammoniac (ammonium chloride, NH_4Cl) from coal soot. This seems not to have been blue skies research: they recognised the commercial implications of their discovery and set up jointly in the business of producing sal ammoniac, a salt widely used in the bleaching trade and also in the tin trade. The business was highly successful and enabled Hutton thereafter to be a financially independent scientist doing research relentlessly for the next forty years in the field that interested him most – geology.

In his geological work he was helped by several luminaries of the Scottish Enlightenment, including at least three from the same family, the Clerks of Penicuik. The family was deeply involved with major Enlightenment figures whose work I have already discussed. For example, Sir John Clerk of Penicuik (1676–1755) had been a major patron of the poet Allan Ramsay, and Ramsay had been a frequent visitor at the family seat of the Clerks. Sir John's son Sir James Clerk had provided funds that enabled the painters Alexander and John Runciman to visit Rome in 1766, and subsequently he had invited Alexander Runciman to paint a series of murals at the new family seat, Penicuik House. Plainly we are speaking here about a family that played a significant part in the Scottish Enlightenment. Two of Sir James Clerk's brothers, George Clerk Maxwell and John Clerk of Eldin, accompanied Hutton on field trips, as did John Clerk's son, John, who was later to be raised to the Bench as Lord Eldin. The lives of these three men were closely entwined with Hutton's.

Hutton's biggest idea concerned the age of the earth. The eighteenth century was heir to a long-standing belief that its age could be calculated from the information disclosed in Holy Writ. Shakespeare wrote: 'The poor world is nearly six thousand years old' (Rosalind in *As You Like It*), Johannes Kepler declared: 'My book may wait a hundred years for a reader, since God has waited six thousand years for a witness.' (McIntyre and McKirdy, *James Hutton*, pp.2–3), and crucially Archbishop James Ussher opened his *Annals of the World* (1658) with the words: 'In the beginning God created Heaven and Earth. Which beginning of time fell upon the entrance of the night preceding the twenty-third day of Octob. in the year 4004.' Ussher calculated the date of every significant event in the Old Testament, the dates were printed in the margins of subsequent printings of the Bible, and for very many people therefore Ussher's dates must have had the status of Holy Writ. Hutton, however, produced overwhelming scientific evidence to support the contention that, as he put it: 'with respect to human observation, this world has neither a beginning nor an end'. (Hutton, *Abstract of a Dissertation*, p.50) In saying this he set his face against the religious beliefs of most people, and of course was duly accused of atheism. But there was no question of his withdrawing his position, for he was as sure of the truth of his scientific insight as he was of his own existence.

Hutton's biographer, John Playfair (1748–1819), successively professor of mathematics and of natural philosophy at Edinburgh, surmises that Hutton early became sure of two things about the earth. One was that most of the present rocks are composed of materials derived from the destruction of earlier bodies, and the second was that there is a continual process of erosion. It takes a long time, but rain, frost, wind and chemical effects of the air take their toll on the hardest bodies. It was Hutton's genius to discern and probe the connection between these two observations. In particular they point to a cyclical process in which material on earth is eroded, carried down to the sea, is then reformed and reappears on the surface of the earth, only to face again those same forces of erosion. In his doctoral thesis, Hutton wrote about the circulation of the blood. In his geology he raised his sights, and wrote about recycling on a planetary scale. The scientific task that arose was the identification of the mechanism by which the cyclical process was effected.

The first stage in the process is the erosion. The observational evidence for this is overwhelming. One only has to see the way the sea has eaten into cliffs of hard rock, the way rivers have cut deep ravines through sandstone strata, the way granite has been reduced to scree on the sides of mountains. These eroded materials are gradually carried by rivers or winds to the sea where, in the second stage in the process, they become deposited as sediment. The third stage is the consolidation of the sediment. Hutton argued that the principal agent of consolidation is heat; in a word, the sediment is cooked. The sediment must be heated because it is plain from the state of exposed rocks on dry land that they have at some stage been in a fluid state. Hutton considered the possibility that the sediment is fluidised by a solvent, but rejected this hypothesis on two grounds, first that there is no solvent that can hold all minerals in solution, and secondly, as Playfair formulates the point, 'in the bodies composed of other bodies, the consolidation is so complete that no room is left for a solvent to have ever occupied'. (Playfair and Ferguson, 'James Hutton & Joseph Black', p.57) The agency that could render the seabed deposits solid would therefore have to be able to act on all sorts of minerals while not occupying any space in them, and the only agency Hutton knew which could do this was heat. From this it followed of course that the interior of the earth must be hot, a fact about the interior of the earth that could easily enough be deduced from the existence of volcanoes and hot springs. But Hutton was arguing from the appearance of ordinary rocks everywhere visible, and he was fitting the point into a grand theory of the earth.

Hutton conceived of the planet as a heat engine, and was well aware of the power of heat to effect change – while Hutton was working out his theory in Edinburgh, James Watt in Glasgow was perfecting his improved version of the Newcomen steam engine. Hutton therefore concluded that the hot consolidated material deep below the surface of the earth, lying under countless millennia of later deposits, could not just lie there. The heat ensured a dynamic, not a static or passive, state, and so the fourth stage in the process, that of elevation of the material, and the fifth stage, that of folding or curvature of the material as different parts of it met with different sorts of resistance, were bound to occur. These then are the stages by which the dry land comes to be there and to have roughly the shape it does: erosion, deposition, consolidation, elevation and folding. This is the process which explains such phenomena as the presence of minerals imbedded in different minerals, and fossil sea creatures imbedded in minerals on mountain tops.

But there were problems to resolve. Coal, deep underground, is subjected to the heating process. We know well what heated coal looks like – ash. Yet freshly mined coal is not ash. If Hutton is right about the earth being a heat engine, then why does coal not look like ash? The answer is compression. When we heat coal, parts of it are dissipated in the atmosphere. But deep underground, in conditions of great compression, the parts that would dissipate cannot do so – there is nowhere for them to escape to. Hutton deduced that the effects of the application of heat to a mineral vary according to whether or not the mineral is in a state of high compression, and he was right about this. His closest friend, Joseph Black, had conducted experiments on limestone. He knew that when limestone was heated it became caustic. Black wanted to know how this happened, and in 1755 published his answer, that the change was due to the fact that carbon dioxide, which forms 40 per cent of limestone, is dissipated by the heat. In the terrestrial depths, limestone is heated yet is not caustic. Why not? Hutton saw that the reply had to be compression. The carbon dioxide cannot escape and so causticity does not occur. This constitutes not a falsification of Black's results, but in a way a confirmation of them. Direct experimental evidence was not, however, forthcoming until 1812 when Hutton's friend and fellow chemist and geologist, Sir James Hall, packed powdered chalk into a sealed gun barrel and heated it. The aim was to discover whether, under conditions of compression, limestone fuses without losing carbon dioxide. The outcome was exactly as Hutton had predicted.

Hutton's theory was a scientific theory of the earth in the sense that it was open to empirical confirmation and also open to empirical refutation. His journeys in search of the scientific evidence were not shots in the dark. He had in each case worked out a good reason why the evidence he was looking for was likely to be in the area to which he had then headed.

Hutton had reasoned that granite, far from being (as commonly supposed) the oldest rock on the earth's surface, was injected upward, while in a molten state, into antecedently consolidated rock. There is a great swathe of granite westward from Aberdeen and across the Grampians. Hutton calculated that that swathe of granite met the older rock, schistus, somewhere near Blair Atholl, and reported his conclusions to the Duke of Atholl, who was sufficiently interested to invite Hutton to his lands during the shooting season of 1785. Hutton went to Glen Tilt, near Blair Atholl, with John Clerk of Eldin, and almost immediately found what he was looking for, veins of red granite in the surrounding rocks, the black schistus. There was no way in which the outer rock could have formed round the granite. The only possible interpretation was that the granite, which must have been the younger material, had flowed, or been injected, into the older material, the black schistus. The discovery was a brilliant confirmation of a scientific hypothesis.

The following year Hutton and John Clerk went to Galloway, and at Sandyhills Bay on the Solway, Hutton was rewarded: 'For here we found the granite interjected among the strata, in descending among them like a mineral vein, and terminating in a thread where it could penetrate no further ... We may now conclude, that, without seeing granite actually in a fluid state, we have every demonstration possible of this fact; that is to say, of granite having been forced to flow, in a state of fusion, among strata broken by a subterranean force, and distorted in every manner and degree.' (quoted in McIntyre and McKirdy, *James Hutton*, p. 36)

Subsequent visits to the Isle of Arran and then to Siccar Point in East Lothian produced further confirmation of Hutton's theory. John Playfair and Sir James Hall were with Hutton on the visit to Siccar Point, where they saw vertical layers of schistus protruding through deposits of horizontal layers of sandstone. (see Plate 11) Playfair's report is justly famous:

> We felt ourselves necessarily carried back to the time when the schistus on which we stood was yet at the bottom of the sea, and when the sandstone before us was only beginning to be deposited, in the shape of sand or mud, from the waters of a superincumbent ocean. An epoch still more remote presented itself, when even the most ancient of these rocks, instead of standing upright in vertical beds, lay in horizontal planes at the bottom of the sea, and was not yet disturbed by that immeasurable force which has burst asunder the solid pavement of the globe. Revolutions still more remote appeared in the distance of this extraordinary perspective. The mind seemed to grow giddy by looking so far into the abyss of time; and while we listened with earnestness and admiration to the philosopher who was now unfolding to us the order and series of these wonderful events, we became sensible how much farther reason may sometimes go than imagination may venture to follow. (Playfair and Ferguson, 'James Hutton & Joseph Black', pp.72–3)

Just as his predecessor in the Edinburgh mathematics chair, Colin Maclaurin, had stood awestruck at the vista of deep space, so Playfair was awestruck at the vista of deep time to which Hutton had introduced him. In his *Abstract* (1785) Hutton focused upon the time required for the processes he described:

> Having thus ascertained a regular system, in which the present land of the globe had been first formed at the bottom of the ocean, and then raised above the surface of the sea, a question naturally occurs with regard to time; what had been the space of time necessary for the

accomplishment of this great work? . . . If . . . no period can
be fixed for the duration or destruction of the present earth,
from our observations of those operations, which though
unmeasurable, admit of no dubiety, we shall be warranted in
drawing the following conclusions; 1*st*, That it had required
an indefinite space of time to have produced the land which
now appears; 2*dly*, That an equal space had been employed
upon the construction of that former land from whence the
materials of the present came; *lastly*, That there is presently
laying at the bottom of the ocean the foundation of future
land, which is to appear after an indefinite space of time.
But, as there is not in human observation proper means
for measuring the waste of land upon the globe, it is
hence inferred, that we cannot estimate the duration of
what we see at present, nor calculate the period at which
it had begun; so that, with respect to human observation,
this world has neither a beginning nor an end. (Hutton,
Abstract of a Dissertation, pp.48–50)

It is notable that in support of his conclusions Hutton always
invokes observation – 'from our *observations* we are warranted in
drawing our conclusions', and 'with respect to human *observation*,
this world has neither a beginning nor an end'. He does not here
deny that the world had a beginning in time, but he does deny
that anything we see indicates such a beginning. The scientific
evidence points to a process by which the present land came to
be formed from the detritus of previous land. But that previous
land got there somehow, and Hutton saw no reason to invoke
a different sort of process to explain how it came into being.
Likewise, our land is eroding and will in due course disappear
into the ocean, to be replaced by new land produced by the same
process. Hutton states: 'The result, therefore, of our present enquiry
is, that we find no vestige of a beginning, – no prospect of an end.'
There is a noteworthy holding back here also: 'we *find* no vestige
of a beginning' – not that there was no beginning, only that no
such vestige has been found. Hutton the scientist was not going

to tangle with the theologians or the religious. He was taking his stand with the scientific evidence alone and therefore had to declare that he could find none that indicated a beginning. If Holy Writ yields up evidence about a beginning then that is another matter, one of divine revelation, and not Hutton's business as a scientist.

This is not to say that Hutton disbelieved in God. Quite the contrary, there is evidence that Hutton was impressed by the so-called design argument for the existence of God. In the opening paragraph of his *Theory of the Earth* he declares of the 'terrestial system': 'We perceive a fabric, erected in wisdom, to obtain a purpose worthy of the power that is apparent in the production of it.' (Hutton, *Theory of the Earth*, p.3) Some lines later he adds: 'there is not any particular, respecting either the qualities of the materials, or the construction of the machine, more obvious to our perception, than are the presence and efficacy of design and intelligence in the power that conducts the work'. Shortly thereafter he affirms: 'We shall thus also be led to acknowledge an order, not unworthy of divine wisdom, in a subject which, in another view, has appeared as the work of chance, or as absolute disorder and confusion.'

Of course it might be said that this is no more than Hutton hiding behind the conventional rhetoric of the day in an attempt to assuage the feelings of the religious. But in that case he hardly needed to go so far as to declare: 'The globe of this earth is evidently made for man. He alone, of all the beings which have life upon this body, enjoys the whole and every part; he alone is capable of knowing the nature of this world, which he thus possesses in virtue of his proper right.' I am unclear how to interpret this passage except as saying that the world has been created for our sake, and our presence therefore reveals the work of a creator. I think Hutton did indeed believe in God, but he did not believe that, for God to have created the world, the world must have had a beginning in time. And while this is no doubt not what the douce citizens of eighteenth-century Edinburgh were taught it is none the less a theologically defensible position with a long and brilliant pedigree.

The presently received scientific wisdom is that the world is about four and a half billion years old, from which it seems to follow that Hutton was wrong in his declaration that there is no vestige of a beginning. I wish to emphasise two points in response to that reasoning. The first is that Hutton chose his words with care: 'we find no vestige of a beginning'. To stress a point made earlier, he did not say that there was no vestige. Secondly, the fact that so much has been learned in the intervening two centuries does not detract an iota from Hutton's achievement in establishing the scientific concept of geological time. Without that breakthrough we would not have had the rest. But it is one thing to be right (or largely right) and another thing to persuade people that you are right. And, as regards the latter, Hutton suffered from two disadvantages. The first was that his literary style was dense, often turgid, and in general obscure and unattractive. The second was that he was not a university professor and so did not gather round him a group of students who would in due course go forth and tell the world about his important discovery. He did however have John Playfair who did a brilliant job as advocate of the Huttonian theory. It is partly as a result of Playfair's advocacy that Hutton's brilliant scientific achievement came to be generally recognised, and that Hutton came to be ranked among the greatest of the extraordinary galaxy of creative thinkers who powered the Scottish Enlightenment.

The End of the Scottish Enlightenment?

It is not easy to date to within a year, or even a decade, the end of the Scottish Enlightenment. By common, though not universal, consent it was a phenomenon contained within the eighteenth century. Nevertheless nineteenth-century Scotland was also intellectually vibrant, and it is necessary to stress the continuities, since it is too easy to see the later century as a sad anti-climax after the days of glory. In important respects there were more days of glory to come after 1800, most spectacularly in the scientific field, where Scotland continued to produce world-beaters, most especially James Clerk Maxwell and Lord Kelvin. Less impressively, but also indicative of important intellectual continuities, Dugald Stewart, who in 1785 moved sideways from the mathematics chair at Edinburgh University to replace Adam Ferguson in the chair of moral philosophy, remained in the post till his death in 1828, carrying forward the project of common sense philosophy first expounded in detail in the 1750s and 1760s in Aberdeen. That same project was carried yet further forward by the occupant of the chair of logic and metaphysics at Edinburgh, Sir William Hamilton. But, unlike Thomas Reid, neither Stewart nor Hamilton was a philosophical genius. I believe that what gave the Scottish Enlightenment its character as a distinct historical moment was the complex set of relations within a group of geniuses and of other immensely creative people, many linked by kinship, who were living in each other's intellectual pockets (as well, often, as in each other's houses). It is because of this close-knit unity that it is possible to accept the term 'Scottish Enlightenment' as a useful tool in historical analysis, and therefore to accept the term as an art-term in writings on history.

There is, however, a different emphasis that might be placed on the term, and a consequent possibility that the term could usefully be exploited in a quite different way. In Chapter Two I argued that Enlightenment has two essential elements. One is autonomous thinking; the enlightened person thinks things through for himself and therefore does not assent to propositions merely on the authoritative word of another. The other element is the high moral value attached to toleration; a society is not enlightened unless it permits people to put their ideas into the public domain without fear of retribution, especially retribution from the political and religious authorities. This description of the elements of Enlightenment does of course need to be greatly finessed, but I am presenting here only the broad outline since that is sufficient for my purpose. Which is to argue, first, that eighteenth-century Scotland was, on the criteria just outlined, a relatively enlightened country, and secondly, that in that respect nothing much has changed since. This concept of Enlightenment therefore does not permit us to say, as some have done, that the Scottish Enlightenment ended with the Napoleonic War, nor that, as others have said, it ended with the death of Walter Scott – I have mentioned here just two of many suggested closure events.

I do not suggest that no good argument may be invoked in support of these claims concerning the Napoleonic War and Walter Scott. As regards the former, it can be said that Scotland, as part of Britain, was confronting a threat to Britain, and that many Scottish regiments played a major part in the confrontation. This, it may be held, would naturally reduce the sense of Scottishness and increase that of Britishness in the Scottish population; and in that case we should doubt that the Scottish Enlightenment survived the Napoleonic War, not because there ceased to be an Enlightenment in Scotland but because the Enlightenment in Scotland, if it continued, was bound to lose its peculiarly Scottish character. As against this, however, there is no evidence that the war with France led the intellectual élite, or the population as a whole, either to be (or to see itself as being) any less Scottish than during the eighteenth century as a whole. There was therefore, despite the war, no reason, from the direction of actual or perceived Scottishness, why the Scottish Enlightenment should not have continued. As regards Walter Scott, he had of course been an immense presence both in Scotland and also more widely in the international republic of letters, for which he was one of the great sources of the European romantic movement, but his death in 1832 was a small matter compared with the continuities across the whole range of Scottish cultural life. It would be utterly artificial to pick out that year as *the* year when one of the great movements of world culture came to an end.

Rejecting therefore these, and similar, suggestions regarding the date of the end of the Scottish Enlightenment, I have followed the common view that the Scottish Enlightenment, considered as a distinct historical epoch, came to an end with the end of that remarkable group of Scottish geniuses who dominated the European intellectual scene across the eighteenth century, and the end should therefore be considered to be around the time of the death of Thomas Reid in 1796 and of James Hutton in 1797.

Of course one has to be vague. For example, Sir John Sinclair's *Statistical Account of Scotland*, a major document of the Scottish Enlightenment, was published over a period of about nine years starting in 1791. Numerous other examples can be quoted, where an appeal to intuition might point to a date beyond 1800. But vagueness about the boundaries does not imply that we do not really have, and cannot operate intelligently with, a concept of the Scottish Enlightenment – any more than the fact that we cannot say precisely when day ends and night begins implies that we cannot operate intelligently with the concepts of day and night. Even if we cannot point to the precise year when the Scottish Enlightenment ended, nobody wishes to say that, for example, James Clerk Maxwell's work on electromagnetism and on the kinetic theory of gases, which was conducted across the middle years of the nineteenth century, was an achievement of the Scottish Enlightenment. James Clerk Maxwell, great grandson of George Clerk Maxwell, one of the Clerks of Penicuik who accompanied James Hutton on his geological expeditions across Scotland, was an heir of the Scottish Enlightenment, not a member of it.

Nevertheless, I do not wish to lose sight of the discussion in Chapter 2 on the nature of Enlightenment considered in terms of autonomous thinking and of the social virtue of toleration. In light of that analysis it seems absurd to ask when Scotland ceased to be enlightened, for it is manifest that Scotland is no less enlightened now than it was in the eighteenth century. The country may not at present boast a disproportionate number of geniuses, but according to the concept of Enlightenment on which I am now focused, a country does not need them to be enlightened. There is a large number of independent-minded thinkers here, and even though they often put into the public domain thoughts that political, religious and other authorities find disagreeable, those thinkers are not silenced by the authorities. I conclude that we, in Scotland, still live in an Age of Enlightenment. The reason why eighteenth-century Scotland was so special, and why the term 'Scottish Enlightenment' has been worked so hard, is that the country produced that extraordinary constellation of geniuses, men who possessed the gift of creativity by means of which they thought their way into intellectual worlds not previously visited by humankind.

Allan, David, *Virtue, Learning and the Scottish Enlightenment*, Edinburgh 1993

Allan, David, *Scotland in the Eighteenth Century*, London 2002

Aspinwall, Bernard, 'William Robertson and America', in Devine and Young, *Eighteenth Century Scotland*, pp.153–73

Berry, Christopher J., 'James Dunbar and the American War of Independence', *Aberdeen University Review*, vol.44, 1974, pp.255–66

Berry, Christopher J., *Social Theory of the Scottish Enlightenment*, Edinburgh 1997

Blair, Hugh, *A Critical Dissertation on the Poems of Ossian*, appended to James Macpherson, *Poems of Ossian*

Blair, Hugh, *Sermons*, Edinburgh 1824

Boece, Hector, *Scotorum Historiae*, Paris 1527

Broadie, Alexander, *The Tradition of Scottish Philosophy*, Edinburgh 1990

Broadie, Alexander (ed.), *The Scottish Enlightenment: An Anthology*, Edinburgh 1997

Broadie, Alexander, *Why Scottish Philosophy Matters*, Edinburgh 2000

Broadie, Alexander, 'Reid, Campbell and universals of language' in Wood, *The Scottish Enlightenment*, pp.351–71

Broadie, Alexander, 'Sympathy and the impartial spectator' in Haakonssen, *The Cambridge Companion to Adam Smith*

Broadie, Alexander (ed.), *The Cambridge Companion to the Scottish Enlightenment*, Cambridge 2003

Broadie, Alexander, see Reid 2005

Broadie, Alexander, see Turnbull 2005

Buchan, James, *Adam Smith and the Pursuit of Perfect Liberty*, London 2006

Cameron, Alasdair, 'Theatre in Scotland 1660–1800', in Hook, *The*

History of Scottish Literature, pp.191–205

Cameron, Alasdair, 'Theatre in Scotland: 1214 to the present', in Paul Scott, *Scotland: A Concise Cultural History*, pp.145–48

Campbell, George, *The Philosophy of Rhetoric*, 2 vols, Edinburgh 1808 (first published 1776)

Carlyle, Alexander, *The Autobiography of Dr. Alexander Carlyle of Inveresk, 1722–1805*, Edinburgh 1910

Carlyle, Alexander, *Anecdotes and Characters of the Times*, ed. J.Kinsley, London 1973

Carter, Jennifer J. and Joan H. Pittock (eds.), *Aberdeen and the Enlightenment*, Aberdeen 1987

Chambers, Robert (ed.), *Biographical Dictionary of Eminent Scotsmen*, 6 vols, London 1864

Craig, David, *Scottish Literature and the Scottish People, 1680–1830*, London 1961

Cuneo, Terence and René van Woudenberg (eds), *The Cambridge Companion to Thomas Reid*, Cambridge 2004

Daiches, David, *The Paradox of Scottish Culture: The Eighteenth-Century Experience*, London 1964

Daniels, Norman, *Thomas Reid's 'Inquiry': The Geometry of Visibles and the Case for Realism*, New York 1974 and Stanford 1989

Davie, George, *The Scottish Enlightenment and other Essays*, Edinburgh 1991

Davie, George, *The Democratic Intellect*, Edinburgh 1982

Davie, George, *The Crisis of the Democratic Intellect*, Edinburgh 1986

Devine, T. M., *The Scottish Nation 1700–2000*, London 1999

Devine, T. M. and J. R. Young (eds.), *Eighteenth Century Scotland: New Perspectives*, East Linton 1999

Donovan, A. L., *Philosophical Chemistry in the Scottish Enlightenment*, Edinburgh 1975

Downie, Barbara L., 'William McGibbon and Niel Gow: Reflections on Tradition and Taste in Eighteenth Century Scotland', unpublished M.Mus. Thesis, Rice University, Houston, Texas 1997

Dwyer, John and Richard B. Sher (eds), *Sociability and Society in Eighteenth-Century Scotland*, Edinburgh 1993

Emerson, Roger L., *Professors, Patronage and Politics: The Aberdeen Universities in the Eighteenth Century*, Aberdeen 1993

Ferguson, Adam, *Reflections previous to the Establishment of a Militia*, London 1756

Ferguson, Adam, *Institutes of Moral Philosophy*, Edinburgh 1800

Ferguson, Adam, *An Essay on the History of Civil Society*, ed. Fania Oz-Salzberger, Cambridge 1995

Ferguson, Adam, *The Correspondence of Adam Ferguson*, 2 vols, ed. V. Merolle, London 1995

Frank, W. A. and Allan B. Wolter, *Duns Scotus, Metaphysician*, Purdue University Press, West Lafayette 1995

Gaskin, J. C. A., *Hume's Philosophy of Religion*, 2nd edn. London 1988

Gibson-Wood, Carol, 'Painting as philosophy: *George Turnbull's Treatise on Ancient Painting*', in Carter and Pittock, *Aberdeen and the Enlightenment*, pp.189–98

Graham, Roderick, *The Great Infidel: A Life of David Hume*, Edinburgh 2004

Griswold, Charles L., *Adam Smith and the Virtues of Enlightenment*, Cambridge 1999

Haakonssen, Knud, *The Science of the Legislator: The Natural Jurisprudence of David Hume and Adam Smith*, Cambridge 1981

Haakonssen, Knud (ed.), *The Cambridge Companion to Adam Smith*, Cambridge 2006

Haldane, John and Stephen Read (eds), *The Philosophy of Thomas Reid: A Collection of Essays*, Oxford 2003

Harris, James, A., *Of Liberty and Necessity: The Free Will Debate in Eighteenth-Century British Philosophy*, Oxford 2005

Hobbes, Thomas, *The Leviathan*, Cambridge 1991

Home, John, *Works of John Home*, 3 vols, ed. Henry Mackenzie, Edinburgh 1822

Hook, Andrew (ed.), *The History of Scottish Literature*. vol.2 1660–1800, Edinburgh 1989

Hook, Andrew and R. B. Sher, *The Glasgow Enlightenment*, East Linton 1994

Hume, David, *Letters of David Hume*, 2 vols, ed. J. Y. T. Greig, Oxford 1932

Hume, David, *New Letters of David Hume*, ed. R. Klibansky and E.C. Mossner, Oxford 1954

Hume, David, *Enquiries Concerning Human Understanding and Concerning the Principles of Morals*, ed. L. A. Selby-Bigge; 3rd edn P. H. Nidditch, Oxford 1975

Hume, David, *Essays Moral, Political and Literary*, ed. Eugene F. Miller, Indianapolis 1987

Hume, David, *A Treatise of Human Nature*, ed. L. A. Selby-Bigge; 2nd edn P. H. Nidditch, Oxford 1978; also ed. D. F. Norton and M. J. Norton, Oxford 2000

Hume, David, *The History of England*, ed. William B. Todd, Indianapolis, 1983

Hume, David, *Dialogues Concerning Natural Religion*, in *Dialogues and Natural History of Religion*, ed. J. C. A. Gaskin, Oxford 1993

Hume, David, *The Natural History of Religion* in *Dialogues and Natural History of Religion*, ed. J. C. A. Gaskin, Oxford 1993

Hume, David, *My Own Life*, in *Dialogues and Natural History of Religion*, ed. J. C. A. Gaskin, Oxford 1993

Hunter, Michael, '"Aikenhead the Atheist": the context and consequences of articulate irreligion in the late seventeenth century', in *Atheism from the Reformation to the Enlightenment*, ed. Michael Hunter and David Wootton, Oxford 1992, pp.221–54

Hutcheson, Francis, *Francis Hutcheson: Philosophical Writings*, ed. R. S. Downie, London 1994

Hutton, James, *Theory of the Earth with Proofs and Illustrations*, Edinburgh 1795; reprinted Herts. 1959

Hutton, James, *Abstract of a Dissertation Concerning the System of the Earth, its Duration, and Stability*, in *Philosophy of Geohistory: 1785–1970*, ed. Claude C. Albritton, Stroudsburg, Pa 1975, pp.24–52

Kames, Lord, (Henry Home), *Sketches of the History of Man*, 2 vols, Edinburgh 1774

Kames, Lord, (Henry Home), *Historical Law-Tracts*, 3rd edn, Edinburgh 1776

Kames, Lord, (Henry Home), *Essays on the Principles of Morality and Natural Religion*, 3rd edn, Edinburgh 1779

Kant, Immanuel, 'What is Enlightenment?' in James Schmidt, *What is Enlightenment?*, London 1996, pp.58–64; also in Kant: *Political Writings*, ed. Hans Reiss, Cambridge 1996, pp.54–60

Keller, Alex, 'The physical nature of man: science, medicine, mathematics', in *Humanism in Renaissance Scotland*, ed. John MacQueen, Edinburgh 1990

Kidd, Colin, *Subverting Scotland's Past: Scottish Whig Historians and the Creation of an Anglo-British Identity*, Cambridge 1993

Kivy, Peter, *The Seventh Sense: Francis Hutcheson and Eighteenth-Century British Aesthetics*, 2nd edn, Oxford 2003

Knox, John, *John Knox's History of the Reformation in Scotland*, 2 vols, ed. W. C. Dickinson, London 1949

McCosh, James, *The Scottish Philosophy*, London 1875

Macdonald, Murdo, *Scottish Art*, London 2000

McIntyre, Donald B. and Alan McKirdy, *James Hutton: The Founder of Modern Geology*, Edinburgh 1997

Macintyre, Gordon, *Dugald Stewart: The Pride and Ornament of Scotland*, Brighton 2003

McKean, Charles, 'James Craig and Edinburgh's New Town', in *James Craig 1774–1795*, ed. Kitty Cruft and Andrew Fraser, Edinburgh 1995, pp.48–56

Maclaurin, Colin, *An Account of Sir Isaac Newton's Philosophical Discoveries*, London 1748

Macmillan, Duncan, *Painting in Scotland: The Golden Age*, Oxford 1986

Macmillan, Duncan, *Scottish Art 1460–2000*, Edinburgh 2000

Macpherson, James, *Temora, An Ancient Epic Poem*, London 1763

Macpherson, James, *The Poems of Ossian*, ed. John MacQueen, Edinburgh 1971

Norton, David Fate, *David Hume: Common-Sense Moralist, Sceptical Metaphysician*, Princeton, NJ 1982

Otteson, James R., *Adam Smith's Marketplace of Life*, Cambridge 2002

Pittock, Murray, *Inventing and Resisting Britain: Cultural Identities in Britain and Ireland, 1685–1789*, Basingstoke 1997

Playfair, John and Adam Ferguson, 'James Hutton & Joseph Black:

Biographies by John Playfair and Adam Ferguson', *Transactions of the Royal Society of Edinburgh*, vol.5, 1805; reprinted Edinburgh 1997

Porter, Roy, *The Enlightenment*, London 1990

Purser, John, *Scotland's Music*, London 1992

Pyle, Andrew, *Hume's Dialogues Concerning Natural Religion*, London 2006

Ramsay, Allan (the poet), *The Works of Allan Ramsay*, 6 vols, ed. B. Martin *et al.*, Edinburgh 1954–75

Ramsay, Allan (the painter), *A Dialogue on Taste*, *1775*; republished in *The Investigator*, 2nd edn, London 1762

Reeder, John (ed.), *On Moral Sentiments: Contemporary Responses to Adam Smith*, Bristol 1997

Reid, Thomas, *The Works of Thomas Reid, DD, FRSE*, ed. Sir William Hamilton, 6th edn, 2 vols, Edinburgh 1863; reprinted Bristol 1994

Reid, Thomas, *Thomas Reid on the Animate Creation: Papers Relating to the Life Sciences*, ed. Paul B. Wood, Edinburgh 1995

Reid, Thomas, *An Inquiry into the Human Mind on the Principles of Common Sense*, ed. Derek R. Brookes, Edinburgh 1997 (first published 1764)

Reid, Thomas, *Essays on the Intellectual Powers of Man*, eds Brookes, Derek R and K. Haakonssen, Edinburgh 2002

Reid, Thomas, *The Correspondence of Thomas Reid*, ed. Paul Wood, Edinburgh 2002

Reid, Thomas, *Thomas Reid on Logic, Rhetoric and the Fine Arts*, ed. Alexander Broadie, Edinburgh 2005

Robertson, John, *The Scottish Enlightenment and the Militia Issue*, Edinburgh 1985

Robertson, William, *History of Scotland*, 2 vols, London 1759

Robertson, William, *History of America*, London 1777

Ross, Ian Simpson, *Lord Kames and the Scotland of his Day*, Oxford 1972

Ross, Ian Simpson, *The Life of Adam Smith*, Oxford 1995

Rothschild, Emma, *Economic Sentiments: Adam Smith, Condorcet, and the Enlightenment*, Cambridge, Mass, 2001

Scott, Mary Jane, 'James Thomson and the Anglo-Scots' in Hook, *The History of Scottish Literature*, pp.81–99

Scott, William R., *Francis Hutcheson: His Life, Teaching and Position in the History of Philosophy*, Cambridge 1900

Shaw, John Stuart, *The Political History of Eighteenth-Century Scotland*, London 1999

Sher, R. B., *Church and University in the Scottish Enlightenment*, Edinburgh 1985

Sinclair, Sir John, *The Statistical Account of Scotland*, vols. 1–21, Edinburgh 1791–9; reissued in facsimile, with parishes arranged into counties, eds. Donald J. Withrington and Ian R. Grant, vols. 1–20, Wakefield 1973–83

Skinner, Andrew S., *A System of Social Science: Papers Relating to Adam Smith*, 2nd edn, Oxford 1996

Smart, Alastair, *Allan Ramsay: Painter, Essayist and Man of the Enlightenment*, Yale 1992

Smith, Adam, *The Theory of Moral Sentiments*, ed. D. D. Raphael and A. L. Macfie, Oxford 1976

Smith, Adam, *An Inquiry into the Nature and Causes of the Wealth of Nations*, ed. R. H. Campbell and A. S. Skinner, 2 vols, Oxford 1976

Smith, Adam, *The Correspondence of Adam Smith*, ed. Ernest Campbell Mossner and Ian Simpson Ross, Oxford 1977

Smith, Adam, *Essays on Philosophical Subjects*, ed. W. P. D. Wightman and J. C. Bryce, Oxford 1980

Smith, Adam, *Lectures on Rhetoric and Belles Lettres*, ed. J. C. Bryce, Oxford 1983

Smout, T.C., *A History of the Scottish People 1560–1830*, London 1998

Stewart, Dugald, *Collected Works*, ed. Sir William Hamilton, Edinburgh 1854

Stewart, Dugald, *Elements of the Philosophy of the Human Mind*, London 1867

Stewart, Dugald, *Account of the Life and Writings of Adam Smith, LL.D.*, in Adam Smith, *Essays on Philosophical Subjects*, ed. W. P. D. Wightman and J. C. Bryce, Oxford 1980, pp.287–332

Stewart, Dugald, *Account of the Life and Writings of Thomas Reid*, in *The Works of Thomas Reid, DD, FRSE*, ed. Sir William Hamilton, 6th edn, 2 vols, Edinburgh 1863; reprinted Bristol 1994, pp.1–38

Stewart, M. A. (ed.), *Studies in the Philosophy of the Scottish Enlightenment*, Oxford 1990

Stewart, M. A., *The Kirk and the Infidel* (Inaugural Lecture), Lancaster 1994

Stewart, M. A. and John P. Wright (eds), *Hume and Hume's Connexions*, Edinburgh 1994

Suderman, Jeffrey M., *Orthodoxy and Enlightenment: George Campbell in the Eighteenth Century*, Montreal & Kingston, 2001

Turnbull, George, *A Treatise on Ancient Painting*, London 1740; repr. without plates, München 1971

Turnbull, George, *The Principles of Moral and Christian Philosophy*, ed. A. Broadie, Indianapolis 2005

Walker, David M. *The Scottish Jurists*, Edinburgh 1985

Withers, Charles W.J. and Paul Wood, *Science and Medicine in the Scottish Enlightenment*, East Linton 2002

Wodrow, Robert, *Analecta: or Materials for a History of Remarkable Providences*, 4 vols, Edinburgh 1842–43

Wood, Paul B., 'Science and the pursuit of virtue in the Aberdeen Enlightenment' in M. A. Stewart, *Studies in the Philosophy of the Scottish Enlightenment*, pp.127–49

Wood, Paul B., *The Aberdeen Enlightenment: The Arts Curriculum in the Eighteenth Century*, Aberdeen 1993

Wood, Paul B., 'Reid, parallel lines, and the geometry of visibles', *Reid Studies*, vol.2, 1998, 27–41

Wood, Paul B. (ed.), *The Scottish Enlightenment: Essays in Reassessment*, Rochester University Press 2000

Adam, Robert 153, 154, member of Oyster Club 27

Adams, John, his description of Gavin Hamilton 49

Advocates' Library, Hume's appointment to 36

aesthetic sense 175–7

Aikenhead, Thomas 33–4

Aikman, John 154

Aikman, William 6

Allan, David, 154, his depiction of the origin of painting 74–5

America, importance of William Robertson's histories in 49

ammonium chloride, Hutton's work on 210

analogy 132–4

Anderson, John, founder of Anderson's Institute 28

Aquinas, Thomas 18

Argyll, Third Duke of 8

Aristotle 149

Aspinwall, Bernard 49

association of ideas 177

authority, arguments from 17, 18

Ayr 9

Balfour, Andrew, co-founder of Edinburgh's Physic Garden 11

ballads, Scottish 13–14

Balliol College, Oxford, Smith's studentship at 192

Baxter, John 154

Beattie, James 7, his criticism of Kames 141, professor of moral philosophy and of logic at Marischal College 28

benevolence, Hutcheson on 116–17, Kames on divine 142–5

Berry, Christopher 96

Black, Joseph 27, 139, 186, his experiments on limestone 213, professor of chemistry at Glasgow 28, member of the Literary Society 28, Smith's literary executor 191

Black Watch regiment 81

Blackwell, Thomas, principal of Marischal College 199

Blair, Hugh 22, 31, 38, 146–50, 167, on authenticity of Ossianic poems 65–6, member of Select Society 26, founder member of Royal Society of Edinburgh 28, his study of language 190, threatened with dedication of Hume's *Dialogues* 140

Boece, Hector, his career 9, as historian 43–4

Bologna, University of 9

Boswell of Auchinleck, Alexander, Lord of Session 26

Boswell, James, his judgment of Hamilton 156, his last interview with Hume 139–40

Boufflers, Comtesse de 162

Boulanger, Nicolas-Antoine 118

Brahe, Tycho 10

Breslau 10

British Empire, its need of a professional army 94, its relation to Scottish identity 59

Brown, John 154

Buchanan, George, associated with Florence Wilson 147, attended

Mair's lectures 9, author of
Rerum Scoticarum Historia 43
Burnet, Gilbert 12
Burnett, James, *see* Monboddo
Burns, Robert 14, 19

Caesar, Julius 70
Calvin, John, attended Mair's
lectures 9
Calvinism 22, 145, Hume's relations
to 130–1, virtue of moderate 51,
scepticism and 137–8
Campbell, Mrs Colin, painted by
Raeburn 173
Campbell, George, principal
of Marischal College 28,
his *Philosophy of Rhetoric*
161–2, 190
Canova, friend of Gavin Hamilton
154
Carlyle, Alexander 28, 31
Carter, Nathaniel 49
causes, knowledge of 55–6
Charlevoix, Pierre-François de 70
Charles II, dedicatee of Stair's
Institutions 12
Christianity, relations between
Enlightenment and 113–15
Clerk, James 154, 210
Clerk of Eldin, John 27
Clerk of Penicuik, Sir John
(1676–1755), patron of
the arts 210
Clerk Maxwell, George 210, 221
Clerk Maxwell, James 219, 221
Colden, Cadwallader 69
College of Justice, Edinburgh 10
Cologne 18
commercial society, moral
dangers in 84–5, self-interested
motives in 97
common sense school, religion
and 123, its dominance in
Scotland 203

Cook, Captain James 70
Cooper, Richard 154
corruption, political 87–9
cosmopolitanism, its relation to
patriotism 95, Hume's 95
Craig, James, his plans for
Edinburgh New Town 8
Criticism, Age of, Enlightenment
as an 20
Cullen, William, 186, professor
of chemistry at Glasgow 27,
member of the Literary Society
28, founder member of Royal
Society of Edinburgh 28

Dalrymple, James (first Viscount
Stair) 12–13
Darien Scheme 7
Davidson, Principal, of Glasgow
25
Davidson, Robert, professor of civil
law at Glasgow
Davie, George, on the generalist
approach to education 111–12
Davie, James, scientific and business
partner of Hutton 210
design argument 132–8
despotism, patriotism opposed to 98
*Dialogues Concerning Natural
Religion*, Hume's 126–40, Hume's
reasons for using dialogue form
128–30, publication of 129–30,
question addressed in 132
Dick, Sir Alexander, president of
Royal College of Physicians 26
Dick, Robert, professor of natural
philosophy at Glasgow 192
Diderot, Denis 118
division of labour, limits to
advantages of 90, moral
significance of 39–40,
professional army the
product of 92
Douglas, a play by John Home 31,

Hume's appreciation of 151, Hume's criticism of 162

Drumoak, Aberdeenshire 11

Dunbar, James, his hostility to slave-trade 96

Dundas, Lord, president of Court of Session 26

Dundee, Boece's home town 9, Wedderburn's home town 10

Dunmore, Earl of 27

Duns Scotus, John 16

Edinburgh New Town, plans for 8, street names of 8

Edinburgh University 9, Sibbald its first professor of medicine 11, James Gregory its first professor of mathematics 11

Ednam in Roxburghshire 7

Education, state funding of 40, 105–6, need for a general 108–12, Dugald Stewart on objectives of 108–9

Elibank, Lord, member of Select Society 26

Elizabeth Gunning, a portrait by Hamilton 153

Elliot, Gilbert 13, 59, received early sight of Hume's *Dialogues* 129, 135–6

English literature, Hume on 61

Enlightenment, concept of 15–20, 23

Episcopalian Church 51

Erasmus, Desiderius 9, 147

evil 145–6

experimental method 61–2, 67, 81

Ferguson, Adam 212, professor of moral philosophy at Edinburgh 27, 167, 219, on comparative history 69, his critique of Hobbes and Rousseau 80–1, on the dangers of a political class 90, on the dying Hume 139, founder of

Poker Club 92, founder member of Royal Society of Edinburgh 28, on importance of study of history 56, on the measurement of progress 99–100, on political corruption 88–9, on the psychopathology of commercial society 84–5, on his qualified optimism 86–7, his support for establishment of a militia in Scotland 90–1, on universality of religious belief 123, on weakness of conjectural history 73–4

Fergusson, Robert 14

Fletcher of Saltoun, Andrew, William Robertson's disagreement with 32

Forbes, Anne, pupil of Gavin Hamilton 154

Forbes, Thomas 11

Frankfurt 10

Franklin, Benjamin 49

freedom, fragility of 85–94, law as ensuring our 86, its relation to the militia issue 93–4

freedom of speech 23, its relation to freedom of thought 23–4

Fyvie Castle 167

Galbraith, Robert, his career 9–10

Galileo 10

Gdansk 10

Gerard, Alexander, professor of moral philosophy at Marischal College, Aberdeen 28

Gerard, Gilbert (son of Alexander Gerard), his opposition to slave-trade 96

General Assembly of Church of Scotland 22, its role in Aikenhead's execution 33–4, its suspension of John Simpson from preaching 116, its timetable disrupted by Mrs Siddons 153

genius, happiness and civic virtue
    more important than 111
Gentle Shepherd, The, play by Allan
    Ramsay senior 29, 152
geological time 218
Glasgow, merchants of 26,
    Presbytery of 34, 36
Glasgow University, its foundation
    9, Mair its principal 9
Glen Tilt, Hutton's trip to 214
Gow, Nathaniel 14
Gow, Niel 14
Grainger, James 7
grammar, philosophical significance
    of 189–90
Grand Tour, 153, 154, Turnbull
    on the educative value of
    54, 157–9
gratitude, its role in morality 102
Gregory, James (1638–75) 11
Gregory, James, professor of
    mathematics at Edinburgh 199
Guild, David, student at St
    Andrews 16–17

Haddington 9
Hall, Sir James 27, his experiments
    on limestone 213–14, his trip with
    Hutton to Siccar Point 215
Hamilton, Alexander 49
Hamilton, Gavin 164, his career
    153–4, studied under Hutcheson
    155, his naturalism 155–6
Hamilton, Patrick 17
Hamilton, Sir William, professor
    of logic and metaphysics at
    Edinburgh 219
happiness, its distribution through
    the generations 99–100,
    Hutcheson's account of its
    relation to morality 117
Helmstedt, Liddel pro-rector of 10
Henry VII 44
heresy, the law on 32

historian, qualities of a good 48–9
historiography, Scottish 43–4,
    Smith on 52–3
history, conjectural 64–75, Hume
    on why we should study it
    46–9, Hutcheson on why we
    should study it 45, Kames on
    the methodology of 68, practical
    value of 57, its relation to moral
    philosophy 61–4, its relation
    to the study of human nature
    190–1, on scientific nature of
    conjectural 73
History of America, impact of
    William Robertson's 49
History of England, Hume's 31
History of Scotland, William
    Robertson's 50, 53, 64
Hobbes, Thomas, criticised by
    Ferguson 80–1
Hogarth, William 7
Holbach, Baron d' 118
Holcomb, Kathleen 28
Home, John, of Athelstaneford,
    his authorship of Douglas 31,
    151, on the need for a citizen
    army 91
human nature, study of history as
    a key to 62–3, Dugald Stewart
    on uniformity of 67, Hamilton's
    portrayal of 156, Hume on
    uniformity of 71
Hume, David 14, 25, 44, his
    battle against superstition 40–2,
    Boswell's last interview with
    139, his correspondence with
    Gilbert Elliot 13, his criticism of
    Home's Douglas 162, eulogised
    by Smith 36–7, his failure to get
    either Edinburgh's chair of moral
    philosophy or Glasgow's chair of
    logic and rhetoric 35–6, on forms
    of atheism 34–5, founder of Select
    Society 26, appointed Librarian

of the Advocates' Library in Edinburgh 36, on miracles 137, proposed dedicating the *Dialogues* to Blair 140, on the qualities of a good critic 182–4, on race 96, on relations between philosophy and toleration 115, secularity of his moral philosophy 117, his reasons for not publishing the *Dialogues* 37, on reasons for studying history 46–9, on his Scottish identity 59–60, on the standard of taste 178–84, his attack on slavery 96, his scepticism on matters of religion 136, his views on the place of liberty in Britain 31–2

Hume, David, (nephew of Hume the philosopher) 37, 130

Hunter of Blackness, David, painted by Raeburn 173

Hurd, Richard 119

Hutcheson, Francis, his aesthetic theory 175–8, his attitude to Calvinist doctrine of depravity 116, his support for Leechman 34, his criticism of Hume 35, on the nature and attractions of history 45, on need to 'put a new face upon Theology in Scotland' 16, teacher of Gavin Hamilton 155, teacher of Smith 192

Hutton, James 27, on the age of the earth 211–18, career of 209–10, on erosion of the earth's surface 211–12, his references to God 217, portrayed by Tassie 165, Smith's literary executor 191

Iliad, Hamilton's portrayals of the 155–6

imagination, history and 46–7

impartial spectator 101, 103, a creature of the imagination 103–4, compared to Hume's concept of the good critic 183

improvement, its role in the Enlightenment 38–42

Inquiry into the Human Mind, Reid's first masterpiece 30, 167–75, 204

Jacobitism, its association with Episcopalian Church 51, a subject banned by Select Society 27, and the militia debate 91, its effect on the Aberdeen colleges 199

James V 44

James VI 6

James, Duke of York 6

Jeans, William 154

Jefferson, Thomas 49

Jews, Emancipation of the 115

Johnson, Dr Samuel, his comment on Mallett 7

Kames, Lord (Henry Home) 25, 31, 44, 148, on assessment of historical evidence 68, on the benevolence of God 142–6, is compared with Judas 141–2, criticism of luxury 99, his disagreement with Ferguson 123, his determinism 141, on historical methodology 73, Hume critical of the *Historical Law-Tracts* of 68, Hume's comment on the *Essays on the Principles of Morality* of 140–1, received Hume's essay on miracles 137, member of Select Society 27, his natural history of patriotism 97–9, on the origin of religion 123, his pessimism 99, his position on the militia debate 93–4, his range of accomplishments 30

Kant, Immanuel, on the nature of enlightenment 15–16

Kelvin, Lord 219

Kenneth II 64
Kepler 10, 211
King's College, Aberdeen 9, Boece
    its principal 9
Kirk (Church of Scotland), its
    attitude to the theatre 152–3
Knox, John, tutee of Mair at St
    Andrews 9, as historian 43
Königsberg 15

La Flèche 118
Lafitau, Joseph-François 69, 70
language, scientific study of 189–90
Law, Scots, Stair's contribution
    to 12–13
Lectures on Rhetoric and Belles
    Lettres, Smith's 52–3, its account
    of the historian's art 101
Leechman, William, professor of
    divinity at Glasgow 28, accused
    of heresy 34, member of the
    Literary Society 28
Leiden 10, 11, 210
Leighton, Robert 12, 30
licentiousness, patriotism opposed to
    98
Liddel, Duncan, his career 10
Lindsay, Sir David 152
Lindsay, Margaret 166
Literary Society of Glasgow, its
    membership 28
Literati, Ferguson on their
    untrustworthiness 88–9
Lobachevsky, N. 208
logarithms, Napier's discovery of 10
Lokert, George, career of 9
Louvain 10
love of neighbour 102
Loyola, Ignatius, attended Mair's
    lectures 9
luxury, Kames's criticism of 99

Macauley, Lord, his response to the
    Aikenhead heresy trial 34

MacFarlane, John, his letter to
    Kames 142
McKean, Charles 8
Mackenzie, Henry, member of
    Oyster Club 27
Maclaurin, Colin 186, 215, his
    anti-Jacobite stance 200, his
    career 199, member of Rankenian
    Club 26, Newton his admirer
    199, on the relation between
    religion and natural philosophy
    201–3, superintended the defence
    of Edinburgh 200
Macmillan, Duncan 154, 163, 166
Macpherson, James 7, 14, the
    literary success of his Poems of
    Ossian 64
Mair, John, career of 9, his reason
    for writing Historia Maioris
    Britanniae 43, his support for
    David Guild 16
Mallett, David 7
Manderston, William, his
    career 10
Marischal College, Aberdeen, Liddel
    founder of its mathematics chair
    10
Mary Queen of Scots, William
    Robertson's portrayal of 53
Masucci, Agostino, teacher of Gavin
    Hamilton 153
Melanchthon, Philip 147
Middle Ages, contrasted with the
    Enlightenment 16–17, 78
militia 97, advantages of 90–4
Militia Act of 1757 91
Millar, Andrew 120
Millar, John 25
miracles, argument from 137
Moderate party 2
Monboddo, Lord, his study of
    language 190
monotheism, the temporal
    successor to polytheism 121–2,

in one respect less good than
polytheism 125
Monro *primus*, Alexander, first
professor of anatomy at
Edinburgh 25
Monro *secundus*, Alexander 25
Montague, Elizabeth 141
Montesquieu, Charles-Louis 118
moral sense 144–5
Morison, Colin 154
Mure, William, former student of
Leechman's 34
music, Scottish 14
My Own Life, Hume's
autobiography 60, 61, 119
mysteries of the Church 114–15

Napier, John, his invention of
logarithms 10
Napoleonic War 220
Nasmyth, Alexander 154
national identity, Scottish 58–61
Natural History of Religion,
Hume's 119–26
natural science, human beings as
object of 55
Nevay, James 154
Newton, Sir Isaac 54–5, 75, 131, 196,
199, 201
non-Euclidean geometry 30, 203–9
North Britain 58

Ockham, William 18
Ossian 14, 64–5
Oyster Club, its membership 27

Padua 10
paintings, difference between Italian
and Flemish 172
Paisley 34
Panama, Isthmus of 7
Paris 59, University of 9, 210,
John Mair's career at 9, Duns
Scotus at 16

parliamentarians, Scottish 8, 58
Parliaments, Union of the 6, 8
particularism, two kinds of 97
patriotism 94–100, its natural
history 97–9
philosophes 118, 140
Philosophical Society of
Aberdeen (the 'Wise Club'), its
membership 28
Philosophical Society of Edinburgh
28
Piranesi 154
Pisa 11
Pitcairne, Archibald 11, 30
Pitt the Younger, William, his
tribute to Smith 21–2
Plato, his classification of atheists as
reported by Hume 35
Playfair, John, his advocacy of
Hutton 218, professor of natural
philosophy at Edinburgh 27, 167,
his description of the Oyster
Club 27, Hutton's biographer
211, 212, his trip with Hutton to
Siccar Point 215
Pliny, on origin of painting 74–5
Poker Club, founded to support
a Scottish militia 91–2, its
membership 92
polytheism, antecedent to
monotheism 121–2, its moral
superiority over monotheism 125
Pope, Alexander 163
Porter, Roy, his criticism of
Smith's doctrine of division of
labour 105–6
Prague 10
Pringle, John, professor of moral
philosophy at Edinburgh 26
propriety, Smith's account
of 101–2
Protestantism, moderate 49
providence, its relation to
historiography 57–8

Rabelais, François 9

Raeburn, Sir Henry 153, 173–5, his portrait of Reid 167, his philosophical relations with Reid 174–5

Ramsay, Allan (the poet) 14, his *The Gentle Shepherd* 29, the raid on his lending library 152, his theatre in the Canongate 152

Ramsay, Allan (the painter) 7, 153, 157, his *A Dialogue on Taste* 29, founder of Select Society 26

Ramsay, Michael 141

Rankenian Club, membership of 26

reason, limits of 130, Hume's critique of powers of 138

reflecting telescope 11

regent master 30

Reid, Thomas 25, on the distinction between real and apparent figure 205, his lectures on the mathematical sciences in Aberdeeen 203, member of the Literary Society 28, member of Philosophical Society of Aberdeen 28, his non-Euclidean geometry 203–9, painted by Raeburn 167, portrayed by Tassie 165, professor of moral philosophy at Glasgow 28, his range of accomplishments 30, on the craft of painting 167–75, on the relation between sign and significate 168–71, on the relation between language and mental powers 189–90, on representation of distance 171–2, on tangible *versus* visible space 207–9, Turnbull's pupil 203

religion, Hume's attitude to 40–2, its origin in fear 121–2, appeasement and the practice of 124

Republic of Letters 14, 20, 21, 24, its relation to patriotism 95

republicanism 90

resentment, its role in morality 102

revelation 131–2

rhetoric 149, painting as 158–9

Riemann, Georg 208

Robertson, John, on the militia question 93–4

Robertson, Hugh 22

Robertson, William 60, 167, principal of Edinburgh University 27, founding member of Royal Society of Edinburgh 28, his historiographic style 53, on the role of providence in defeat of Spanish Armada 57, on start of Scottish history 64, supporter of John Home 31, on the value of the Union 32, 50, on uniformity of human nature 69, on comparative history 69–70

Robison, John, professor of natural philosophy at Edinburgh 28, 167, discovered inverse square law of electric force 186

Rosebery, Third Earl of 30

Rousseau, Jean-Jacques, criticised by Ferguson 80–1

Royal College of Physicians of Edinburgh 11

Royal Society of Edinburgh, its founding members 28

Rule Britannia 7

Runciman, Alexander 154, 210, his depiction of the origin of painting 74

Runciman, John 154, 210

Rush, Benjamin 49

Russell, Bertrand 132

science, its effect on religious belief 124–5, unity of 186–91, its aim according to Smith 197

scientific discovery, psychology
    of 191–8
Scotland, its economic state before
    the Enlightenment 7
Scott, Walter, his *Bride of
    Lammermuir* 12, his relation to
    the Scottish Enlightenment 220 -1
Scougall, Henry 12, 30
Seasons, The, James Thomson's
    masterpiece 7
Seget, Thomas, career of 10
Select Society, its membership 26–7
Shakespeare 211
Shepherd, Lady Mary 20
Sibbald, Robert, career of 11, 30
Siccar Point, Hutton's trip to 214–15
Siddons, Mrs Sarah 152–3
Simpson, John, professor of
    sacred theology at Glasgow
    116, his rejection of dogma of
    Incarnation 116
Simpson, Robert, professor of
    mathematics at Glasgow 192
Sinclair, Sir John, his range
    of accomplishments 30, his
    Statistical Account 38–9, 221
Skirving, Archibald 154
slavery, Smith's hostility to 96
Smart, Alastair 166
Smibert, John, career of 6–7
Smith, Adam 14, 25, 44, 139, on
    the aim of science 197, on the
    American war 92, his arguments
    against monopolies 21, on the
    care of his literary papers 191,
    his concept of sympathy 101,
    his *Dissertation on the Origin of
    Languages* 66, on division of
    labour 105–7, founder of Oyster
    Club 27, founder of Select
    Society 26, founder member of
    Royal Society of Edinburgh
    28, and the impartial spectator
    101, 103, 183, Joseph Black

and James Hutton his literary
    executors 191, his letter on the
    death of Hume 36–7, 138–9,
    on merit and demerit 102–3,
    on motivation 193, on need
    for state funded education 105,
    portrayed by Tassie 165, on
    propriety and impropriety 101–3,
    on the psychology of scientific
    discovery 191–8, 201, his range of
    accomplishments 30, on scientific
    motivation 193, on slavery 96,
    his stadial theory 75–6, his
    study of the origin of language
    190, his support for American
    independence 22, and the
    publication of Hume's *Dialogues*
    37, on the writing of history 52
Societies, Enlightenment 24–8
St Andrews University, its
    foundation 9, its low profile
    during the Enlightenment 25–6
St Giles, High Kirk of, Hugh Blair's
    association with 22, 146
St Salvator's College 9, 16, 17
stadial theory of human
    development, 84, its relation to
    patriotism 97–8, Smith's version
    of the 75–6
Stair, first Viscount 12–13
standard of taste, Hume's account of
    the 178–84, Hutcheson's account
    of the 177
Statistical Account of Scotland, Sir
    John Sinclair's 30, 38–9
Stevenson, John, professor of logic
    at Edinburgh 26, teacher of
    Hutton 209–10
Stewart, Dugald, professor of moral
    philosophy at Edinburgh 25, 219,
    his account of conjectural history
    66–8, member of Oyster Club
    27, on need for a well-balanced
    education 108–12, gives

philosophical basis of George
Davie's *Democratic Intellect*
111–12, his report on Raeburn's
portrait of Reid 174, his report
on Smith's mathematical abilities
192, on two kinds of progress
72–3, 77, on the unity of
science 187
Stewart, John, professor of natural
philosophy at Edinburgh 119–20
Stewart, Matthew, professor of
mathematics at Edinburgh 25
Stirling, John, principal of Glasgow
University and brother-in-law of
John Simpson 116
stoicism, Christian 146–7
Strahan, William, Hume's publisher
in London 37, 127
surprise, its role in scientific
discovery 194–6
sympathy, its importance
for historiography 53, its
nature 101–8

Theory of Moral Sentiments, Smith's
69, 193, its attack on slavery 96,
its account of sympathy 101–2
Tacitus 70
Tassie, James 165
Thomson, James 7
Thurso, the new town planned by
Sir John Sinclair 30
time, deep 209, 215
toleration 115, 118, 222, polytheism
and 125
Treatise of Human Nature, Hume's
31, 164, 187–8, 193
Turnbull, George, an ally of
Maclaurin's 203, his concept of
the picturesque 184–5, on the
design argument 200–1, on the
educational value of paintings

156–61, on freedom and slavery
24, member of Rankenian Club
26, on need to give history a
prominent place in syllabus 53–4,
on questions to ask about a
painting 180

understanding, historical 54–8
Union of the Crowns 6
Union Jack 8
Ussher, Archbishop James 211

Vitoria, Francisco, Mair's lectures
attended by 9
Voltaire, François-Marie 118

Wade, General, his road system as a
product of public works 93
Walker, Revd. Robert, painted by
Raeburn 173
Warburton, William 119–20
Watt, James, inventor of improved
version of Newcomen steam
engine 28, 186
Wealth of Nations 26, 56, Ferguson's
criticism of 92, Smith's motive
for writing 38, its doctrine of
division of labour 104–5
Wedderburn, John, acquaintance of
Galileo 10
Westminster Confession 115
Westminster Parliament 8
Wilberforce, William 21
William of Orange 6
Wilson, Florence 147
Wishart, William, principal of
Edinburgh 26, 147
Wodrow, Robert 152
wonder, its role in scientific
discovery 195–6
Wood, Paul 199, 203, 207

BIRLINN LTD (incorporating John Donald and Polygon) is one of Scotland's leading publishers with over four hundred titles in print. Should you wish to be put on our catalogue mailing list **contact**:

Catalogue Request
Birlinn Ltd
West Newington House
10 Newington Road
Edinburgh EH9 1QS
Scotland, UK

Tel: + 44 (0) 131 668 4371
Fax: + 44 (0) 131 668 4466
e-mail: info@birlinn.co.uk

Postage and packing is free within the UK. For overseas orders, postage and packing (airmail) will be charged at 30% of the total order value.

For more information, or to order online, visit our website at **www.birlinn.co.uk**

Birlinn *Limited*
Other Imprints – JOHN DONALD • POLYGON